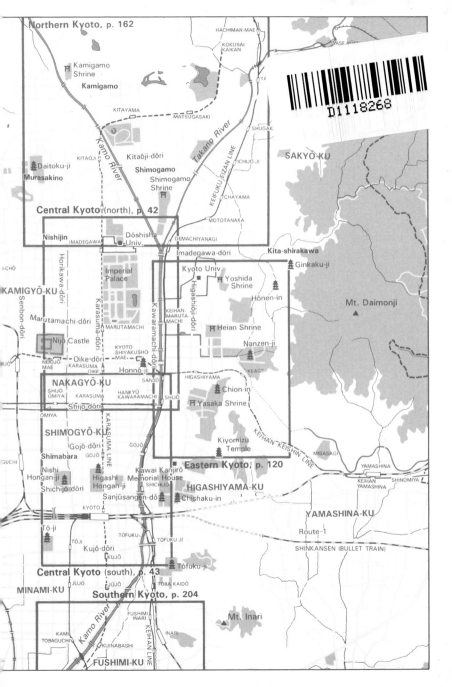

HACHIMAN-MAE

KOKUSAI KAIKAN

YASE YUO

Kamigamo Shrine

Kamigamo

KITAYAMA

MATSUGASAKI

SHUGAK

SAKYŌ-KU

Daitoku-ji

Murasakino

KITAŌJI

Kitaōji-dōri

Shimogamo

Shimogamo Shrine

CHAYAMA

ICHIJŌ-JI

Kamo **River**

Takano River

KEIFUKU EIZAN LINE

MOTOTANAKA

Nishijin

IMADEGAWA

Dōshisha Univ.

DEMACHIYANAGI

Imadegawa-dōri

Kita-shirakawa

Kyoto Univ

Ginkaku-ji

Yoshida Shrine

KAMIGYŌ-KU

Imperial Palace

Hōnen-in

Mt. Daimonji

Horikawa-dōri

Karasuma-dōri

Higashiōji-dōri

I-CHŌ

Marutamachi-dōri

MARUTAMACHI

Heian Shrine

Senbon-dōri

Nijō Castle

KYOTO SHIYAKUSHO-MAE

Nanzen-ji

Oike-dōri

KARASUMA OIKE

Honnō-ji

NIJŌJŌ MAE

HIGASHIYAMA

KEAGE

KEIHAN MARUTA-MACHI

SANJŌ

NAKAGYŌ-KU

SHIJŌ ŌMIYA

KARASUMA

HANKYŪ KAWARAMACHI

SHIJŌ

Chion-in

Yasaka Shrine

Shijō-dōri

ŌMIYA

SHIMOGYŌ-KU

KARASUMA LINE

Kiyomizu Temple

KEIHAN KEISHIN LINE

MISASAGI

YAMASHINA

Gojō-dōri

GOJŌ

Shimabara

Nishi Hongan-ji

Higashi Hongan-ji

Kawai Kanjirō Memorial House

HIGASHIYAMA-KU

SHINOMIYA

KEIHAN YAMASHINA

GUCHI

Shichijō-dōri

SHICHIJŌ

Sanjūsangen-dō

Chishaku-in

YAMASHINA-KU

KYOTO

Tō-ji

TŌFUKU-JI

TŌFUKU JI

Route-1

SHINKANSEN (BULLET TRAIN)

TŌJI

Kujō-dōri

KUJŌ

Tōfuku-ji

MINAMI-KU

JŪJŌ

JŪJŌ

TOBA KAIDŌ

FUSHIMI INARI

KAMI TOBAGUCHI

KUINABASHI

INARI

KEIHAN LINE

Mt. Inari

FUSHIMI-KU

OLD KYOTO

OLD KYOTO

A Guide to Traditional Shops,
Restaurants, and Inns

REVISED AND UPDATED

DIANE DURSTON

PHOTOGRAPHS BY Lucy Birmingham

FOREWORD BY Donald Richie

KODANSHA USA

Here's to you Anita Durston,
My mother, my teacher and my friend.

NOTE: The Japanese personal names of historical figures who lived in or before the Edo period are written in the Japanese manner, surname preceding given name. Post-Edo names follow the Western order.

Maps updated by Tadamitsu Ōmori.
Original maps by Michio Kojima.

PHOTO CREDITS: Kenneth Hamm 5 (bottom), 163, 164, 181, 182, 205, 206, 213 (left), 222, 228, 229. Tsuyoshi Itō 34, 35, 217, 218, 219 (top), 220, 221, 226. Stephen Futscher 111, 116, 153–59, 201. Gekkeikan 208, 209. Kodansha Photo Library 16–17, 115, 219 (bottom), 223, 224, 225 (top). Bon Color Photo Agency 214–15.

■ ■ ■

Published by Kodansha USA, Inc.
451 Park Avenue South
New York, NY 10016

Distributed in the United Kingdom and continental Europe
by Kodansha Europe Ltd.

First edition published in Japan in 1986 by Kodansha International
Revised edition 2005 by Kodansha International
First US edition 2013 by Kodansha USA

21 20 19 18 17 16 15 14 13   6 5 4 3 2 1

The Library of Congress has cataloged the earlier printing as follows:

Library of Congress Cataloging-in-Publication Data
Durston, Diane
    Old Kyoto
    Bibliography: p.
    1. Kyoto (Japan)—Description—Guide-books. Title.
DS897.K83D87   1986   915.2'18640448   85-45709

www.kodanshausa.com

Contents

Foreword

Kyoto—a fact well publicized—is very special. It holds the imperial past and the cultural best—temples, gardens, cuisine, kimono, crafts.

What is not generally recalled is that Kyoto is what it is because, almost alone among Japanese cities, it was not bombed, remaining undestroyed during World War II. Thus the old capital looks as all Japan might have, had it not been destroyed.

This being so, Kyoto—or at least parts of it—is still made of wood. It is the only city in Japan, perhaps in the world, so made. To walk the backstreets of the old capital is to stroll in a carpentered forest.

Thus Kyoto is more than the official traditional Japan one reads about in ordinary guidebooks and takes guided tours to see; it is also these warrens of backstreets with their inns and restaurants and shops, the buildings still made of wood and stone and tile.

As we walk these streets we see the grain, the hue, the texture of wood, watch its changing color, feel its warmth, sense nature. If you half close your eyes and look at these streets you will see how natural they are—the varied textures, the different shapes, the lines of roofs, all natural, all organic as though growing there.

Here, too, the last of the urban natural. Elsewhere, still, rice paddies harmonize and contrast with the valleys and the hills. The very materials—straw, wood, plaster, paper—are natural; when the dyed cloth was washed in the stream it delineated the current, emphasized the banks, seemed a part of the water itself.

And so even now there are backstreet corners in Kyoto where a harmonious accommodation is made between what man has built and what he found there—the line of a tree reflected in the line of a pillar, the grain of the rock, the grain of the stone wall.

Even now that concrete is cheaper than stone and metal is cheaper than wood and plastic is cheaper than anything, the warrens of old buildings—shops, inns, eateries—have no pretensions, do not aspire to becoming monuments. They can never become a part of the official traditional Kyoto. They are still in use. People live in these old buildings, work in them, always have.

The blank, anonymous postwar look of most Japanese cities is due not only to their having been destroyed by war. They are also being destroyed by the high price of land, the necessity for larger and more efficient buildings, the price of building materials and the necessity of building with cheap prefab modules, by the national preoccupation with the making of money.

Indeed, even sections of Kyoto look like Osaka or Nagoya, and in time the resemblance will be closer still. None of the great sights will go—this or that palace, that pavilion or this. There may well be some who would prefer a useful modern apartment block to a useless ancient temple, no matter how famous, but the official attitude is against them. The Kyoto city government would never permit this.

But there is no one to speak for these old-fashioned streets where the possibly dangerous wooden buildings are so inefficiently occupying valuable land.

Consequently, some of the finest environments, those which speak most truly of living Kyoto—these will vanish. This part of the living fabric of tradition will disappear. "Old Kyoto" will, of course, survive—it is, after all, a city on display where all, Japanese and foreigner alike, come as they would to an exposition.

But traces of the quiet, traditional backstreets of Kyoto will not vanish. One of these is the book you are holding. Here the look, the feel, the smell, the tastes of real traditional Kyoto have been preserved.

In her eighteen years in Kyoto, Diane Durston lived with this true, living tradition. With affection and understanding she has given us the only account of these streets and their inns and shops and places to eat and to drink.

More than any other book it captures with care, with precision, and with love those qualities which make the real Kyoto what it still remains.

Donald Richie

Beginnings

Dusk settles over the backstreets of Kyoto, tucking in the rows of old wooden houses for another peaceful night's sleep. The glow of sunset deepens and hangs between the sagging tile rooftops; telephone lines and pine branches are silhouetted against an indigo sky. Someone's grandfather, bucket and washrag under one arm, clacks down the alley in wooden *geta* on his way to the public bath. The cackle of old women gossiping in doorways echoes in the quiet night air. An old man in white gauze pajamas squats on his doorstep amid a circle of impatient children begging him to light another sparkler to celebrate an ordinary summer night.

One of the only shops left open on the street is the corner saké shop, where a boisterous caucus of day laborers and pensioners wash down the day's grievances with a cold bottle of beer. The reassuring whir of an electric fan (and the shopkeeper's amazing skills of arbitration) tempers the injustices of eight hours in the relentless Kyoto heat. "*Oideyasu!*" she calls out in Kyoto dialect, welcoming another weary pilgrim into the fold.

The bathhouse is still open, and the curtains at its entryway wave enticingly at simmering neighbors with promises of relief. The noodle shop two doors down feeds the last of the day's ravenous boardinghouse students, who sit slurping noodles with the cook in front of the TV set, kibitzing the outcome of the ball game.

The vegetable stand, the tofu shop, and the flower vendor have all closed down for the night. So have the knife sharpener, the seal carver, and the lacquerer—their electric fans the only ones working overtime tonight. An hour past supper and the smell of grilled fish still clings to the air. Lights go on behind the latticed paper windows of the houses, making them glow like a corridor of two-story wooden lanterns in the deepening twilight. A temple bell tolls the passage of another day. The local cop bicycles past on his evening rounds, humming; trouble is still a surprise in old Kyoto neighborhoods like these.

If it weren't for the surveyor's stakes in the vacant lot down the street, it would be easy to suppose that this neighborhood looks much the same today as it did a hundred years ago. Within two weeks a three-story concrete apartment building will wedge its way between the gray tile rooftops of these "bedrooms of eels," the local nickname for the elongated wood-frame houses whose narrow façades line the streets of Kyoto. The *apaato*, the latest modern addition to the old neighborhood, though a disappointment to some, at least is no longer a surprise.

The old wooden buildings, the homes of craftsmen and merchants whose shopfronts open right onto the streets, are disappearing one by one; extracted hygienically, like aching teeth, leaving cavities in the landscape and the heart of the ancient city. Made simply of wood, clay, and sand, they are easily demolished, gone within hours on any hot Kyoto afternoon. But with them goes much of the history and charm of this thousand-year-old city. The old shops and houses gave shelter to a different world. A poorer world economically, but one in which the common people learned, if only out of sheer necessity, how to live peacefully in cramped quarters, how to turn disaster into progress, and poverty into an aesthetic ideal. During ages in which the aristocrats sank in their own decadence and the samurai fought their way to destruction, it was the common people of Kyoto, the merchants and craftsmen, who kept many of the arts and crafts, customs and traditions of their civilization alive.

The old shops of Kyoto, some of whose families boast over twenty generations in the same trade, continue to house the spirit of the ancient capital, quietly tending the simple businesses of their grandfathers, as if the essence of what they represent were tucked safely away in family shrines behind the urns that hold their ashes.

Wooden buckets and paper umbrellas are still made in the old shops as they were in the seventeenth century, but the citizens of twenty-first-century Kyoto haven't much use for them anymore, preferring the "advantages" of plastic and nylon. Most homes in Japan now have their own baths, and people no longer relish the pleasures of a soak in the communal tubs of the city's old-fashioned *sentō*, or public baths. Shops and restaurants specializing in *Kyō-ryōri*, the exquisite local cuisine, must now compete with German delicatessens and French cafés for customers among Kyoto's increasingly cosmopolitan populace.

No one begrudges the improvements in the quality of life the last century has brought to Japan—modern transportation, better medical care, more of the luxuries once reserved for the upper classes. But a sigh escapes at times, bemoaning the inevitable loss of old-world charm.

Down Kyoto's narrow, quiet backstreets there are still many glimpses of an elegant past to be found. The luster of a hand-painted vermilion lacquer bowl with an inlaid mother-of-pearl dragonfly carefully removed from a signed wooden box by a solicitous old shopkeeper's wife . . . the moment's hesitation before you slice into a sweet bean cake the fragile shape and color of a cherry blossom . . . the unexpected pleasure of discovering the intricately woven pattern on a common house broom. The aura of classical Japanese living does still exist in Kyoto. It can be found in the windows of old fan shops, on the curtains of confectioneries, in the tiny gardens of the neighborhood inns. The spirit of the city lives on in the hearts of its shopkeepers.

Thousands of people flock to Kyoto year after year in search of the old spirit. They take bus tours to famous gardens and ancient temples; they visit museums and read pamphlets on religions and warlords to try to find it. They walk past it without blinking twice on their way to catch the train.

The dark façades of the traditional Kyoto shops at first seem all alike with their curtain veils and no signs in English. Even the seasoned traveler finds it awkward to venture further. But what you'll find inside is often a warm-hearted shopkeeper eager to be at your service. My hope is that this book will help you to find what you're looking for in Kyoto, help you locate the heart of the city.

The traditional shopkeepers of Kyoto have taken great pains to maintain the old wooden buildings with their sagging beams and sinking stone floors. They insist on making the same fine products with the best materials they can buy, as if they were still purveyors to the imperial household, as many of them once were. They stubbornly cling to old wood-burning stoves, convinced, as their grandfathers were that they boil a tastier pot of rice. They shun power tools, knowing nothing can match the character of a surface that has been laboriously polished by hand. They are aware that the twenty-first century has made many of their products passé and search for ways to show modern customers that the quality of one's life does not depend entirely on the number of electric appliances on the kitchen counter. They hope their children will take over when they die, but live in the knowledge that, for many of them, their shop's legacy will be buried with them as their sons hurry off to Osaka in search of fashionable office jobs.

The famous temples and manicured villas may define the rarefied soul of feudal Japan, but the old noodle shops and inns, the teahouses and tofu makers, are the marrow of its bones. Walk around Kyoto; part the curtains of the old shops; step inside . . . "*Oideyasu!*"

Diane Durston
Kyoto

CHRONOLOGY

NARA
710–94

HEIAN
794–1185

KAMAKURA
1185–1333

MUROMACHI
1333–1568

MOMOYAMA
1568–1600

EDO
1600–1868

MEIJI
1868–1912

TAISHŌ
1912–26

SHŌWA
1926–89

HEISEI
1989 to present

History

The folk that have been attracted thither and the poets do all with one voice acclaim this Heiankyō, the capital of peace and tranquility.
——Emperor Kanmu
794, eleventh month, eighth day

When the emperor Kanmu brought his court to this valley in the eighth century, he could not have known that the title he bestowed on the city held an irony that would one day be as classic as the grand imperial city itself. For over a thousand years, Kyoto (as it is known today) was the capital of Japan, and, like most capital cities, was the scene of endless wars and political strife, and the site of more than its share of devastating natural disasters. Although it was indeed the birthplace of one of the most refined and sophisticated cultures on earth, in reality it was far from the peaceful citadel Kanmu originally envisioned. Still considered the center of traditional culture in Japan, Kyoto and the people who live there have a long and difficult history behind them.

Kanmu chose this site for a number of reasons: it was surrounded on three sides by mountains that made it a natural castle, it had an endless (if capricious) supply of water from the river that divides it in half, and, conveniently enough, it had 130,000 members of the Hata clan, who as the descendants of Korean immigrants could teach his craftsmen how to weave (and lend him the money to build his palace).

His dream was to create an imperial city that would rival the glorious capital of the Tang dynasty, Chang-an. He called for a comprehensive plan for the layout of his city, branding the valley floor with a permanent grid pattern of streets, which divided the area into rectangular blocks, just like the Chinese model he sought to outdo.

During the 390 years of relative calm now known as the Heian period, Kanmu's descendants led a life of luxury and elegance inside the palace walls characterized by languid afternoons sipping saké and breaking romantic promises beneath the willows in an atmosphere of isolated splendor that rivaled the excesses of Versailles. The "Golden Age" also resulted in the weakening of imperial determination to deal with the mundane business of governing the land, a duty that powerful local clans would fight over for the ensuing several centuries. The Fujiwara clan dominated this first age of scrambled Kyoto politics, assuming the role of regents by marrying into the imperial family.

The presence of the emperor and his squabbling entourage made Kyoto not only the center of the political scene, but also a bustling hub of commerce. Artisans, skilled in the sophisticated techniques of Chinese craftsmanship, were called to the new capital to provide the accoutrements and luxuries required to maintain the extravagant lifestyle of the imperial court. Merchants flocked to Heiankyō to provide the materials, foods, and commodities necessary to build and support the growing city. Two marketplaces were established in the southeast and southwest of the city where merchants could exchange their wares. The markets were lively places where people of all ranks, from noblemen to peasants, walked about examining the latest products and wares. The eastern market, where Kyoto Station now stands, flourished, while the western market died out, establishing the eastern half as the city center as early as the tenth century.

By the twelfth century, however, it had become obvious that the townspeople would have to stick together in order to defend themselves against an endless stream of military and natural disasters. Neighborhoods formed around shrines and temples in tightly knit communities for self-defense. Some communities even built moatlike ditches around their neighborhoods, not just for protection, but for the purpose of flood control, crop irrigation, and defense against the frequent fires that plagued the city built entirely of wood and thatch.

It was during this era of natural (and man-made) disasters that Kamo no Chōmei, the hermit poet, sat alone in his hut on a mountainside near Ōhara foretelling the fate of the city he loved:

> The flow of the river is ceaseless:
> Its waters never the same . . .

He watched as the torrents of political turmoil swept away the elegance and refinement of what later would be called the Golden Age of Japanese history. He mourned the devastating price the people of Kyoto paid for the honor of inhabiting the ancient capital of Japan. And perhaps he realized that constant "change" would be the only element upon which the populace could depend.

The military government established by the Minamoto clan that took over when the Fujiwara family went into decline was so busy holding down its own fort that it had not the time, inclination, or means to help the commoners rebuild their row houses after every battle, fire, or flood. By the time Minamoto no Yoritomo was proclaimed the first shogun in 1192, a large portion of the city had been devastated, and the starving townspeople were left to their own devices when he moved his camp to Kamakura in the east.

The ability of the merchants and craftsmen to band together in mini town-ships enabled them to undertake reconstruction on their own. The crisscross pattern of the city streets provided manageable blocks of approximately forty dwellings each, in which groups of merchants and craftsmen worked together to rebuild their homes and shops. The unity and self-determination that evolved in these neighborhoods at the beginning of the twelfth century helped them survive the rise and fall of a succession of military leaders over the next four hundred years.

The arrival of Zen from China in the early thirteenth century was an event that had a great impact on Japanese culture. The austere sect of Buddhism with its emphasis on personal training of body and mind was attractive to the shogun and his samurai for the strength and discipline it encouraged, a wel-come change from the weak life of luxury they saw as a primary factor in the decline of both the emperor and his regents. The great Zen temples that were built in the following century became centers of culture in Kyoto. Zen priests encouraged continued contact with China, offering Kyoto merchants the opportunity to begin a prosperous trade network that gave them the economic strength, not only to survive, but to flourish while other sectors of the society collapsed. They began to form guilds called *za*, which were under the protec-tion of shrines and temples on whose grounds they held regular markets in return for the payment of special taxes.

Yet another coup took place in the early fourteenth century, bringing the Ashikaga shogunate to power and reestablishing Kyoto as the political center of Japan. The 235 years of Ashikaga reign were characterized by unparalleled cultural development, but also by political and social disasters on a scale hith-erto unseen. The Ashikaga shogunate, a firm follower of Zen, was a great patron of the arts. The Muromachi period, named for the palace built by the shogu-nate near the emperor's quarters in Kyoto, was an age in which ink painting, calligraphy, and tea ceremony flourished in Japan. The third shogun, Yoshi-mitsu, ordered the construction of the magnificent Kinkaku-ji, the Golden Pavilion, in the northwest of Kyoto in 1397.

But by the middle of the fifteenth century, Kyoto was again the scene of a power struggle between warlords from the provinces who flocked to the capital city with cravings for a taste of the notorious life of luxury at court.

The realm inherited by Ashikaga Yoshimasa, the grandson of Yoshimitsu, was in a state of total chaos; 1449, the year he was born, marked the beginning of a terrible plague that took the lives of a thousand citizens a day. It was as if the mid-fifteenth century had been singled out for disaster by a legion of angry gods. In 1442 the Kamogawa River had flooded, washing away two major bridges. In 1444, the merchants took over Kitano Shrine in an appeal for just government. The military government slashed their way in, forcing the mer-chants to commit group suicide, but not before they had set fire to the shrine,

burning it to the ground. Throughout the decade before Yoshimasa's birth, the warrior-priests of Enryaku-ji Temple on Mt. Hiei stormed down the mountainside on a number of occasions, wielding the feared portable shrine (said to possess the power of life and death) and making demands on the imperial court. The year 1447 saw severe earthquakes and floods, and by the time Yoshimasa was ten years old, a massive famine had left great funerary mounds all over the besieged capital city.

Depressed (though probably not the word for it) by the condition of the kingdom he had inherited, Yoshimasa chose to abandon his duties as shogun at the age of thirty-five. He pined away the rest of his days at Ginkaku-ji, the Silver Pavilion, an exquisite if less glamorous villa than his grandfather's, on the opposite side of the city. The villa "turned its back on the city" and faced the Higashi-yama Mountains. The aesthetic ideal it represents was named after them— *Higashiyama bunka,* the "culture of the Eastern Mountains," referring to a wealth of aesthetic endeavors that flourished under the patronage of a timorous warlord who refused to deal with the world outside his exquisite villa.

For the city's craftsmen and merchants, the Muromachi period saw the development of the tea ceremony, a practice whose popularity stimulated the production of ceramic bowls and flower vases, bamboo basketry and utensils, cast-metal teakettles, and lacquerware. It also created a need for skilled carpen-

Bird's-eye view of Kyoto, 1808

ters and gardeners capable of building and caring for tearooms and landscape gardens, establishing an aesthetic basis for Japanese architecture from then on.

The succession dispute Yoshimasa left behind started the Ōnin War (1467–77), a disastrous ten years of battles that leveled the city, ruining all parties involved, and ironically failing to settle the original dispute. Hardly a building was left standing. The need for citywide reconstruction following the Ōnin War provided another (if tragic) source of work for the common people. The merchant townships set about rebuilding their city with little or no help from either the shogunate or the noblemen, who were either disinterested in the fate of the peasants or in nearly as desperate shape themselves. A recorded eighty-two thousand citizens died of starvation in 1480. Even the imperial court fell into a state of poverty, with the emperor himself at one point resorting to the sale of calligraphy to survive.

By this time, the merchants had acquired the acumen to take advantage of the constantly shifting political winds, and had accumulated the wealth to put the city back on its feet by supplying both sides of an endless string of competing armies with food and supplies. For the talent of hiding their true sympathies, Kyoto merchants earned the reputation for being "two-faced"—never answering directly, never giving a clear yes or no—a trait they are still accused of from time to time today.

By the middle of the sixteenth century, the winds of war had once again begun to blow. When St. Francis Xavier arrived in Kyoto in 1551, he was the first Western traveler to see the ancient city, or what was left of it. He wrote: "Today much of Kyoto lies in ruins because of the wars; many people have told us that it once had eighteen thousand houses, and it seems to me that this must have been true, to judge from the very large size of the city." When the Ashikaga shogunate fell, the rough-and-tumble Oda Nobunaga was there to grab power. Although he did much to unify the country that had for so long been at the mercy of warring factions, he did not endear himself to the people of Kyoto. He burned down over four hundred temples at Enryaku-ji on the top of Mt. Hiei,

The inn Kinmata (page 93), ca. 1900

Gion, the entertainment district

Kyoto's sacred mountain, because of the threat its powerful priests presented to his own regime. He then proceeded to wipe out a large portion of the north-eastern sector of the city (not well organized into communities) for the inability of the inhabitants to pay his exorbitant taxes. He was not a popular fellow.

Toyotomi Hideyoshi, Nobunaga's successor, did the most to rebuild Kyoto, if only to add to his own power and glory. During this period at the end of the sixteenth century the merchants and craftsmen came to his aid by helping with the reconstruction of the many temples that had been destroyed during the Ōnin War. Hideyoshi had dreams of restoring the capital city to an even higher level of grandeur than Emperor Kanmu himself could have imagined. In 1591, he ordered the construction of the Odoi, a wall that would surround the entire city. Only a few crumbling mementos of the great wall survive today. Hideyoshi enlisted the aid of Kyoto merchants and craftsmen, not only in the rebuilding of temples and shrines, but also in the construction of a magnificent pleasure palace, Juraku-dai, which he built on the ruins of the Imperial Palace itself.

During this period groups of townspeople organized themselves into neighborhood communities called *machi* (or *chō*) and undertook much of this reconstruction on their own. The rebuilding of the city proved much to their advantage, and the merchant class became so prosperous that they started to create their own separate world of art and extravagance, the "floating world" depicted in woodblock prints, a world of pleasure and often excess, but a world that existed for the first time for the common people.

With substantial wealth around them now, the townspeople were in a position to begin refining their existence. Aware of the aesthetics of tea, the merchants employed master carpenters (formerly only available to samurai warriors and the nobility) to create a living environment that embodied the finest aspects of all the levels of society whose presence could be felt in Kyoto: the spiritual qualities of the Zen priesthood, the refined tastes of the nobility, the austere restraint of the warriors, the skill of the finest craftsmen, the simplicity of the farmers, and the sense of unflagging practicality that had brought the prospering merchant class this far.

The death of Hideyoshi and the rise of Tokugawa Ieyasu, who moved his government to Edo (now Tokyo) in 1603, may have taken politics to the east, but it left Kyoto's merchants and craftsmen to spend the next two hundred years developing the arts and crafts for which the city is famous. The merchants aspired to raise their lowly social status by imitating all the trappings of the upper-class samurai, who by then were practically out of work with no wars left to wage. The merchants patronized the arts—pottery, weaving, lacquering, papermaking, painting, gardening, and architecture.

By the middle of the Edo period, the shogunate was feeling the waves of social change resulting from the rise in power of the merchant class and began legislating every detail of the merchants' lives, right down to the size of dolls their children were allowed to own. Not only did they close all traffic with foreign countries by edict in 1639 in the hope of stemming the merchants' access to goods from abroad, but they issued a long list of restrictions intended to keep the merchants down. No elaborate hair combs, no parasols, no silk kimonos, no "selling of peculiar things to hit the public fancy," to name a few. But these at least were based on the assumption that the merchant class was a force to be dealt with. The rules of conduct issued for the peasants were even more abusive: get up early, don't buy saké or tea, don't smoke, and divorce a wife who drinks too much tea and wastes time on casual excursions.

In spite of the rigid codes, it was, by the middle of the eighteenth century, too late for the shogun to control the merchants any longer. They were well on their way to becoming the powerful economic wizards that run the country today. The townhouses, or *machiya*, they lived in grew bigger (sometimes overnight) during the confusion of rebuilding after every fire that plagued the tinderbox city. With each reconstruction, the now powerful merchants extended their property lines farther into the streets (making it a real art for cars today to navigate between telephone poles planted right on the shoulder and children on bicycles with no other place to play). The servants and employees of the merchants were relegated to dwellings much humbler than the grand abodes of their masters that faced the main boulevards. They were set back off the roads on narrow alleys, hidden away behind the *machiya* of their employers. The merchants owned the property on which their employees lived, and at the same time relied upon them to work in their shops and to make the products they sold, establishing a pattern of mutual dependence within each community in Kyoto, which has survived to the present day.

The shops of Kyoto and their keepers flourished in the late Edo period . . . until one bone-chilling morning late in the winter of 1788. A wind suddenly blew in from the east, knocking over street stalls, peddlers, even horses with a force unheard of in Kyoto, a city usually thankful for the slightest breeze to break the stillness of its captive basin air. Somewhere along the west bank of the Kamogawa River, a fire broke out in a moneychanger's shop that gave way to the hurricane gusts. By dawn the next day the entire city was in flames. Three days later 183,000 homes, 909 temples, and 37 shrines had been reduced to ash. Virtually no wooden structure in the city center remains that predates the monstrous Tenmei Fire. Again the townspeople had a city to rebuild.

The end of the eighteenth century was a difficult time not only for the citizens of Kyoto, but for the entire country. The military government was in disastrous economic straits, having borrowed the funds to finance the extravagant tastes of the increasing population of samurai who played a nonproductive role during the politically stable Edo period, when the need for their services had all but been eliminated. The samurai had begun to borrow money from the merchants, and fell further and further into debt.

A series of major famines occurred during the late eighteenth and early nineteenth centuries. Over a million peasants died of starvation during the great famine of 1780–86. The Tokugawa shogunate was ineffectual despite the new laws calling for a return to austerity among the samurai, who were by now accustomed to leading an indolent life of luxury. A succession of weak Tokugawa shoguns noted for administrative incompetence assured the decline of the shogunate's power throughout the land. An impoverished and restless populace, with the aid of dissatisfied feudal lords (*daimyō*), began plotting the overthrow of the shogunate and the restoration of the emperor as ruler of Japan.

When Commodore Perry's ships sailed into port on July 8, 1853, the country was ready for change. His demands for the opening of trade with the United States ended over two hundred years of self-enforced isolation. Renewed commerce with the West was to have a major impact on Japanese culture from then on. Intrigued by the guns and machinery the foreigners brought with them, the Japanese sought to acquire much of the "advanced" accoutrements of Western life. The new word for chic in Japanese was *haikara*, the Japanese phonetic rendition of "high collar," a popular fashion among Western men in the late nineteenth century.

Shintarō Morita, Kagoshin (page 125), in formal dress on the day he was honored by the emperor

Weaving, Kagoshin, ca. 1920

For Kyoto, still the home of the emperor, this era of change and confusion meant that it would once again be the site of a major battle. Unrest in the provinces brought vassals to Kyoto to "save the emperor" from the hands of the shogun, who by now was struggling to maintain control. Plotters with hopes of restoring the emperor to power held clandestine meetings at some of the city's famous inns; deep gashes in beams and corner posts in some of those inns today attest to the amount of swashbuckling that preceded the shogunate's surrender. One such skirmish led to a fire in the Kyoto hideout of a provincial clan leader, again leaving much of the city devastated in 1864. But within four short years the people of Kyoto had once again rebuilt the entire city.

Lacking the support of most of the *daimyō*, the last shogun surrendered power in 1868 and the court of the emperor Meiji moved to Edo in the same year, renaming it Tokyo, the eastern capital.

The loss of their emperor broke the hearts of the people of Kyoto. All their civic pride was bound to an image of Kyoto as the "Imperial City." An air of depression hung over the valley for over a decade, leaving its mark on the local arts and crafts, which suffered a great decline in production in the years that followed.

But 1894 marked the 1100th anniversary of Kyoto, and the people commemorated the event by building Heian Shrine, a replica of the original Imperial Palace and a memorial to the deified soul of Emperor Kanmu, whose dream had created their proud city so long ago.

The period that followed was a time of welcome peace for the people of Kyoto. Craftsmen continued to hone the skills for which they had become world famous. The caste system prescribed by the Tokugawas was finally abolished, leaving citizens of all classes freer than ever before to pursue the livelihood of their choice; a number of new shops opened around the turn of the century.

World War II was the next (and hopefully the last) catastrophe to disrupt the lives of the citizens of Kyoto. Fortunately, the United States opted to save the ancient capital city, and it was not destroyed in the firebombing that leveled Tokyo and Osaka. Uncertainty, however, caused city fathers to order the widening of Kyoto's most important thoroughfares to act as possible firebreaks if such a tragedy should occur. This resulted in the loss of over eighteen thousand fine old shops and houses. Many merchants and craftsmen enlisted by the Imperial Army were also lost in the war, causing a drastic decline in the number of shops left open when Japan surrendered in 1945. After the war, materials were scarce and difficult to obtain, forcing many craftsmen to seek other employment. Before World War II there were over a hundred bucket makers in Kyoto; today their number can be counted on one hand.

The trend for Americanization after the war also left its mark on Kyoto arts and crafts. Young people preferred American-style products, mass-produced in five shades of plastic, to the studiously handmade breakables their grandfathers crafted. Fast food and fast cars represent the latest hazards to life in Kyoto. What is left of old Kyoto must contend with this latest threat to its existence, a more insidious foe than fire or famine. The old shops must find ways to adjust to changing Japanese tastes, to fit their products to twenty-first-century life, or fade away. With luck, the strength of will and stubborn determination the shopkeepers of Kyoto have shown over the past eleven centuries will help them through this most recent "minor difficulty."

The prediction of Kamo no Chōmei was not far from wrong. The people's legacy has always been one of change . . . a history of elegance and disaster . . . always flowing, never the same.

Kyoto Crafts

For years . . . ages . . . the rivers of Kyoto flaunted their brilliant Yūzen colors, the long streamers of hand-painted silk giving up their excess dye to the cold, clear waters. In the Gojōzaka district near Kiyomizu-dera, the huge climbing kilns puffed and snorted their black smoke into the Kyoto skies, turning the efforts of local potters into gleaming porcelain. The great Thousand-Armed Kannon, the goddess of mercy, and her 1,000 equally-armed companion images stood watch over rows and rows of open fans that were laid out to dry in the courtyard before her. The constant *katan-koton* clanking of thirty thousand looms vibrated the wood-frame houses along the narrow streets of Nishijin, the weaving district.

Far to the north, woodsmen carefully trimmed the towering cedar trees, shaving them as today's college girls shave their legs, flawlessly preparing them to decorate the homes of the wealthy. Kyoto bustles today as it did in the seventeenth century; the skies and waters are colored now with a different sort of affliction. The sights, like the sounds of the city, have synthesized.

The crafts of Kyoto have changed, but they have survived. Baskets are still woven, scrolls mounted, incense prepared with formulas that are still family secrets. Knives and fine carving tools are forged, and statues of Buddha are still cast in bronze and gilded in Kyoto. What has changed is not so much the objects that are produced, but the role they play in Japanese society. Today the craftsman decorates where once he filled a daily need; his products are costly where once they were commonplace; he has become an artist where once he was a nameless craftsman. There was no word for "art" in the Japanese language until the nineteenth century.

Adjectives like rustic and rough-hewn have no place in the vocabulary of Kyoto crafts; the word is *miyabi*, the elusive element of refinement and elegance that characterizes even the most common of everyday objects produced in the ancient capital city.

Kyoto crafts evolved out of certain cultural phenomena that developed over the centuries and can be grouped accordingly. The presence of the imperial court in Kyoto; the development of the tea ceremony; the position of the ancient capital as the center of Buddhism in Japan; and the lavish entertainment world of geisha and kabuki were some of the primary factors that influenced the extraordinary level of craftsmanship that developed throughout the long history of Kyoto.

Purveyors to the Imperial Household

From the time the emperor Kanmu arrived in Kyoto in the eighth century, the strongest influence on Kyoto craftsmen was the presence of the imperial court. From then on the privilege of being selected as *kunaichō-goyōtashi*—a purveyor to the imperial household—was an honor unparalleled among the craftsmen, merchants, and chefs who were at the exclusive disposal of the court. Throughout the Middle Ages these purveyors were given special wooden placards granting them admittance to the Imperial Palace compound. Though the practice was abolished after World War II, many old shopkeepers still proudly keep their original placards as family heirlooms and as symbols of the "royal" quality of their traditional products.

Several *kunaichō-goyōtashi* shops can be found in the area around the old Imperial Palace, between Imadegawa and Oike, from Kawaramachi to Horikawa. (See Fūka and Kagoshin in the shop listings.)

Among the crafts that developed under the influence of the Heian court were the fine silk brocades for the twelve-layered robes of the courtiers; painted and natural-wood folding fans; musical instruments like the *koto* (zither), the *biwa* (lute), the large *taiko* (drum), the *tsuzumi* (hourglass-shaped hand drum), and a variety of *fue* (flutes). Lacquerware (*shikki*) was so popular at court that it replaced pottery as the most popular type of serving vessel. One of the aspects of Kyoto cuisine, or *Kyō-ryōri*, that adds elegance to the overall sensory experience is the continued use of fine lacquerware. *Maki-e*, the technique of sprinkling gold and silver dust on a lacquer ground, was developed during the Heian period for the exclusive benefit of the imperial court.

Religious Reflections

Shinto and Buddhism, the two major religions of Japan, have always been centered in Kyoto, and many great monuments to both are located here. The Five

Great Temples of Zen (Nanzen-ji, Daitoku-ji, Kennin-ji, Tenryū-ji, and Tōfuku-ji, though others vied for the title) were located in Kyoto. So were a number of powerful shrines (Kamigamo-jinja, Shimogamo-jinja, Kitano-jinja, Yoshida-jinja, and Yasaka-jinja). Both shrines and temples acted as places of relative stability during times of war in the capital. Merchants and craftsmen conducted regular fairs at the major shrines and temples, which were considered a kind of central gathering place for many of the guilds, offering them protection from the shogunate in exchange for special taxes, and thus keeping the priests in a position of power.

Craftsmen and merchants built their homes and shops in front of the gates of temples, creating townships called *monzen-machi*. They produced religious articles (*butsugu*), including Buddhist home altars (*butsudan*) constructed of lacquered wood with elaborate gilded carvings and chased metal fittings; and sculptures (*butsuzō*) in carved wood or cast bronze.

Hundreds of small religious objects—like incense burners (*kōro*) and incense (*kō* or *senkō*), bronze bells (*kane*) and wooden gongs (*mokugyo*), candles (*rōsoku*) and prayer beads (*juzu*)—can still be found in front of the main gates of both Nishi and Higashi Hongan-ji temples north of Kyoto Station. These two powerful temples are the headquarters of two branches of the powerful Jōdo sect of Buddhism, and worshipers from rural prefectures make frequent pilgrimages here, buying Buddhist articles made by Kyoto craftsmen to take home to their local temples.

At least one shop in almost every neighborhood makes Shinto household altars (*kamidana*) and the portable shrines (*mikoshi*) for neighborhood festivals. The smooth, natural finish of a Shinto shrine and its smaller representations epitomizes the Japanese love of simple, unadorned beauty. The fine Japanese woodwork and joinery that goes into the making of these diminutive spirit houses was handed down by the highly specialized craftsmen (*miya-daiku*) who built (and rebuilt) the shrines, temples and teahouses of Japan. Today, the skills are known to only a few, and one craftsman is reportedly booked with orders for more temple repairs than he could possibly accomplish in his lifetime.

The Illustrious Influence of Tea

One of the strongest and deepest influences on the arts and crafts of Kyoto is that of the tea ceremony. When tea was first brought to Japan from China in the eighth century, it became a permanent item on the list of exotic luxuries reserved for members of the imperial court. They imbibed the heady beverage with formal pomp and ceremony, collecting the treasured utensils of the Chinese, and holding lavish tea parties in the pavilions of the aristocracy.

Not until the time of Murata Jukō (1422–1502) did ceremonial tea take on the spiritual aspect that gave it a central role in the development of Japanese culture. Following the teachings of Ikkyū, the legendary Zen priest, Murata developed a concept of ritual tea as a discipline for the mind and body, combined with the same aesthetic values promoted by the Zen priests—simplicity, refinement, and restraint. These were qualities that the samurai sought as a counterbalance to the decadence and excesses they saw as having caused the decline of the aristocracy.

The popularity of the tea ceremony stimulated the development of crafts that could not only produce the many specialized utensils that became an aspect of central importance to the tea ceremony, but that could meet its unique aesthetic demands for *wabi*, the sensibility of rustic refinement sought after by the great tea masters of Kyoto, such as Sen no Rikyū, who designed the first Raku-ware tea bowls made by the Korean potter Chōjiro in the sixteenth century.

The tea bowl (*chawan*) was of primary importance, though bamboo tea whisks (*chasen*), tea scoops (*chashaku*), lacquered tea caddies (*chaki*), fresh-water containers (*mizusashi*), waste-water containers (*kensui*), bamboo ladles (*hishaku*), iron teakettles (*kama*), flower vases (*hana-ire*), and an assortment of other objects all fall under the category of *cha-dōgu*, the necessary utensils for the tearoom.

Bamboo ware, ceramics, lacquerware (for the service of *cha-kaiseki*, the meal that accompanies a formal tea ceremony), metalwork, and textiles (both for garments worn by *chajin*, or "tea people," and for wrapping the precious utensils before they are placed in their wooden storage boxes) all became essential elements to the practice of tea.

Other skills required were the making of special charcoal (*sumi*) for heating the tea water, the preparation of aromatic woods and subtly blended incense (*o-kō*) burned before the guests arrived, and the making of tatami mats, *shōji* paper windows, and *fusuma* sliding doors—all of which evolved from the tearooms of the shogun Ashikaga Yoshimasa at Ginkaku-ji. His Silver Pavilion in the northeast of Kyoto and the tiny four-mat room called the Dōjin-sai were the settings for countless tea ceremonies, and created a standard for those that followed.

The Ashikaga shogunate also promoted a solemn form of theater called noh drama, which conformed with the Zen principles of economy of expression and restraint admired by the samurai. Many of the masks (*nō-men*) and ornate costumes in silk damask or embroidered silk gauze made by craftsmen in the seventeenth and eighteenth centuries are still in use today.

Reflections from the Floating World

A more down-to-earth, if equally esoteric, influence on the arts and crafts of Kyoto came from the bawdy night world of the geisha quarters. The peaceful seventeenth and eighteenth centuries brought prosperity and leisure time to the merchant class, who created their own colorful world of entertainment.

Considered vulgar by the upper classes, the "floating world" in *ukiyo-e* wood-block prints of the day was one of willowy courtesans arrayed in exuberantly decorated kimono, draped languidly over balconies, sighing under a midsummer moon.

The brilliantly dyed and embroidered kimono of the geisha; the elaborate hair ornaments (*kanzashi*) of lacquer, gold, silver, tortoiseshell, and glass; the tall platform clogs (*geta*) of their *maiko* apprentices; the sweeping kimono sashes (*obi*); the oiled paper umbrellas (*wagasa*); and a long list of accessories, including everything from round *uchiwa* fans to long, slender tobacco pipes (*kiseru*)—all were a part of the romantic world of Gion, the main geisha quarter of Kyoto.

Kabuki, the people's theater, with its boldly patterned costumes, exotic makeup, and swashbuckling flamboyance, provided Kyoto craftsmen with ever-new challenges in pattern design and color composition.

Threatened by the economic prowess of the rising merchant class, the Tokugawa shogunate forbade those of this rank to wear the costly silk brocades that were the pride of the upper classes. But not to be easily dismissed, the merchants urged dyers to match the extravagance of woven fabrics with dyeing techniques that produced an equally sumptuous effect. Yūzen, the paste-resist technique of fabric dyeing invented by a former fan painter, was developed during this era, achieving fine-lined results that must have aggravated the floundering lawmakers beyond words.

Objects for Every Day

To the rich and powerful of every culture go the finest of its arts and crafts, but the refinement and skillfulness of even the most common household objects in Kyoto are a clue to the level of craftsmanship the society attained. A simple hand-cut, hand-polished boxwood comb (*tsuge-kushi*)—something no bride would be without in old Kyoto—is an object of delicate beauty. Buckets (*oke, taru*) with staves that have been carefully planed to fit the proper angle, then joined with tiny bamboo pegs, seem as suitable for displaying on a shelf as for carrying sushi. The same goes for handmade wooden *geta* carved from a single block of paulownia.

The everyday necessities of life for the common people of Kyoto—the butcher knives (*hōchō*), the sewing needles (*hari*), the roof tiles (*kawara*), the workmen's coats (*hanten, happi*), the shop curtains (*noren*), the farmwomen's trousers (*monpe*), the chests of drawers (*tansu*), the name stamps (*hanko*), the paper lanterns (*bonbori, chōchin*)—all possess an undeniable sense of gentility not ordinarily associated with something like an ordinary pair of socks, until you've had the pleasure of being fitted for a dazzling white pair of cotton *tabi* that button neatly at the ankle.

The Traditional Local Cuisine

Western food—
Every damn plate
is round.

—Anonymous
modern *senryū* (satirical poem)

A length of split green bamboo, a three-layered ceramic serving dish the shape of a gourd, a red and black lacquered tray with the single bough of a cherry tree in full bloom painted delicately in the center in gold . . . Japanese food is never boring. Kyoto, as the old imperial capital, was also the birthplace of *kaiseki*, the formal cuisine that doesn't forget the other four senses.

Environment is the first consideration. Seated on cushions in a private tatami-mat room overlooking a meticulously groomed garden with only the sound of water trickling from the stone basin just outside to accent the silence . . . you are ready to begin.

The door slides open and a lady in kimono (sometimes jolly, more often demure) enters to hand you a hot towel to wipe your hands—a simple, civilized custom that's hard to live without, once you've been regularly spoiled.

A *kaiseki* meal is served in courses (from seven to twelve), each prepared in a different manner, using seasonally appropriate ingredients. The range of flavors, from sweet to sour, from salty to plain, is subtly planned so that each succeeding flavor complements the last. Only ingredients in the peak of season are used, and accents of seasonal color—a maple leaf in autumn or a sprig of plum blossoms in spring—inevitably appear. One particularly "Kyoto" touch is that only the lightest seasoning is used. Kyoto restaurateurs believe that the natural flavor of the finest ingredients available speaks for itself.

A typical course might include appetizers (*zensai*), raw fish (*otsukuri*), a seafood and vegetable "salad" (*aemono*), one or more soups (*suimono* or *shirumono*), simmered foods (*nimono*), steamed dishes (*mushimono*), broiled or grilled foods (*yakimono*), deep-fried tidbits (*agemono*), vinegared "salad" (*sunomono*), rice (*gohan*), pickles (*tsukemono*), and perhaps a bowl of fruit for dessert. The combinations are endless and left up to the discretion of the chef, though a very formal order of dishes and ingredients appears in the case of *cha-kaiseki*, which is the meal that accompanies a tea ceremony.

Cha-kaiseki is actually a concept all its own. The word *kaiseki* in this case is written with characters that mean "a stone in the folds of a kimono" and refers to an old Zen practice of sending priests to bed with nothing but a hot stone tucked into their kimonos to keep their bellies warm. A *cha-kaiseki* meal served in "artful proportions" is intended to be just enough to do the same, while complementing the flavor of thick green tea.

The *kaiseki* served in most restaurants is of the other variety, written with characters that mean "banquet." This style of *kaiseki* evolved from the saké parties at teahouses that were popular in the nineteenth century and often required the services of geisha.

Part of the magic of a *kaiseki* meal for the novice is having no idea what you are eating, much less what comes next. The possibilities are so vast that warlords and wealthy merchants of the Edo period (experts in the realm of the senses) even made a game of guessing which foods they had been presented during an evening's entertainment and drinking. A spirit of adventure is a prerequisite; the reward is a sensory experience you will not soon forget.

A *kaiseki* meal in one of Kyoto's finest *ryōtei* restaurants can be very expensive, though ¥20,000 is not thought to be exorbitant, considering the long hours involved in making such a wide variety of delicate dishes. In addition, the best of Kyoto's restaurants make it a rule never to serve a guest the same meal twice. The proprietress (often the owner's wife) takes careful note of each guest's likes and dislikes, catering to the guest's every whim and presenting a memorable meal every time.

One retired restaurant owner confessed that customers paying top prices for *kaiseki* cuisine are not merely being charged for the food. They are paying for the fine porcelain on which the meal is served and the treasured appointments (hanging scrolls by famous calligraphers and flower vases two centuries old) of the private room. The connoisseur of Kyoto cuisine looks forward with each visit to which priceless serving dish will appear that evening.

Much less expensive options do exist, and one marvelous alternative is the elaborate Kyoto box lunch (*Kyō-bentō*) served at many of the best places for a fraction of the cost. Usually served between 11 A.M. and 2 P.M., prices range from ¥3,000 to ¥10,000, providing you with an excellent sampler of the cuisine offered at each restaurant, though often (but not always) you must forgo the private room and the luxury of spending a minimum of two hours over a full-course *kaiseki* meal.

Although most people think only of *kaiseki* when they hear *Kyō-ryōri*, the essential elements of an old-fashioned Kyoto-style meal were simply salted fish and pickled vegetables. Living far from the nearest sea, the people of Kyoto found it necessary to invent a thousand ways of preparing both. For a "real" Kyoto meal in the old style, Hirano-ya in Maruyama Park comes closest to the essence of traditional local cuisine with its preserved fish and boiled potato meal (*imobō*). *Kyō-tsukemono*, the pickled vegetables served with rice, are famous throughout Japan and are one of the most popular souvenirs among visitors from other districts.

Shōjin ryōri, the vegetarian food served in Buddhist temples, also developed in Kyoto from its prototype, *fucha ryōri*, brought by priests from China. Both styles are still served and the best place to try them is in the temples themselves. Local specialties like *yuba* (skimmed soybean milk), *nama-fu* (a wheat gluten delicacy), and an assortment of tofu dishes are all a part of *shōjin ryōri*. These high-protein, low-calorie foods served in a variety of unusual dishes make vegetarian eating a pleasurable as well as healthy experience.

Though sushi and sukiyaki are popular in the West, many people hesitate to try the more exotic foods of Japan because of understandable misgivings about squid, fish roe, and sea urchin. Skipping a night at one of Kyoto's top *ryōtei* is like going to New York without trying the lox and bagels. I recommend swallowing it first and asking questions later. You'd be surprised how good a sea urchin can taste.

A Night in a Traditional Inn

A night in a traditional Japanese inn, or *ryokan*, is an experience not to be missed, no matter how much easier it may sound to seek refuge in one of the major hotels. A hotel is a hotel whether you are in St. Louis or St. Moritz, but a *ryokan* is a sample of traditional Japanese living at its finest.

Stone walkways lead off narrow side streets to one- or two-story tile-roofed inns in which hand-polished wooden corridors twist and turn past peaceful interior gardens to your room. Tatami mats, an alcove (*tokonoma*) in which a bamboo basket of fresh flowers was placed this morning in anticipation of your arrival, a hanging scroll (one that's been in the family for generations), a small lacquered writing box, and a closet full of thickly quilted futon bedding . . . a combination of small things surround you with comfort and the sense of being a true guest. Acclaimed internationally for their warm hospitality, fine service, and excellent cuisine, the traditional inns of Kyoto offer a chance to experience first-hand the amenities once reserved for noblemen and feudal lords.

For this singular pleasure, however, there are certain minor difficulties that must first be surmounted, and this is where the real cultural adventure begins.

There's the one about the American who walked into his immaculate tatami-mat room at the *ryokan* to find the maid, who had just arrived with a fresh pot of tea, staring down at his feet in horror. After what seemed an eternity of shocked silence, the man asked himself if perhaps she had never seen foreign toes before. Then suddenly, much to his chagrin, came the stark realization that he was still wearing the toilet slippers! Stories like these have kept Japanese in stitches (and Westerners in the Holiday Inn) for years. There are a few classic intricacies to "*ryokan* life" that once unfolded could put an end to an entire school of contemporary Japanese humor. Let's give it a try:

1. *Take off your shoes and relax.* If you spend any amount of time at all in Japan, this becomes a way of life. Shoes are considered dirty and should always be left at the door. This seems reasonable enough—until you carry the principle to the matter of slippers.

2. *Slippers fall into two basic categories: corridor slippers and toilet slippers . . . and never the twain shall meet.* When you take off your shoes in the entryway to a traditional home, restaurant, or inn, you will be given a pair of slippers to walk down the wooden corridor to your room. Take them off before you walk on tatami. Stockinged feet are preferable to bare feet in Japan, but even bare feet are better than slippers on tatami. Put your slippers on when you leave your room to shuffle down the corridor to the toilet, take them off, and step into the wooden slippers you'll find inside the restroom door. The catch is to remember to reverse the process on your way back to your room.

3. *Take a bath before you take a bath.* In other words, bathtubs in Japan are for soaking, not for washing, which is done seated on a little stool before you get in. Soap up, rinse off, and then step into the tub, which is usually torrid enough to make you think that someone has mistakenly left the hot water running. (This is a carry-over from the days when a two-story Japanese home was heated by a single charcoal hibachi and the heat you absorbed from the bath was intended to keep you warm long enough to get inside your futon and go to sleep before frostbite set in. Modern gas heaters are taken for granted in many homes today, but lots of old customs have yet to be replaced.)

4. *Don't let the term "communal bath" frighten you.* Though there is generally only one bath in each *ryokan*, it doesn't mean that everyone jumps in at once. There is usually one for men and one for women, or a time for women to use the bath and a time for men. Many *ryokan* call guests to the bath one family at a time so you have all the privacy you like. A few of the most expensive inns have installed private baths in some of the rooms to accommodate their more modest guests, but there is a fine custom in Japan called *hadaka no tsukiai*, or naked friendship, which refers to the great ice-breaking effect of taking a bath with a roomful of strangers. You meet the nicest people and have the opportunity of starting a new friendship with no secrets.

5. There really aren't any more rules to remember, but four is an unlucky number in Japan, so I've added one more suggestion to round things off. You usually pay by the person at a *ryokan*, rather than by the room. At a moderately priced inn you'll pay up to ¥15,000 each, but this includes breakfast and dinner.

Nowadays, many of the old inns do permit guests to stay overnight without meals (*shokuji nashi*), which often brings the price down to less than ¥5,000 per person. When in doubt ask the Kyoto Tourist Information office (see Getting Around) to call for you. They will check prices, service charges and whether or not you can stay without meals. It is, however, true that many of the finest inns in Kyoto are noted for their excellent cuisine, and passing up a chance to sample it (served decadently in your own room) can be a definite loss when you consider that comparable meals elsewhere in town often end up costing you more.

None of this matters in the least when you wake up in the morning, snuggled inside a thick futon, to watch the snow fall in the garden just outside your room. In a few moments, the maid will arrive with the breakfast tray, bowing politely as she begs your pardon for disturbing an elegant night's sleep.

Machiya, the Bedrooms of Eels

Local people call the old wooden row houses of Kyoto *unagi no nedoko*, the bedrooms of eels. Casting no aspersions on the character of residents, the dubious nickname given the long, narrow dwellings (often less than thirty feet wide and up to ten times as long) is certainly a title well-earned. The *machiya*, or city houses, as they are formally called, have been the homes and workplaces of the townspeople of Kyoto for hundreds of years, and as such they reveal much about the nature of this city.

The *machiya* that remain intact in Kyoto today are monuments to a complicated system of cooperation and interdependence between the people of the miniature townships they formed. These neighborhoods were made up of orderly blocks of forty family units each and were called *chō* (the same character that reads *machi*). The *chō* were formed originally between members of a particular craft—weavers, dyers, lacquerers, and so on—or grew up near the gates of the city's many temples and shrines, among groups of innkeepers who housed the throngs of pilgrims that arrived to worship each year, or among candle and incense makers, for example, whose products were required there.

Each *machiya* is but one part of an overall community whole, both socially and physically. Neighboring dwellings are grouped into a five-family cooperative unit that is called a *gonin-gumi*. About eight of these units make up a whole *chō*, which then relates to the nearest local shrine, whose activities it supports. The local shrine is not only a religious center, but a social gathering place at which regular festivals and ceremonies are held, bringing the whole neighborhood together several times a year.

Before the ground is broken for construction of a new house in the neighborhood, a priest from the shrine must conduct a ceremony on the site to appease the spirit of the land, who just might resent another intrusion. These ceremonies are observed today, in the building of a five-story bank or a small private residence.

Geomancy, a determining factor in former days in deciding things such as the proper orientation of entrances, ovens, and even toilets, is still in use today in Kyoto, though not as widely practiced as in the past. Many people still consult priests or seers in choosing the most auspicious location and orientation for their new homes.

Historically, the *chō* were formed in self-defense against the constantly warring political factions that periodically left the city in ruin during the Middle Ages. Remnants of moats that were built originally by residents to defend their *chō* can still be found in some of the old neighborhoods. An even more formidable enemy of the wooden *machiya* and its inhabitants was that of fire; a thousand years of Kyoto history reads like a list of regularly scheduled conflagrations; the last major fire of the eighteenth century destroyed nearly eighty percent of the city. In fact, virtually no examples of *machiya* remain in downtown Kyoto that are more than 120 years old, since a fire that started during the struggle to restore the emperor to power swept through the matchstick wooden row houses again in 1864. Through repeated destruction and rebuilding, the bonds among the townspeople and merchants grew stronger. The communities that were formed as a result each had their own special customs, rules, and architectural features that symbolized the unity within each neighborhood.

The architectural style of a particular *chō* was determined by the requirements of the group's trade and its proximity to a shrine or temple. With harmony as the keynote, similarities within a township were demonstrated in a unified style of elements like the type of roof tiles, the depth of the eaves, and even the pattern and number of slats in the window grates. It was considered a breach of propriety to flaunt one's personal wealth by outdoing the neighbors in the adornment of a façade, so the prosperous merchant displayed his success with lavish touches to the interior such as hand-carved transoms, lacquered trims, or the use of elaborately decorated paper on sliding paper doors (*fusuma*).

But tact and good taste were not the only considerations that determined the restrained visage of the homes of Kyoto's merchants. Strictly enforced edicts were handed down by the shogunate during the Edo period (1603–1868) forbidding any extravagant displays in the merchants' houses, inside or out, in an attempt to keep the rising merchant class in their place at the lower end of the class system. For example, no merchant was allowed to build a house over two stories high.

Nonetheless, by the middle of the Edo period, the merchants had achieved a powerful enough position financially to manifest their individual tastes, regardless of the shogunate and its ludicrous edicts.

Every *machiya* is essentially constructed on one basic unit of measure—a single tatami mat—roughly three by six feet. Rooms are measured by the number of mats they contain, which then determines the width and length of every house. This uniform system of measurement, by which not only elements within an individual house but in the neighborhood and city as a whole are determined, makes the *machiya* unique in the world of architecture.

The façade of a typical *machiya* in Kyoto (although styles differ from neighborhood to neighborhood) has certain design features that are interesting to note. Many houses have curved bamboo covers over the gutter in front. This is called an *inu-yarai*, which literally means a dog barrier, though it was used as a sort of buffer to keep all kinds of pests (even the two-legged kind) and street traffic at a distance since *machiya* were built right on the edge of the road. Some of the houses still have a *komayose*, the now decorative wooden railing that was used originally as a hitching post.

The heavy, somber façade of a typical kimono merchant's house, for example, often seems aloof at first as you approach from the street. The dark, slatted windows called *kōshi-mado* were a means of creating privacy amid the hustle and bustle of city life that went on outside just inches away. Originally, the front windows of merchant dwellings opened up to reveal the *misenoma*, or shop room.

Mushiko-mado, literally "insect cage window," is another characteristic of Kyoto city houses and refers to the porthole-type windows cut out of the walls

Machiya, exterior view

of buildings in which the second-floor façades were made of clay. Oblong or rectangular in shape, these windows have thick vertical clay bars and appear to be used for ventilation. Appearances being very important in Kyoto, the *mushiko-mado* were actually used as hidden vantage points from which the merchants could observe the goings-on in the neighborhood without being seen by passers-by in the streets below. Strict rules of deportment enforced by the Tokugawa shogunate during the Edo period forbade members of the lower class ever to have their heads above those of their superiors. The *mushiko-mado* enabled merchants to "look down" on the snooty samurai, without being arrested for impudence.

Customers entered via the sliding door in front and stepped into the *tōri-niwa*, a stone walkway that led back through the kitchen all the way to the interior of the house. A *noren* curtain hanging in place over the entry would indicate that the shop was open for business, a custom which remains today. Another curtain, often a *nawa-noren*, or rope curtain, separated the kitchen from the shopfront. Stepping up from the *tōri-niwa* to the raised shop room, customers sat down on tatami to discuss business with the proprietor over a cup of green tea.

Except for the *tōri-niwa*, which often had a plain dirt floor, all the rooms of the house were raised about two feet above ground level to provide adequate ventilation during Kyoto's humid summers: there is nothing worse than a moldy tatami mat. Every *machiya* in Kyoto is designed with the idea of keeping cool in the summer. Though the winters are cold, it is easier to bundle up than to

Machiya, interior view

survive the hot and humid months. The use of woven tatami mats as flooring material throughout is said to allow the floor to "breathe." The sliding paper doors which act as room dividers are replaced with reed screens during the summer to help ventilation, or can be removed completely, creating as much of a breeze as possible. The rooms of *machiya* are lined up in a row, one behind the other, parallel to the *tōri-niwa*, creating the famous "eel" effect. The ancient division of the city into a tidy grid pattern determined the long, narrow subdivision of lots within each city block, as did the fact that taxes were once levied based on the amount of street frontage each dwelling had.

Unlike the more spacious *yashiki* homes of the privileged samurai, where a garden separated the entrance from the street, *machiya* gardens were a private, limited space located deep in the interior—always a refreshing surprise. Here the master of the house could create a little piece of paradise all his own.

Guests, parting the *noren* curtain to wait in the *genkan* (a welcoming room where visitors were officially greeted), waited for the invitation to literally "come up" into the house proper with the words *o-agari kudasai*.

The quieter recesses of the house are a startling contrast to the business world of the shop quarters. The homes of prosperous merchants often had more than one interior garden, one of which acted as a divider between the shop room and the living quarters in the back. Polished wood verandas run along the edges of these interior gardens, linking inside and out. The deep eaves make this a fine location for contemplating the harvest moon in comfort, protected from the possibility of an unexpected evening shower.

To the left of the little garden is the *zashiki*. This is the heart of the house. The *zashiki* is used as a room for entertaining guests, though the function of rooms in a *machiya* can change instantly with the addition or subtraction of the easily removable *fusuma* doors that take the place of walls. This makes for the flexible environment that was necessary in houses in which there were often only two rooms for every possible family function.

The *zashiki* is the most elegantly designed room in the house. Facing the main garden, the *okuniwa*, this room more than any other shows the influence of the tea ceremony on *machiya*. Just like the traditional tearoom, the *zashiki* has a *tokonoma*, the recessed niche of honor where a single scroll painting and one small ceramic vase are the only embellishments. They sit quietly in the shadows of which novelist Junichirō Tanizaki once wrote so fondly: "The quality we call beauty must always grow from the realities of life, and our ancestors, forced to live in dark rooms, presently came to discover the beauty in shadows, ultimately to guide shadows to beauty's end. And so it has come to be that the beauty of a Japanese room depends on a variation of shadows, heavy shadows against light shadows . . . it has nothing else. Westerners are amazed at the simplicity of Japanese rooms, perceiving in them no more than ashen walls bereft of ornament. Their reaction is understandable, but it betrays a failure to comprehend the mystery of shadows." (A failure, I might add, that is shared by most modern Japanese as well.)

Beyond the gracious refinement of the *zashiki*, the most impressive room is, surprisingly, the kitchen. Built to one side of the stone-floored *tōri-niwa*, the ceiling of this room stretches high above, leaving the massive curved beams that support the heavy tile roof exposed to view. Light streams down through the skylights overhead. An old well, no longer in use, sits in one corner and a large clay oven, the *kamado*, with its giant iron cauldrons, squats in the other. Near the oven is one of the very special features of the *machiya*, the one that has to do with "soul." No *machiya* kitchen would be without a tiny shrine to the god of fire. The roots of ancient Japanese culture are founded in a deeply spiritual, highly superstitious tradition of paying respect to the *kami*, or gods, who protect everything from ovens to rice fields. Not to be meddled with even today, the *kami* are sure to receive their daily due of flowers and votive candles, just to be safe.

In old Kyoto, there were no automatic dishwashers, no electric toasters, no microwave ovens . . . just simple two-burner stoves, and tiled sinks. Not even a refrigerator disturbed the old order, when the lady of the house went out each morning to the local market street to buy just enough food to last the day. Dry goods and housewares were kept in the long wooden cabinet called a *mizuya* that lined one wall of every kitchen. Pickling, salting, and drying were the only means of food preservation available to housewives in the days before the refrigerator became a standard household appliance after the Tokyo Olympics in 1964.

Behind the main garden at the back of the property of most merchants was the *kura*, or storehouse. The thick walls and heavy doors provided a place to keep the family treasures safe from fires and thieves. Many merchants used their *kura* as warehouses to store goods for sale, since the small shop room in front usually provided only enough space to display samples and conduct business.

Many of the old shops in this book were chosen not just for the fine traditional products they sell, but for the beauty of the *machiya* that house them. Although the government, both on national and local levels, has made some effort to preserve the few isolated *machiya* that have been maintained in original condition, every day they fall under the bulldozers of progress in Kyoto. Most of the shopkeepers who have maintained their old shops have done so at their own expense, and it is due largely to them that bits and pieces of old Kyoto are still around for us to enjoy.

A Few Helpful Notes

Closing Time

Punctuality is a blessing and a hindrance in Japan. Trains are unfailingly reliable. It takes something nearly catastrophic to stop them, and an earthquake or flood will often only result in a short delay. Shops too, and most particularly restaurants, are conscious of the clock. Though shopkeepers may stretch to accommodate a last-minute customer, restaurants follow a strict regime, and the posted closing time refers to the hour in which the shop locks its doors for the night, with all customers on the outside.

So if you wish to linger over your meal, allow yourself ample time by arriving several hours before closing. Because the cleaning up procedures are time-consuming, kitchens frequently shut down thirty to sixty minutes prior to closing. You will be asked if you have any "last order," which, depending on the establishment, may also include alcoholic beverages. If you are still seated as the evening draws to a close, your waiter or waitress will most likely whisk away your bill to tally it up. Sometimes done as early as thirty minutes before closing, this standard procedure is meant as a gentle reminder. An eye to the other clientele will suffice as a guideline to the uninitiated.

The Price You Pay

The prices at restaurants and hotels increase with the times. Rather than quoting individual prices of the moment, the approximate price per person at each establishment is indicated as follows:

- RESTAURANTS

¥	inexpensive	less than ¥3,000
¥¥	moderate	¥3,000–¥6,000
¥¥¥	expensive	¥6,000–¥12,000
¥¥¥¥	very expensive	over ¥12,000

- ACCOMMODATIONS (per person per night; often includes two meals)

¥	inexpensive	less than ¥5,000
¥¥	moderate	¥5,000–¥15,000
¥¥¥	expensive	¥15,000–¥25,000
¥¥¥¥	very expensive	over ¥25,000

The majority of shops in the book are *shinise* (old shops that have been in the same family for a hundred years and three generations), and their prices reflect the high quality and impeccable service that reflect the status of "purveyors to the imperial court" which many of them held in days gone by. Hence, most Kyoto shopkeepers do not barter. The price you are quoted is the price. Period. Attempts to negotiate can result in an icy glare and a loss of goodwill.

Credit was never a custom in traditional Kyoto, where the townspeople are still notoriously frugal and cautious with strangers. While changing financial customs on the international scene have made the credit card ubiquitous throughout Japan, do not be surprised if some establishments accept payment only in cash. Likewise, some places will frown upon cashing traveler's checks. Prepare for this by inquiring through the concierge at your hotel and taking the requisite cash. Always check before you enter for the logos of major card companies prominently displayed outside places that accept them.

ATMs which accept foreign credit cards are few and far between at the time of this writing. Machines where international credit cards can be used and which have English instructions are located in Kyoto Central Post Office in front of Kyoto Station (open from 0:05 to 23:55 on weekdays and Saturdays, and from 0:05 to 20:00 on Sundays and holidays), and on the basement floor of Kyoto Tower (open daily from 10:00 to 21:00).

A Crash Course in Suffixes

Though a working grasp of a foreign language is not feasible for a short stay, a quick lesson in the common suffixes that sprinkle the tourist literature of Kyoto will go a long way in helping you navigate. Helpful suffixes include the following:

SUFFIX	ENGLISH	EXAMPLE
-dōri	street	Gojō-dōri
-ku	ward	Higashiyama-ku
-kawa/-gawa	river	Kamogawa

As any first-time visitor soon discovers, Kyoto abounds with temples and shrines. At times it seems there is one around every corner and down every alley. Attention to the suffixes will allow you to decipher what stands before you.

-tera/-dera	temple	Kiyomizu-dera
-ji	temple	Daitoku-ji
-jinja	Shinto shrine	Yasaka-jinja

RAKU-CHŪ

Central Kyoto

As the heart of the old capital city, Raku-chū is still the busiest, most densely populated area in Kyoto. Most of the shops for which the city is famous, both old and new, are here in a broad area that runs from Kita-ōji in the north to just below Kyoto Station in the south, and from Nishi-ōji in the west to the Kamogawa River in the east. This is roughly the district that the emperor Kanmu branded with a grid pattern of streets that has existed since 794. The Imperial Palace was located in the center of that grid until the eleventh century, when it was moved a few blocks east, where it remains today.

With the Imperial Palace as the center of both politics and commerce, the area around it was inhabited by aristocrats and religious leaders, as well as by the merchants and craftsmen who were kunai-chō-goyōtashi—official purveyors to the imperial household, an honor some of the shops in this book still proudly boast of today.

The Nishijin textile district is located in the northwestern part of Raku-chū. Downtown, near Kawaramachi-Shijō, you'll find Pontochō, the geisha quarter; Nishiki, the city's oldest market street, and Teramachi, a Buddhist temple district, part of which now lies hidden, along with a sprinkling of wonderful old booksellers, antique dealers, restaurants and traditional shops, in the midst of a modern shopping arcade.

With the contrast (and sometimes conflict) between old and new, Raku-chū is the heart of Kyoto—bustling, vibrant, and eclectic. Exploring the old shops that nestle here and there along its backstreets could keep you busy for years.

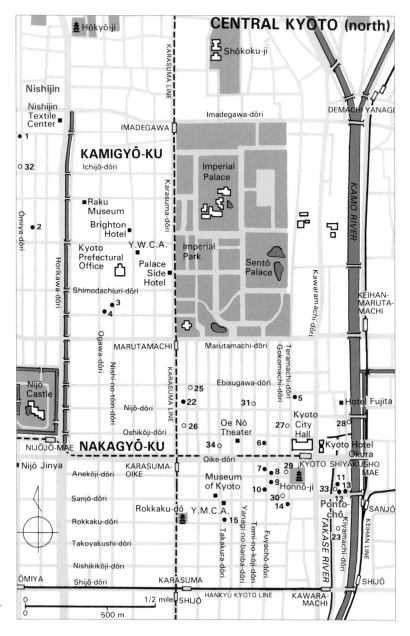

CENTRAL KYOTO (north)

Hōkyō-ji

Shōkoku-ji

DEMACHI YANAGI

Nishijin

Nishijin Textile Center ■
● 1

IMADEGAWA

Imadegawa-dōri

KAMIGYŌ-KU

Ichijō-dōri

○ 32

■ Raku Museum

■ Brighton Hotel

Kyoto Prefectural Office

Y.W.C.A. ■

Imperial Palace

Imperial Park

Sentō Palace

KEIHAN-MARUTA-MACHI

● 2

Palace Side Hotel ■

Shimodachiuri-dōri

● 3
● 4

MARUTAMACHI

Marutamachi-dōri

Nijō Castle

○ 25
● 22

Ebisugawa-dōri

31 ○

● 5

■ Hotel Fujita

26 ○

Nijō-dōri

Oshikōji-dōri

Oe Nō Theater

27 ○

Kyoto City Hall

28 ○

Kyoto Hotel Okura

NIJŌJŌ-MAE

NAKAGYŌ-KU

34 ○

6 ●

Oike-dōri

■ Nijō Jinya

Anekōji-dōri

KARASUMA-OIKE

Museum of Kyoto

7 ●
8 ●
9 ●
10 ●

30 ○
14 ●

29 ●

Honnō-ji

KYOTO SHIYAKUSHO MAE

11 ●
13 ●
12 ●

33 ○

Sanjō-dōri

SANJŌ

Rokkaku-dō

Y.M.C.A.

● 15

Ponto-chō

23 ○

Rokkaku-dōri

Takoyakushi-dōri

Nishikikōji-dōri

ŌMIYA

Shijō-dōri

KARASUMA

SHIJŌ

0 —— 1/2 mile
0 —— 500 m

HANKYŪ KYOTO LINE

SHIJŌ

KAWARA-MACHI

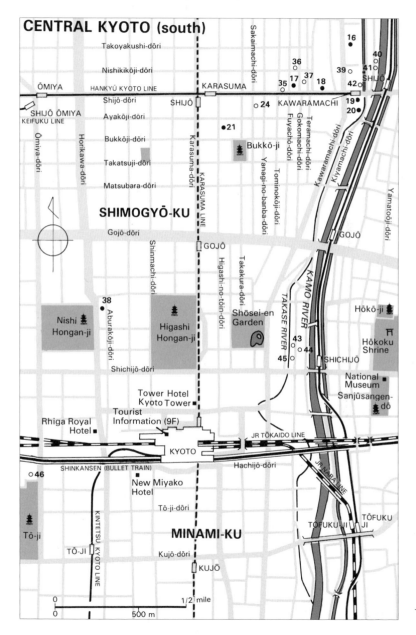

CENTRAL KYOTO (south)

Takoyakushi-dōri

Nishikikōji-dōri

ŌMIYA HANKYŪ KYOTO LINE KARASUMA

SHIJŌ ŌMIYA
KEIFUKU LINE

Shijō-dōri SHIJŌ

Ayakōji-dōri

Bukkōji-dōri

Takatsuji-dōri

Matsubara-dōri

Sakaimachi-dōri

16

36
17 37
35 18

39
40
41
SHIJŌ
42

●24 KAWARAMACHI
19
20

●21

Bukkō-ji

SHIMOGYŌ-KU

Gojō-dōri

GOJŌ

GOJŌ

38
Nishi
Hongan-ji

Aburakōji-dōri

Higashi
Hongan-ji

Shōsei-en
Garden

Hōkō-ji

Hōkoku
Shrine

43
44

45 SHICHIJŌ

Shichijō-dōri

National
Museum
Sanjūsangen-
dō

Tower Hotel
Kyoto Tower
Tourist
Information (9F)

Rhiga Royal
Hotel

JR TŌKAIDO LINE

KYOTO

SHINKANSEN (BULLET TRAIN)

Hachijō-dōri

○46

New Miyako
Hotel

Tō-ji-dōri

MINAMI-KU

Tō-ji

TŌ-JI

Kujō-dōri

KUJŌ

TŌFUKU-JI TŌFUKU
JI

0   1/2 mile
0   500 m

AIZEN KŌBŌ
indigo textiles

愛染工房

Ōmiya Nishi-iru, Nakasuji-dōri, Kamigyō-ku

上京区中筋通大宮西入 TEL: (075) 441–0355 (English spoken) FAX: (075) 414–0355

OPEN: Daily, 10 A.M.–5:30 P.M. (Saturdays and Sundays phone first)

Down a narrow backstreet in Nishijin, the heart of the textile district in Kyoto, is Aizen Kōbō, the house of an old kimono-sash (*obi*) weaving family established over a century ago. Today they specialize in indigo dyeing, or *aizome*, a traditional folk technique most often found in remote areas of the Japanese countryside.

A century ago, the Utsuki family were masters of *tsuzure-ori*, the tedious fingernail weaving technique that produces the complicated relief brocade patterns seen in the finest Kyoto-style *obi*, often laced with threads of silver and gold. With the introduction of the jacquard loom and the decline in popularity of kimono and *obi* for everyday wear, there was less call for the costly *tsuzure-ori obi* and the Utsuki family was faced with a dilemma that has become a fact of life for traditional craftsmen all over Japan.

It was then that the late Shōzō Utsuki had the good fortune to join up with members of the Mingei (Folk Art) Movement in Kyoto. Kanjirō Kawai, renowned potter and one of the leaders of the group, persuaded Shōzō to learn the old

folk ways of indigo dyeing and *sashiko* embroidery, crafts that were then considered lowbrow and seemed destined to become extinct. Few Japanese appreciated folk crafts in the 1920s and 1930s when the deluge of manufactured goods from the West caused them to turn their backs on crafts they saw as crude or outmoded. Kawai saw that the beauty of natural indigo dye and the quality of simple handwoven, handmade garments would one day again come into its own. Fortunately, Shōzō agreed and began to change the complex production methods of his large *obi* business to the simple folk-methods of weaving cotton and linen using only 100 percent natural dyes.

Though indigo dying has now seen a renaissance in Japan, at the time Utsuki-san took this step it was nothing short of revolutionary in the tradition-bound Nishijin district of Kyoto. Shōzō Utsuki was succeeded by his son Kenichi, who with his wife Hisako, carries on his father's work and takes it in ever-new directions. Today his shop is one of the only places in Kyoto where handwoven, hand-dyed, and hand-embroidered garments of *hon-ai*, or "real" indigo, are available.

One of the most popular garments made at Aizen Kōbō is still the traditional *samu-e*, a loose-fitting, two-piece garment worn by Zen priests and local craftsmen. Dyed with *hon-ai*, they look and feel better after five years of regular wear than they do the day you first put them on. The color fades gracefully and the durable fabric becomes softer and softer.

Aizen Kōbō makes not only fine *samu-e*, but also *happi* coats (workmen's jackets), *monpe* (farmwomen's pants), and a newer line of Western-style clothes designed by Hisako-san. Skeins of natural-dyed threads are available, as are a number of accessory items, such as handbags and coin purses, at reasonable prices. The best *samu-e* woven with the finest cotton fiber and dyed with natural indigo come in all sizes (even extra-large). Although the price is higher than the machine-made variety, considering the beauty of natural indigo dye (and dividing the price by the number of years the handmade garment will last) it is still a bargain. The Utsukis say

that most of the indigo-blue colored fabrics you find today in department stores and boutiques in Japan are produced from synthetic indigo dyes. He recommends letting your nose find the *hon-ai*, which has a very pungent smell before it has been washed.

The much photographed building that houses Aizen Kōbō was built in the Meiji period. It is one of a few *machiya* in the Nishijin district that has been carefully restored, and it has been officially recognized as a Cultural Asset by the Kyoto prefectural government.

Many of the beautiful doorway curtains (*noren*) you see hanging outside traditional Kyoto shops were made at Aizen Kōbō. They also have a selection of antique textiles, including several dyed coverlets (*tsutsugaki*) once used to cover wedding chests for delivery to the bride's new home, decorated in colorful turtle and crane patterns that are traditional symbols of good luck. Two decades ago, Aizen Kōbō's resident weaver, Hiroshi Matsuguchi, was among those who began a revival of the *tsutsugaki* resist paste dyeing technique, a folk tradition that had nearly died out in Japan. *Ramii*, a rare linen-like fiber that becomes feather soft with use, is also woven here and is available by the meter.

It is now a rare pleasure to hear the once familiar *katan-koton* sound of Nishijin brocade looms—most of which have now fallen silent. In an age when the kimono and *obi* are no longer garments for everyday wear, Aizen Kōbō is one of the few Nishijin weavers that has found a "new" old medium in which to survive the transition to modern times.

SHIOYOSHI-KEN
Kyoto confectionery

Nakadachi-uri-agaru, Kuromon-dōri, Kamigyō-ku
上京区黒門通中立売上ル　TEL: (075) 441–0803　FAX: (075) 451–2008

OPEN: 9 A.M.–6 P.M. ■ CLOSED: Every third Wednesday

In the fall of 1587, the great feudal lord Toyotomi Hideyoshi pulled his gilded boats into port at Yodo to begin his grand procession northward to his residence at Juraku-dai, the "Palace of Gathered Pleasures" which legions of workers had built for him atop, significantly, the ruins of the old Imperial Palace. The luxurious gardens of the walled palace were filled with plants requisitioned from the gardens of the local citizenry. The doors of its gates were of solid copper, and the pattern of its tiles brought to mind "jewelled tigers breathing in the wind, and golden dragons intoning in the clouds." Hideyoshi had outdone his own reputation as an extravagant showman with Juraku-dai.

Juraku-dai was destroyed in a succession squabble just ten short years later, but Shioyoshi-ken has captured for posterity the legendary palace that once dominated this district in its sweet bean cakes, dubbing them "*Juraku manjū*." Each bun is branded with "Tenchō," the name of the era in which the palace was constructed, and is individually wrapped in handmade paper that bears Hideyoshi's family crest, the five-pointed paulownia leaf.

Kyoto confectionery, or *Kyō-gashi*, is known not only for its delicate flavor and imaginative seasonal shapes and colors, but also for the poetic names contrived for each variety. These often allude to legendary characters, events, or places in Japanese history, or to quotations from memorable passages in Japanese literature. As sweets are an important part of the tea ceremony, recognition of the particular allusion in the name of the confection offered at a tea gathering adds to the pleasure of appreciating the theme that the host wishes to convey. The history of the tea served, the scene depicted for the arrangement in the *tokonoma* alcove—all relate to the subject of the hanging scroll which gives the guests a hint as to their host's unstated scheme. The more obscure the relationships between the "clues," the more delighted the guest feels for having discovered it.

It is the business of Shioyoshi-ken to indulge the fantasies and tastes of Kyoto's tea masters, a task they have

spent a good hundred years refining. Another of their sweets, a *hi-gashi*, or dry sweet, has been named after the beautiful Princess Kōgō, an imperial concubine who was banished from the palace when the emperor tired of her. She lived out her days in sorrow in a nunnery in Arashiyama. The real key to the allusion contained in the name of the confection is the tiny bit of salty Daitoku-ji *nattō* hidden in the center—the irony of love, the inevitable shock of finding a teardrop at the heart of an experience so sweet.

Shioyoshi-ken is noted for the wide variety of confectionery it offers. There is the hard ribbon candy called *aruheitō* made from an old Portuguese recipe, and *yōkan*, a jellied sweet–bean paste wrapped in sheaths of dried bamboo leaves. In addition to these, Shioyoshi-ken has a selection of *nama-gashi*, the soft, uncooked sweets, jellies, pastes and doughs whose form and flavor are designed to match the season. The owners pride themselves on using only the best available ingredients, including a specially hand-processed sugar called *wasanbon* made at an ancient refinery on Shikoku Island in the Inland Sea. The old-fashioned process by which the cane sugar is refined produces a delicate powdery white sugar that melts in your mouth.

Sweetness aside, the other quality for which Shioyoshi-ken is known is the beauty of their Taishō-period building. The traditional *machiya-zukuri*, or townhouse construction, of Shioyoshi-ken has the shop (with family living quarters and interior garden in the rear) on the right side and the kitchens on the left. The *mushiko-mado* windows on the second floor overlook a large wrought-iron gas lantern typical of Kyoto shops that date from the Meiji or Taishō period.

The large six-paneled *noren* curtain gives the shop's name and also lists its most famous products.

Be sure to examine the floral arrangement inside the glass case that lines the wall on the left. Camellias, peonies, plum blossoms, maple leaves, and even wisteria are fashioned out of sugar by Takaya-san, a master of *kōgei-gashi*, the shaping of elaborate floral designs from confectionery, one of Kyoto's most esoteric art forms.

FŪKA
wheat gluten

Sawaragi-chō-agaru, Nishi-no-tōin-dōri, Kamigyō-ku
上京区西洞院通椹木町上ル   TEL: (075) 231–1584   FAX: (075) 231–3625
OPEN: 9 A.M.–5 P.M. ■ CLOSED: Mondays

Leave it to the people of Kyoto to take a food as simple as *fu*, the wheat gluten product which once provided Zen monks in China with needed protein in their vegetarian diets, and turn it into a dainty sweet to be served with ceremonial tea or used as a decorative touch in Kyoto cuisine, a different color and shape for every season: pink cherry blossom *fu* in spring, bright purple eggplant *fu* in summer, red and yellow maple leaf *fu* in autumn, and festive New Year's ornament shapes for January 1. Although an accurate translation, "wheat gluten" hardly seems adequate in describing the fanciful Kyoto specialty known as *fu*.

Fūka, just west of the Imperial Palace grounds, has been making *fu* for 130 years. Shōji Kobori, the present owner, is the sixth-generation master of a shop once designated as an official purveyor to the imperial household.

Fūka is famous for its *nama-fu*, the chewy variety made of half gluten and half *mochi* rice flour, which is most frequently used in the making of confections. *Sasamaki-fu* is one variety of *nama-fu*, filled with sweet bean paste and beautifully wrapped in bamboo leaves to be served with green tea. *Nama-fu* is used in soups and sauces, in special shapes and colors that evoke the seasons.

Rikyū-fu, named after the tea master Sen no Rikyū, is a variety of regular *fu* that is boiled in a spicy broth and then deep-fried. It can be sliced and served cold as an appetizer with saké or beer. Sen no Rikyū was the tea master who popularized both *fu* and *nama-fu* for use in the tea ceremony in the sixteenth century. During the Edo period (1603–1868) *fu* and *nama-fu* became so popular that an entire street in downtown Kyoto still bears the name Fuyachō-dōri, after the many *fu* shops that once lined it. Today, only a few shops that specialize in this little-known treat remain in Kyoto.

The traditional method of making *fu* is both quintessentially simple and backbreakingly hard work. A plain wheat dough is made of flour and water, and kneaded for two long hours. Next the dough is placed under water and kneaded again until it separates into its two basic elements, starch and gluten. The gluten is removed and allowed to rest for several hours.

Nama-fu is made from a combination of this gluten and *mochi* rice flour that is not allowed to rise, giving it a smooth, chewy consistency suitable for forming into different shapes. Traditional flavorings for *nama-fu* include herbs or seaweed, and today Kobori-san and his staff experiment with such ingredients as pumpkin or even bacon, to the applause of many dyed-in-the-wool traditional connoisseurs. Filled with sweet bean paste, *nama-fu* becomes a confectionery unlike any to be found in the West.

Only enough *nama-fu* is made each day at Fūka to fill the orders of the tea masters and restaurateurs who are their regular customers, so it is best to place your order a day ahead of time. Sometimes there is just enough left to sell over the counter, but not always.

Like his predecessors, Shōji Kobori pays little attention to the fuss made over *shinise*, the name given to revered old Kyoto shops. The late Kōichi Kobori once said, "Too many places rely on an established name and use the *Kyō* pre-

fix on their products as if that were enough to ensure quality. My family has been making *fu* for many generations, and our shop has become famous for it. But good *fu* is now made in many places all over Japan. Saying 'Kyō-this' and 'Kyō-that' doesn't mean it's the best. I just try to make the finest product I can . . . people who like *fu* can be the final judge."

IRIYAMA TŌFU
tofu

入
山
豆
腐

Abura-no-kōji-kado, Sawaragi-chō, Kamigyō-ku
上京区椹木町油小路角   TEL: (075) 241–2339

OPEN: 10 A.M. until sold out ■ CLOSED: Sundays

Mame de   Made of beans
Shikaku de   Squarely cut
Yawarakaku te   And soft.

When the priest Ingen wrote this poem in 1661, he was not only praising the qualities of good tofu, but implying something about the human spirit. *Mame* means both beans and diligence, *shikaku* means honest (or square); and *yawarakai* means soft or gentle—a desirable combination, in bean curds and people.

Tofu is as much a part of the diet in Japan as cheese is in the West. High in protein and low in calories, this soybean product was first made in China over two thousand years ago. Tofu can be fried, simmered, grilled, and even eaten fresh, dipped in soy sauce and covered with diced green onions. Tofu is a simple food that absorbs and enhances the flavor of soups and broths, adding vital protein to the traditional Buddhist vegetarian diet. The most frequent dishes in which it can be found in modern-day Japan are miso soup, *yudōfu* (a one-pot simmered dish), *oden* (a stew-like dish with tofu and other specialties simmered in broth), and *hiya-yakko* (cold fresh tofu, popular in summer).

Few shops in modern Kyoto persist in the traditional methods of making tofu, but at Iriyama Tōfu (if you rise early enough in the morning) you can watch a ninth-generation tofu-maker whose ancestors made tofu for the imperial court in the early nineteenth century. Today the shop specializes in "cotton" tofu (*momen-goshi*), a more coarsely textured variety than "silk" tofu (*kinu-goshi*) that has become popular supermarket fare in recent years. Cotton tofu has the ring of farmhouses and home cooking that makes most fancy chefs in the pursuit of Kyoto-style elegance tend to turn up their noses, according to the unaffected Mrs. Iriyama. "We don't make pretty tofu here," she says, fanning the charcoal fire with one hand as she turns the skewered tofu with the other. An occasional charcoal cinder on the surface of Iriyama's grilled tofu (*yaki-dōfu*) just adds to the flavor. Unlike many of the tofu shops in Japan today, the Iriyamas use no chemical

additives to gel their tofu, preferring the use of refined *nigari* sea brine as a coagulant even if it is less predictable (especially in hot weather), for the subtle sweetness it imparts.

Two large vats of soybeans simmer over the old wood-burning cookstoves inside this 120-year-old building on the same site where the Iriyamas' ancestors cooked soybeans in the late Edo period. The sagging stone floors, old well, and crumbling clay ovens comfort each other in modern times when most other tofu-makers have turned to concrete and stainless steel. Mrs. Iriyama tells the story of the time when a delivery truck barreling down the narrow backstreet took out the west wall of the shop, plowing into the back of the old clay ovens in the process. It would have been easier to replace them with new gas-burning stoves, but the Iriyamas felt that the traditional stoves cooked a better-tasting batch of beans. Finding someone who still knew how to make an old cookstove was a task in itself (almost as difficult as it was to find a tofu shop like this one in an age when many Kyoto housewives buy tofu at the supermarket), but they did, and though they resemble giant anthills with a chimney, the "new" ovens crackle and shoot off sparks through the early morning hours at Iriyama Tōfu just as the old ones did.

Mr. Iriyama is somewhat of a history buff. Working here from dawn to dusk since he was a small boy, he had to give up any dreams of academia. Nonetheless, he has memorized the names of all the eras in the Edo period (more than fifty) and can recite the history of this neighborhood back to the great Nishijin Fire in 1730. Not far from the Imperial Palace, the neighborhood (formerly a guild of fishmongers) was the scene of constant battles between warring militant factions in their struggles for control of the capital. Iriyama-san tells of fierce samurai with flailing swords destroying wells and terrorizing the peasants two hundred years ago, as if he had been there himself. In the rafters at the back of his shop is a wooden pole about six feet long used by his great-great-grand-father over a hundred years ago to carry giant dangling buckets of tofu door-to-door on his rounds.

Cotton, or regular, tofu, deep-fried plain tofu (*o-age*), and deep-fried tofu mixed with sesame or chopped vegetables (*hirosu*) are available at Iriyama Tōfu year round. The grilled tofu made fresh daily from autumn through spring may have a coarser texture than that sold in local supermarkets, but the aroma of fresh soybean curd and the homemade old-fashioned flavor (not to mention the free history lesson) are well worth the wait for neighbors who bring their own containers and wait in line, sharing the latest local gossip, while Mrs. Iriyama and her husband grin and sweat and grill their delicious tofu.

IPPŌ-DŌ tea

Nijō-kita, Teramachi-dōri, Nakagyō-ku
中京区寺町通二条北 TEL: (075) 211–3421 (English spoken) FAX: (075) 241–0153
OPEN: 9 A.M.–7 P.M., Tearoom: 11 A.M.–5 P.M. ■ CLOSED: January 1–3 ■ CREDIT: Major cards

It is Ippō-dō's fault that everything on Teramachi-dōri within two blocks is permeated with the enticing aroma of freshly roasted tea leaves. In fact, Ippō-dō has been perfuming the neighborhood for 140 years with the finest green tea from Uji, the most famous tea producing region in Japan, just south of Kyoto.

Uji, where the round, carefully trimmed hedgerows of tea plants color the hills a vivid green, has the perfect climate for growing tea. Situated on the foggy banks of the Uji River, the misty air and rich soil give forth the best tea in the country—with the help of what Mr. Watanabe, the present owner of Ippō-dō, calls his secret ingredient—the addition of herring to the soil as a natural fertilizer.

Ippō-dō was once designated by the Imperial Household Agency as a purveyor to the imperial family (though such designations were officially discontinued after World War II).

Until the twentieth century, tea was a luxury in which only the upper classes indulged. Said to have been brought back from China by the Buddhist monk Eisai in 1191, tea gained prominence as a beverage among the samurai when Sen no Rikyū perfected the tea ceremony some four centuries later. For the next five hundred years it was drunk in its powdered form, called *matcha*. In the mid-eighteenth century the process for making *sencha*, the rolled-leaf type of green tea, was discovered. When a tea processing machine was introduced in the early 1920s, the common people were finally initiated to the formerly exclusive pleasures of green tea.

There are several different types of tea (*o-cha*) available at Ippō-dō: *matcha*, the powdered tea of the tea ceremony; *gyokuro*, a sweet, fragrant leaf tea using only the finest leaves at the top of the best plants; *sencha*, a leaf tea from the same plants as *gyokuro*, but with a sharper astringency (*sencha* is the type most often served to guests in Japan today); *bancha*, a coarser green leaf tea, the most common roasted variety; *hōji-cha*, a lightly roasted blend of *bancha* and *sencha*; *mugicha*, roasted with barley; and *Uji-shimizu*, a powder used for making iced green tea. Within each type of tea there are also many varieties and grades to be sampled. Over thirty varieties of *matcha* alone are available, with indications given as to which tea is preferred by which tea master. Watanabe-san says that fine tea should not be stored for more than two weeks and therefore recommends buying only forty-gram containers of *matcha* at a time. Many of Ippō-dō's foreign customers prefer the aromatic *hōjicha* or the delicate *gyokuro*.

Every year in May, the tea leaves are hand picked in Uji, and connoisseurs look forward to sampling the season's fresh *shincha*, or "new tea." In the seventeenth and eighteenth centuries, the Tokugawa shogunate halted all other traffic along the Tōkaidō Highway when the convoy bearing the annual shipment of *shincha* from Uji made its way to Edo.

The trademark fluttering shop curtains at Ippō-dō veil a remarkably unchanged interior lined with old tea jars along the north wall. The present building was constructed in 1864 after war had destroyed a large part of the city. The original shop, called Ōmiya, was established in 1717 and was located across the street. But in 1846, a nobleman who purchased tea there exhorted the shopkeeper to carry on his fine trade with the words "*Cha hitotsu o tamotsu yō ni*," or "Promise you'll never sell anything but fine tea." From that day forward the shop took the name Ippō-dō, using Chinese characters that mean "one promise."

Attentive clerks wait behind the old counter to steep a sample cup of whichever tea the customer would like to try, and then carefully measure out the requested amount. The airtight canisters with their turn-of-the century green and orange labels in which the leaf teas are sold are a treasure in themselves. A lovely tasting room now adjoins the original main shop room—an excellent place to sample teas before you buy.

O-cha has all the eye-opening, mind-clearing effects of coffee, without the strain on the stomach. The fresh astringent flavor and aroma of a cup of the finest tea from Ippō-dō may convert even the most inveterate coffee drinker to the fold of tea.

NOTE: Many of the shops along Teramachi-dōri near Ippō-dō specialize in both antique and new tea utensils. (Hōrai-dō, another tea shop on Teramachi about a block north of Shijō, offers a variety of ceramic bowls, teapots, whisks, and accessories, along with a selection of fine Uji teas. See Day Trips to the Countryside.)

YUBAHAN
yuba (soy milk "skin")

Oike-agaru, Fuya-chō-dōri, Nakagyō-ku
中京区麩屋町通御池上ル   TEL: (075) 221–5622   FAX: (075) 231–3625
OPEN: 8 A.M.–6 P.M. ■ CLOSED: Thursdays

One brisk autumn morning, not long after I arrived in Kyoto, I came upon a sight I shall never forget: an old wooden rowhouse whose heavily gridded front windows were open wide to the street, with its crisp linen shop curtain flapping softly in the breeze, and a scene that had to come right out of another era.

Hard at work was a man pulling sheets of a paperlike substance out of steaming vats to hang dripping wet in the morning air to dry. Walking from vat to vat he repeated the process, one, two, a dozen times, rhythmically like a machine, but not like a machine, like a man performing a very old task his bones knew by heart. He stopped from time to time to stoke brick furnaces beneath the rows of vats with more saw-dust (sawdust burns more evenly than firewood, though it is more expensive to use). Steam rose and spun its lazy way up through the heavy curved rafters to the skylight twenty feet overhead. I asked if he was making paper. He snorted a laugh. "No, it's *yuba*," he said, knowing where that would leave me. "*Yuba?*" I repeated to be sure I'd heard

him right. He looked at me with proud amusement, wiped his hands on his apron, and disappeared into the back. Soon he was back with a tiny dish and a cruet of soy sauce. "*Yuba.* Try some." I don't remember what else he told me then. All that lingers is the fragrance of wood smoke, and the memory of my first taste of *yuba*, the pale yellow soy milk skimmings that look an awful lot like paper—but aren't.

To make *yuba*, soybeans are soaked overnight, ground in a giant stone mor-tar, and then boiled for hours over an old clay *kamado* stove. Next they are placed in a cheesecloth bag and pressed in an old lever contraption weighted with huge stones that have been in the family for longer than anyone can remember. The extracted soy milk is then placed in long, flat, open vats over a fire which must be constantly stoked with sawdust to keep the milk at an even simmer. As the vats begin to heat, thin sheets form over the steaming soy milk; they are lifted gently off in one even piece and hung to dry on a wooden stick suspended above.

When I returned several years later, the man and his wonderful old shop hadn't changed—but I had. I'd come to love the popular Kyoto specialty, having tasted it a hundred times in the soups and subtle sauces of Kyoto-style cuisine. He had one surprise left for me, though—this time he asked his wife to fry up some *yuba*, potato chip style, which she promptly did and brought us a sample basket of the crunchy delicacy which we proceeded to devour with lust and speed.

He dusted off a spot for me to sit amid the stone grinding mortars, the giant wooden tubs, and old clay *kamado* and went on with his work. (I was there this time for an interview, but boiling soy milk waits for no woman.) Each sheet of *yuba* takes eight to ten minutes to form; no clocks or timers are involved, just one continuous motion of lifting, hanging, moving on to the next vat, all day long. To comment on the difficulty of this kind of work, Tomizō Asano, the ninth-generation *yuba* maker, volunteered one of his family's most guarded trade secrets. "Standing over these steaming trays all day is enough to make a man sweat even in the middle of winter . . . the extra salt is actually one of our trade secrets," he grinned. He even wisecracked that "it's no big deal" to keep on in an age-old tradition like this. He's been making *yuba* since he was thirteen years old. "It's just what I do," he said.

Yuba can be purchased fresh (*hikiage yuba*) or dried flat (*ita yuba*) or in rolls (*kiri-komaki yuba*). The dried variety lasts a year, but the sooner it is eaten the better. Sliced and added to soups, it absorbs the flavor of any seasoning and contains the highest concentration of protein found in any natural food, making it an important part of *shōjin*

ryōri, the Buddhist vegetarian cuisine.

Yubahan started making *yuba* in 1716, but all family records were lost in the huge fire of 1864 that destroyed much of the city, a result of the battles that took place at the time of the Meiji Restoration. The 140-year-old building was reconstructed not long after the fire, but apart from that, little is left of the shop's history but the priceless hand-me-down tales.

Lifting yet another sheet of *yuba* onto a rack to dry, Asano-san shot me a nonchalant grin when I asked why his shop name "Yubahan" is written with Chinese characters meaning "half a wave of hot water," rather than with the usual characters for *yuba*. "Who knows," he shrugged. "Guess there were a couple of things I just never thought to ask."

HIIRAGI-YA
inn (ryokan)

Oike-kado, Fuya-chō-dōri, Nakagyō-ku
中京区麩屋町通御池角　TEL: (075) 221–1136 (English spoken)
CHECK-IN: 3 P.M. ▪ CHECK-OUT: 11 A.M. ▪ RATES: ¥¥¥¥ ▪ CREDIT: Major credit cards

Somehow Hiiragi-ya still bears the ambience of an inn that caters to samurai. Something in the scale and aesthetics of each room—the black lacquered trim of an alcove, the ornate gilded detail on a painted screen—join to create an air of the luxury and privilege that belonged exclusively to the upper classes in Edo-period Japan.

Indeed, it was the samurai who were among Hiiragi-ya's most frequent guests in the mid-nineteenth century. The inn was founded in 1861 by a renowned metalsmith whose sword guards (*tsuba*) were sought after by the samurai. The craftsman's father had left his hometown on the Japan Sea to establish a trading post in Kyoto. He set up a boarding house for his porters there (as well as for others who came to the capital in search of work). He named the house after Hiiragi-jinja, his favorite shrine, which stands on the grounds of Shimogamo Shrine, just north of the fork in

Charlie Chaplin participates in a tea ceremony at Hiiragi-ya

the Kamogawa River. The name is in keeping with the Japanese love of double entendre—*hiiragi*, written with different Chinese characters, means "holly," which is a symbol of good luck and the inn's trademark.

In 1853, the metalsmith's son was urged by his samurai friends to open an inn to accommodate the lords and their retainers from the provinces who made frequent trips to the capital. The decade leading up to the revolt that ousted the shogunate and reinstated the emperor as ruler of Japan was a time of political unrest in Kyoto. *Daimyō*, the rulers of the provinces, converged on Kyoto, prepared to fight for one side or the other. Hiiragi-ya, in those days, was undoubtedly the scene of many a midnight plotting between samurai determined to champion their cause. Like most diplomatic Kyoto families, the present proprietress refrains from saying which side her samurai guests were on—perhaps both.

At various times in the inn's 145-year history, noted politicians and ministers of state, as well as several famous writers, such as Yukio Mishima and Yasunari Kawabata, have been guests at Hiiragi-ya. In one room you may sit at the same desk from which Mishima gazed out over the beautiful gardens with pen in hand. More extravagant in its tastes than its reserved neighbor, Tawara-ya, whose subdued decor calls to mind the philosophy of the tea ceremony, Hiiragi-ya has the decorative sense of elegance associated with the old ruling class.

The exterior of Hiiragi-ya, whose long clay walls run all the way to the corner of Oike-dōri, has the old *komayose* wooden hitching post reminiscent of the days when samurai arrived in a flourish on horseback. Inside, the lobby has a few modern touches, and each room has a private bath, although family-size baths are also available, with large Meiji-period stained-glass windows to enjoy.

Another unique "modern" feature at Hiiragi-ya is a push-button automatic control box which dims lights, opens and closes curtains, and calls the maid—an exotic-looking device invented by the last-generation proprietor long before the push button-phone or the computer arrived in Japan. Hiiragi-ya, with its samurai flair and old-fashioned charm, is certainly among the most beloved inns in Kyoto, and has attracted foreign guests for over fifty years.

TAWARA-YA
inn (ryokan)

Ane-kōji-agaru, Fuya-chō-dōri, Nakagyō-ku

中京区麩屋町通姉小路上ル   TEL: (075) 211–5566 (English spoken)

CHECK-IN: 2:00 P.M. ▪ CHECK-OUT: 11:00 A.M. ▪ RATES: ¥¥¥¥ ▪ CREDIT: Major credit cards

"I would call back this world of shadows we are losing. . . . I would have the eaves deep and the walls dark . . . I would strip away the useless decoration. . . . I do not ask that this be done everywhere, but perhaps we may be allowed at least one mansion where we can turn off the electric lights and see what it is like without them."

■ ■ ■

The nostalgia Junichirō Tanizaki felt for the loss of the sense of shadowy beauty that was once characteristic of the Japanese house is understandable when you look at how rapidly modernization has changed the face of Kyoto. Even in the so-called traditional Japanese inns, it is not unusual to find a coin-operated TV set in the *tokonoma* alcove, formerly a place of honor in a Japanese room in which only a classic hanging scroll and a simple flower arrangement would be placed.

There is a place in Kyoto where the beauty of the play of light and shadow is tended as carefully as a dying flame. Tawara-ya is such a place—so precious that reservations are taken a year in advance for a night in Kyoto's quintessential inn.

Three hundred years ago, Wasuke Okazaki, a textile merchant from a village called Tawara sent his son to establish a post in Kyoto from which he could conduct business and provide lodging for his own employees and eventually for others whose lot it was to be on the road. Gradually Tawara-ya, as the inn was named, gained a reputation for excellence. For more than a hundred years the inn has been host to people of nobility and fame from all over the world. Members of the imperial family have stayed at Tawara-ya, as did Hirobumi Itō, the first prime minister of Japan. The guest book bears the names and inscriptions of Rothschilds and Rockefellers—even of Marlon Brando.

The present owner, Toshi (Okazaki) Satō, has ten generations of tradition to uphold. Glaring fluorescent light bulbs, coin-operated television sets, and refrigerators have no place of honor in the alcoves at Tawara-ya. Instead, Satō-san maintains a classic Japanese inn with all the traditional elements of beauty,

but without the usual accompanying inconveniences: no need to share the bath, no bone-chilling mornings without proper heat, or sweltering afternoons with droning electric fans.

Nowhere but here do the corridors flicker with the soft candlelight of a dozen lacquered antique lamps. In every other inn in Kyoto, candles have been disposed of as hazardous and inconvenient, but the conscientious maids at Tawara-ya never leave their candles (or their customers) unattended for a moment.

It is possible to lose yourself down the long, twisting corridors of Tawara-ya, where each turn reveals another intimate touch: a folding screen adorned with a mountain scene in the Zen style of brush painting, an arrangement of wildflowers in a natural salt-glazed ceramic vase, a stone water basin into which cold, clear water drips oh so slowly from a bamboo spout. King Carl Gustav XVI of Sweden once nearly missed his officially scheduled tour of the city, having lingered so long in the morning light of Tawara-ya's splendid gardens.

Every room is different, furnished simply but elegantly with fine antiques that have been in the Okazaki family for generations—lacquered tables, brocade armrests, intricately woven bamboo basketry. Each has a private bathroom done in ceramic tiles from a local kiln, and cedar bathtubs whose fragrance when heated scents the air like a mountain breeze.

With all this to speak for it, Satō-san says that the key to the success of Tawara-ya is simply the service. Even the elderly gardener bows as you pass the stand of new bamboo where he is busily snipping off a leaf that has outlived its time.

A night at Tawara-ya is quite expensive, but the price includes breakfast and dinner. Where else can you bathe in a cedar soaking tub, dress in a crisp cotton *yukata*, and then sit down to one of Kyoto's finest meals, impeccably served by candlelight in a private room overlooking your own intimate garden?

Saul Bellow summed up the sentiments of all the guests who've spent a peaceful night at Tawara-ya: "I found here what I had hoped to find in Japan—the human scale, tranquility, and beauty." How Tanizaki would envy his good fortune.

SAIUN-DŌ
Japanese painting supplies

Fuya-chō Higashi, Ane-kōji, Nakagyō-ku
中京区姉小路麸屋町東　TEL: (075) 221–2464 (English spoken)
OPEN: 9 A.M.–6 P.M. ■ CLOSED: Wednesdays

Saiun-dō (Painted Clouds) was named by Tessai Tomioka (1837–1924), one of the great masters of Japanese literati painting, and once one of Saiun-dō's best customers.

In 1863, Tsukio Fujimoto, himself an accomplished Kyoto painter, succumbed to the urgings of his painter friends and opened a shop selling the special colors he had formulated for use in his own work. Preparing them in separate porcelain dishes, Fujimoto called them *gansai* (face colors), for the subtle, transparent quality that his formulas produced. Unlike the cumbersome mineral colors (*iwa-enogu*) which must be ground with a mortar and pestle and mixed with a special medium (*nikawa* hide glue), before they can be applied, Fujimoto's colors were obtained from plant pigments and were water soluble, making them ideal for the delicate washes applied to *suiboku-ga*, or ink paintings.

Saiun-dō sells all the supplies necessary for Japanese painting—brushes (over a hundred kinds), inks, paints, water containers, brush holders, even handmade papers. They have brushes for every imaginable purpose, from a six-inch-wide *hake* flat brush for temple-door-sized washes, to a one-millimeter-wide *kegaki* fine line brush for painting the hairs on a brow. There are even special *ten-tsuki* brushes for painting dots or tears. Ask to see the brush catalog, which has some notation in English as to type of bristles, and name and function of each principal type of brush. One brush thought to be unique to Japan is the *renpitsu*, actually five separate brushes bound together with a single handle. The *renpitsu* is used for large sweeps of color where a gradation of shades is desired with one stroke. Unlike the broad, flat *hake* brush, the combination of individually pointed brushes in the *renpitsu* is designed to produce a clean, sharp edge of deep color that fades to a lighter overall wash with one stroke.

Saiun-dō's guest book lists world-famous painters and designers from New York, Paris, and Tokyo—artists who have come to appreciate the beauty of a handmade badger-hair (*tanuki-ke*)

brush for fine detail work, or a sheep-hair (*hitsuji-ke*) brush for applying color washes.

Aside from specialized supplies for professional painters, Fujimoto-san, the great-grandson of Tsukio Fujimoto, can also provide the novice with everything needed to begin painting in the *suiboku-ga* (or ink painting) style. *Sumi-e*, refers to paintings that do not have color, while *suiboku-ga* includes ink paintings with light washes of color. Here you can purchase an all-purpose *tsuketate* brush that is capable of producing a fine line as well as a fully gradated wash; a traditional *shitajiki* felt cloth to place under paper; *sumi* ink sticks ranging in tones from blue to brown; a *suzuri* ink grinding stone; a square *hissen* water vessel for rinsing brushes; a set of small white porcelain bowls for mixing colors; a package of off-white *gasen-shi* paper for practicing, and a twelve-to-sixteen color set of *gansai* paints that provide the full range of traditional Japanese colors from the original secret formulas developed by Tsukio Fujimoto over a hundred years ago. Everything necessary to start will total around ¥10,000—unless the glass display cases overpower you with temptation. There you'll find beautiful cast-metal paperweights, handmade bamboo brush cases, painted porcelain water containers, and hand-braided silk scroll tassels.

Saiun-dō's one-room shop was built in the late Edo period, and has the intimate atmosphere of the traditional Kyoto-style establishment dealing in very specialized products for a limited clientele. Seated on tatami behind a low wooden desk, the Fujimotos weigh small packets of powdered mineral colors (*iwa-enogu*) and chunks of dissolving colors (*suihi*) to fill the stack of orders from the many artists of the contemporary Nihonga school of Japanese painting, who prefer the thick, crystalline texture that the mineral paints provide. Fujimoto-san is knowledgeable and friendly and though he says that he barely manages in English, the number of foreign artists in his guest book attests to his ability to communicate. It gives him as much pleasure to advise beginners as to serve Japan's greatest master painters.

MISOKA-AN KAWAMICHI-YA
buckwheat noodles (soba)

Sanjō-agaru, Fuya-chō-dōri, Nakagyō-ku
中京区麸屋町通三条上ル TEL: (075) 221–2525, 231–8507 (English spoken)
OPEN: 11 A.M.–8 P.M. ▪ CLOSED: Thursdays ▪ PRICES: ¥–¥¥ ▪ CREDIT: Major credit cards

Though acrobatics do not qualify for a mention on the list of the revered martial arts of Japan, the sight of a delivery boy on a bicycle frantically dodging taxi-cabs, buses, and pedestrians with a tray overflowing with steaming bowls of *soba* noodles balanced on one shoulder is proof that juggling is indeed high art in Kyoto.

The making of *soba*, or buckwheat noodles, served in a variety of delicious soups is another traditional art form too often overlooked. Found everywhere—on train station platforms, next door to movie houses, down the street or around the corner in everybody's neighborhood—*soba* can range in flavor from dishwater to delicacy. Connoisseurs in Kyoto frequent the two or three old *soba* shops that have survived several generations of discriminating customers by continuing to serve the finest handmade buckwheat noodles in homemade broth.

Kawamichi-ya is one of the best. Not far from the center of town, it serves a wide variety of noodle dishes in a shop that is as wonderful as the menu (available in English). It is difficult to tell whether Kawamichi-ya is in a garden or vice versa. The long, narrow Kyoto-style building has three gardens: a front garden with a beautiful plum tree that drapes its blossom-laden branches over the gateway in spring, a central courtyard garden with tables where you may sit outside if the weather permits, and a lovely garden that surrounds the small open-air room at the back, all to assure that you are surrounded by greenery in any season. Light streams in through the windows to catch the sheen of polished wood in the interior—a hanging scroll depicts a crow huddled on a snowy branch in mid-winter, a flower arrangement of graceful pampas grass heralds early fall, or the sound of a tiny porcelain wind chime catches the slightest breeze on a sultry August afternoon.

The tradition of *soba* noodles in Japan dates back to the early seventeenth century, and Kawamichi-ya traces its own history to a time some three hundred years ago when it provided noodles for pilgrims climbing Mt. Hiei to pray at Enryaku-ji, the great Tendai Buddhist temple at the top. Every year on May 16,

the birthday of Emperor Kanmu, who founded the city of Kyoto, the people at Kawamichi-ya set up stalls on top of the holy mountain, serving *soba* to faithful worshipers who scale the steep slopes to attend memorial services. The emperor Kanmu apparently gave aid to the ancestors of the Kawamichi-ya family way back in the ninth century (just what he did has become obscured over the ages), but even in the twenty-first century, their descendants have not forgotten to thank him each year with this special service in his memory.

The full name of the shop is Misoka-an Kawamichi-ya. *Misoka* refers to a long-neglected custom of eating noodles for good luck on the last day of every month. There is still a custom of eating noodles called *toshi-koshi-soba* on the last day of the year, and every New Year's Eve at midnight, the shop is full of well-wishers slurping out the old, while listening for the temple bells to ring in the new.

The specialty at Kawamichi-ya is a one-pot noodle dish called *hōkōro*, prepared at your table in an interesting metal pot which more than one customer has coveted.

Kawamichi-ya also makes cookies out of the buckwheat flour for which they are famous. The cookie shop, built in the late Edo period is located around the corner from the noodle shop. Its dark, heavy façade and long *mushiko-mado* window slats are characteristic of Kyoto merchant house architecture, and the Kawamichi-ya cookie shop is one of the oldest in the neighborhood.

Just inside the rope curtains that separate the kitchen from the cookie shop you'll find another of the secrets to Kawamichi-ya's long success—a row of round-bellied grinning Hotei, the customary guardian deity of traditional Kyoto kitchens. Though only a few of the set of fifteen are on display above the old cookstove, the remainder may now be seen across the street in a niche on the wall of the new garage to which they have recently been relegated. Perhaps they'll learn to adapt to their new (if less glamorous) role of guarding delivery trucks. In modern times we all must make adjustments.

Visit Shōgo-in Kawamichi-ya, a sister shop located just north of the Kyoto Handicraft Center near Shōgo-in Temple, if you are in the area. It is actually a *noren-wake* shop, or a "split-curtain" shop, a common practice among Kyoto restaurateurs in which a former apprentice goes into business for himself with the blessing of the original shop's master. The new shop is run independently, but retains the spirit of the original and has the same fine *soba*, traditional atmosphere, and lovely gardens for which the parent shop is famous.

TSUKIMOCHI-YA NAOMASA
baked bean-cakes

Sanjō-agaru hachi-ken-me, Kiyamachi-dōri, Nakagyō-ku
中京区木屋町通三条上ル八軒目   TEL: (075) 231–0175   FAX: (075) 231–0176
OPEN: 9:30 A.M.–8:00 P.M. ■ CLOSED: Thursdays (or Friday, if Thursday is a holiday)

The moon may be made of blue cheese in the West, but in Japan it's just a lunar bean-cake. "Tsukimochi" means "moon cake," and the flavor too is extraterrestrial. Whether the shop took its name from the small baked bean-cakes or vice versa is a question that the years have obscured, for when the first toasted cake was baked on this site five generations ago, neither family, nor bean-cake, nor shop had a name. In fact, commoners in Japan were not allowed to have family names until after 1868 when the Tokugawa shogunate was ousted and the rigid feudal class system was officially denounced. People were often known by what they made. Although the family name is now Kimura, the shop's formal name, Tsukimochi-ya Naomasa, means "Naomasa, the moon-cake baker." It is said that Naomasa invented the type of cake from which he and his shop once took their name. Rather than simply steaming his cakes like ordinary *manjū*, Naomasa decided to try placing them in a small clay oven just long enough to give them a light, golden crust. The

resulting bean-cakes, known as *geppei* (or *tsukimochi*) are as tempting to the Western palate as to the Japanese. Another baked specialty of the house, *yaki-guri tsukimochi*, has a chestnut in the center of a *koshi-an* (pureed sweet bean) filling with the same light crust. A set of five of each kind (the *hitokuchi geppei*, or bite-sized moon cakes, are best) makes a mouth-watering souvenir, but should be eaten within a week as no preservatives are added.

Wa-gashi, the general term for Japanese sweets, refers to a wide variety of confectionery that includes *nama-gashi* (jellies, pastes, and doughs), *han-nama-gashi* (steamed, paste-filled buns), *yaki-gashi* (lightly baked cakes, like *tsukimochi*), and *hi-gashi* (sugary wafers). The main ingredients used in all *wa-gashi* are sweet potatoes, chestnuts, red and white beans, brown or white sugar, and, rice (or wheat) flour. No animal products (butter, lard, milk) or chocolate are used, and *wa-gashi* are never served as dessert after a meal. They are snacks to accompany a cup of green tea when guests drop by, or with *matcha*,

Central Kyoto

the thick powdered tea of the tea ceremony. Sweets are occasionally served before a meal—as appetizers—rather than after dinner when fruit is considered the appropriate finishing touch.

Tsukimochi-ya uses two special kinds of sugar in the making of their sweets: Okinawan brown sugar (*kurozatō*), said to be the best, and a specially processed cane sugar (*wasanbon*) from Shikoku. Their "moon cakes" have a *koshi-an* filling and a thin egg and flour crust.

Tsukimochi-ya also offers a selection of *nama-gashi*, the uncooked type of bean-cake, which changes according to the season. In a variety of colors and shapes and with poetic names that elicit spring, winter, summer, and fall, seasonal *nama-gashi* decorate the windows at Tsukimochi-ya in turn—delicate doughy peaches, flaky white snowballs, or maple leaves tinted yellow and crimson. *Nama-gashi* can be purchased individually, and should be eaten the same day, perhaps with the cup of green tea that awaits you at your inn.

The shop, like the delicate sweets presented, possesses an air of miniature perfection. Soft light from a Meiji-period glass lamp glows through the

stained-glass "moonscape" border on the front window that was a decorative touch added around a hundred years ago by the flamboyant great-grandfather of Hironao Kimura, the present owner. Apart from the display of seasonal specialties, there is always a different *mame* (or "bean-sized") bonsai placed discreetly in the window. The cultivation of miniature plants in small containers is a little-known art form, but one at which Kimura-san is a respected local master.

In 1989, the family were forced to leave their old shop, with its intricate bamboo work and wooden pantries, to make way for a high-rise building that the owner of the property decided to construct in its place. Kimura-san fought city hall for the right to rebuild a traditional wood-frame shopfront on a site next door, but fire ordinances now forbid the addition of any new wooden structures in the downtown area. Thus the shop is now a modern building, but you can still sit on a low bamboo bench and watch the owner and his family roll out one by one the sweet cakes you have ordered, just as their predecessors used to do.

Note the original *kanban* shop sign that hangs inside on the north wall. It hung outside until World War II, when rumors that Kyoto was the next city to be bombed forced Tsukimochi-ya to bring their old treasure indoors. On the same wall hangs a small painting showing business as it was in 1804—two ladies in kimono side by side making bean-cakes while the baker slides another paddle-full into the glowing oven. Not much different from today, really.

NAITŌ brooms

Sanjō-ōhashi Nishi-zume, Nakagyō-ku
中京区三条大橋西詰   TEL: (075) 221-3018
OPEN: Daily, 9:30 A.M.–7:30 P.M.

*Anna otoko wa hōki de haku hodo aru. (That kind of man is as
plentiful as broom sweepings; i.e., men like him are a dime a dozen.)*

A good broom (just like a good man) is getting harder and harder to find these days, and they usually cost a good deal more than a dime a dozen. But one shop in Kyoto still has the real thing. Across the Sanjō Bridge from Keihan Sanjō Station, on the north side of the street, the Naitō family has been dealing in handmade brooms and brushes for over one hundred years.

The shop was built in 1869 and is typical of Kyoto merchant shops dealing in practical items for everyday use. Open to the street, its wares are displayed hanging from walls and rafters, with a raised tatami mat area in one corner at the back where the proprietress sits chatting with customers over a cup of tea, helping them choose "the right tool for the right job." Unlike many similar shopkeepers whose businesses now face a crowded modern thoroughfare, Mrs. Naitō has never found it necessary to enclose her shop in metal-frame sliding glass doors. It remains as

it always has been—a part of the bustling activity of Sanjō-dōri just outside. Mrs. Naitō insists that her old shop will hold its own until she herself leaves this world behind. She remembers a time when the shop sold dozens of brooms a day. Now only a shadow of the former selection hangs from hooks along its precious old walls. When her husband Rikimatsu Naitō, a fifth-generation broom maker, passed away, no one was left to carry on the family trade, a difficult and time-consuming process that requires strong muscles and calloused hands. Now the shop sells brooms made by his former apprentices and friends, who are among the last remaining traditional broom makers in Kyoto. According to Mrs. Naitō, when these men pass on, their trade dies with them. The advent of the vacuum cleaner and the rising popularity of carpet over tatami mats in Japan, have left few people who appreciate the value of a hand-tied hemp palm *shuro-bōki* broom these days.

Soft enough to sweep tatami, *shuro-bōki* come in a variety of sizes made to fit the job (as well as the sweeper). There is a broom or brush for everything: one for cleaning your *hanko* (seal), another for ashtrays, one for the corners of desk drawers, toilet bowls, the collars of shirts, rusty iron kettles, the wooden frames of *shōji* windows, or simply for brushing the crumbs off your kitchen table. The palm fibers used in making them must be brought in from the outlying prefectures where they are grown. Their soft bristles are designed especially for sweeping tatami mats, and though they are more expensive than mass-produced brooms, they last a good twenty years and are a particular favorite in Kyoto, where housewives are notoriously meticulous.

The other kind of broom featured at Naitō's is the *kibi-bōki* (millet-stalk broom). Resembling their Western counterparts, the *kibi-bōki* last only three to five years and are less expensive than *shuro-bōki*, but they are hand-tied with colorfully dyed cord, making them quite unexpectedly an art form all their own.

In the display boxes at the front of the shop there are specialty brushes for Yūzen dying that are made of animal hair. There is also an assortment of wonderful body brushes made of either *shuro* or horsehair, to which many of the elderly residents of Kyoto attribute their long-standing good health.

The largest broom in the shop hangs in a dark corner at the back and is Naitō-san's most valued keepsake from days gone by. It was made by her great-great-grandfather a hundred years ago and has taken on a deep brown patina and a lot of character. Although it's been grasped by a thousand hands and swept as many floors, it still looks like new. The bristles of a handmade *shuro-bōki* never fall out; they just gradually wear down.

The *shuro-bōki*, however, are on the endangered species list in the world of Japanese crafts. Passing the old broom shop amid the dense traffic on Sanjō-dōri, it is a comfort to glance in and see Mrs. Naitō engrossed in the morning paper and firmly ensconced as usual amidst her simply beautiful brooms.

FUNAHASHI-YA
rice crackers

舩はしや

Sanjō-ōhashi Nishi-zume, Nakagyō-ku
中京区三条大橋西詰　TEL: (075) 221–2673　FAX: (075) 221–2683
OPEN: Daily, 9 A.M.–9 P.M. ■ CREDIT: JCB, VISA

When Yasuyuki Tsuji was eight years old, he could stand outside his grandfather's shop and listen to the *karankoron* of wooden *geta* across the old bridge at Sanjō. But wooden footgear is no longer in fashion, and when the giant wooden planks of the Sanjō Ōhashi could no longer bear the weight of modern traffic, it was replaced with reinforced concrete.

Established in 1885, Funahashi-ya still stands on its original site beside the bridge on the west bank of the Kamogawa River. Funahashi-ya was named after the long wooden flatboats that plied the river for centuries, carrying loads of charcoal and cotton back and forth to Osaka in the south.

Funahashi-ya has long been a landmark for tourists returning home via the Sanjō-Keihan train on the east bank of the river. It is an inevitable last stop to pick up a souvenir of Kyoto for family and friends: a sampler of Funahashi-ya's rice crackers carefully packaged in handmade paper or wooden boxes.

Rice crackers are known as *o-kaki* in Kyoto dialect (they are called *arare* or *senbei* in other regions). Originally, they were a midday snack for farmers working in the fields to accompany a cup of green tea during their afternoon break. Crisp, flavored with soy sauce, sesame, or wrapped in a sheet of dried seaweed, the rice crackers at Funahashi-ya are baked fresh locally. Over fifty varieties are available, including several exotic flavors such as curry, chili pepper, and *wasabi* (the green horseradish paste found on sushi). Tsuji-san's suggestion for health-conscious customers are the *daizu*, or dried soybeans—roasted, salted, battered, or plain.

Despite the gleaming rows of cracker jars that first catch one's eye at Funahashi-ya, their real specialty is a confectionery called *go-shiki-mame*. These "five-colored beans" have been a popular Kyoto treat for over five hundred years. With a flavor for every color (plum pink, citrus yellow, cinnamon brown, seaweed green, and the elusive "snow" white), these bite-size sweets are actually dried green peas in a naturally flavored sugar coating. Samples are available for the skeptic, and Mr. Tsuji guarantees fresh-

ness since he makes them himself from the original family recipe.

The shop is open to the street in typical Kyoto style. The fact that theft has never been a problem may reflect either the ethics of traditional Japanese society in general or the vigilance of Shōki, the guardian figure whose clay likeness can be seen on the lookout for trouble in his perch above the first floor eaves. Though the kitchen has been modernized and the lighting improved, Mr. Tsuji has kept the fine wood, bamboo, and tile details of the interior, making Funahashi-ya an excellent example of how an old Kyoto shop can be adapted to fit modern times without giving up its traditional beauty. Notice the old wooden *kanban*, or signboard, hanging on the back wall of the shop. It once hung outdoors on Sanjō Street, until the threat of bombing during World War II prompted the owner to bring his hand-carved zelkova wood treasure indoors, as did many of the merchants in Kyoto at the time.

Funahashi-ya, like most old Kyoto shops, has living quarters upstairs and to the rear of the kitchen. The wooden-slatted *kōshi* that cover the windows on the second floor are also typically Kyoto, a means of providing privacy in a crowded city where houses and shops were built right on the street.

Early every morning, the Tsujis can be seen in front of Funahashi-ya sweeping the sidewalks and splashing them with water in another of Kyoto's traditional customs. Not only does the water keep the dust away from the open shopfront, but it serves as a symbol of welcome to the day's first customers.

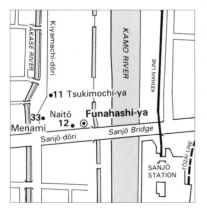

NISHIHARU
woodblock prints

Teramachi-kado, Sanjō-dōri, Nakagyō-ku
中京区三条通寺町角 TEL: (075) 211–2849 (English spoken)
OPEN: Daily, 2 P.M.–7 P.M.

Ukiyo-e—images of the floating world—the tawdry, mortal world that slips from our hands and leaves us with only the memory of squandered fortunes and ill-spent youth. Beautiful winsome women, the light of neglected oil lamps flickering out at daybreak, the painted flowers of a priceless silk kimono lying in disarray on the floor where it was flung in a moment of careless passion—the excesses of a world that no longer exists—except in *ukiyo-e*, the woodblock prints which depict life in the entertainment quarters of Edo-period Japan.

Nishiharu is the oldest shop in Kyoto dealing exclusively in antique woodblock prints (*moku-hanga*). It has stood for sixty-five years on the corner of Teramachi and Sanjō streets (once the hub of downtown activity), silently watching the transformation that has left it and one or two of its old neighbors amid a circus of new souvenir shops and glittering *pachinko* parlors.

Mr. Tōru Sekigawa, the owner, believes in doing business in the old style. He has no random piles of prints stacked here and there on glass showcases, just one small tatami-mat room, with a single scroll hanging in the alcove, and a cup of tea and courtesy waiting for every customer. His carefully selected collection of antique *ukiyo-e* prints are tucked neatly away in lacquered boxes and old cabinet drawers waiting to be unveiled, one by one, at the customer's request.

Although this style of business was intended for the buyer who knows what to ask for, Mr. Sekigawa is happy to bring out dozens of prints for any novice who shows a real interest in this fascinating art form. You can ask to see prints by specific artists: Hiroshige, Utamaro, Kuniyoshi, Hokusai, Sharaku and others. Or you may ask to see those of a particular genre: *bijin-ga*, portraits of beautiful women; *yakusha-e*, portraits of kabuki actors; or *fūzoku-ga*, prints depicting the scenery or way of life in the city. *Yokohama-e* prints, done around 1860, focus on foreigners, Western ships, and fashions in Yokohama after the port was opened for trade by Admiral Perry in 1854, ushering in the Meiji period. The most popular

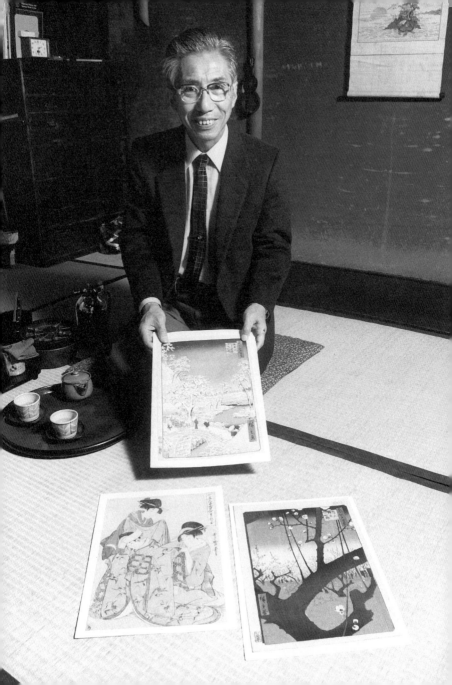

Meiji artist was Yoshitoshi Taiso.

Ukiyo-e were not considered works of art in eighteenth- and nineteenth-century Japan. They were sold as affordable souvenirs of the entertainment quarters, when kabuki actors and geisha were the celebrities of their day. There are several different types of prints, one technique developing out of another over a period of about two hundred years (c. 1680–1850). The oldest are the *sumizuri-e* (Sekigawa-san's personal favorites), printed simply in black ink. Next are the *tessai-shiki*, or hand-colored prints in which the red *tan-e*, or red and yellow *beni-e* colors were applied to the prints with a brush. *Urushi-e* refers to the kind of prints in which details are colored with a shiny black ink that gives objects like hats the look of real lacquer. *Benizuri-e* are prints in which three to six colors are printed, rather than painted, and *nishiki-e*, or "brocade" prints, are elaborately printed in six or more colors.

Mr. Sekigawa says that the value of a woodblock print is determined by the artist's name, the era in which it was printed, the beauty of the composition, the quality of the printing impression, and the state of preservation. He sells no print that cannot be identified as to age and artist, and every print is tagged with this basic information in Japanese and English, as many of his regular buyers are collectors from Europe and America. *Ukiyo-e* were first recognized as works of art by European artists and collectors, who discovered them used as packing material for shipments of Japanese porcelain in the latter half of the nineteenth century.

Mr. Sekigawa guarantees every piece he sells to be authentic. His advice on the care and display of *ukiyo-e* is simply to keep them out of direct sunlight because ultraviolet rays cause color changes, particularly in the green hues. Hang your print for no more than three months out of the year, but don't store it too long without airing it for a few days in a dry place. Dry climates are better than wet for the preservation of woodblock prints, which are highly sensitive to humidity. The best *ukiyo-e* are sought after not only by art collectors, but by rodents and insects who devour them with unparalleled zeal. Store them with ordinary mothballs in a pest-free location.

Mr. Sekigawa has no plans to modernize his shop in the future, beyond making structural repairs when necessary. He tried carpeting the tatami and moving in a desk after his father retired. But, sliding out an elegant lacquered tray with a fresh cup of tea, he says, "In the end, I decided tatami was the best place to spread out my prints and chat with customers. Besides, nothing pleases me more than talking with a middle-aged lady on a trip to Kyoto from the countryside who stops in to tell me how happy she is to find my shop just as she remembered it fifty years ago on a school excursion to Kyoto."

MIYAWAKI BAISEN-AN

fans

宮脇売扇庵

Tomino-kōji Nishi-iru, Rokkaku-dōri, Nakagyō-ku
中京区六角通富小路西入   TEL: (075) 221–0181   FAX: (075) 221–0439
OPEN: 9 A.M.–6 P.M. ■ CLOSED: New Year's holidays ■ CREDIT: Major credit cards

---

*Art has surely sounded its lowest depths when it comes to portraying
a lager-beer bottle on one side of a fan, and to providing a railway
timetable on the other.*

—B. H. Chamberlain (1904)

For more than a hundred years, West-erners have been upbraiding the Japa-nese for busying themselves with modernization while age-old traditions die at their feet. Chamberlain missed out on the real tragedy; television com-mercials do all the advertising these days and fans are no longer needed at all. Once commonplace in Kyoto, the old round *uchiwa* fans now appear only dur-ing annual festivals or as wall decora-tions for those who delight in nostalgia.

Miyawaki has been making beautiful fans since 1823 and, fortunately for Kyoto, still believes in the reason they exist. Fans in Kyoto are important, not only as a means of fighting off the sum-mer heat, but as an indispensable ele-ment of traditional Japanese dance, and as stylish accessories no elegant lady should be without. For the most part, the Japanese have no tradition of wear-ing jewelry. The earrings, brooches, pendants, bracelets, and rings that adorn beauties in the Western world are not acceptable accessories for the simple lines of the kimono. Apart from elaborate hair ornaments worn by geisha, a Japanese woman's most ele-gant accessory has always been a hand-painted, delicately scented folding fan.

Although many of the arts now associated with Japan actually origi-nated in China, the *sensu*, or folding fan, is said to be an invention of the Japanese. (The Japanese even accused the Chinese of pirating technological secrets when they adopted the *sensu* in the fourteenth century.) Legend tells of a beautiful young woman who entered a nunnery after the unfortu-nate death of her warrior husband not long after their marriage. Once when the abbot of the temple fell sick, she made a fan of folded paper to ease his fever. A folding-cypress fan called a *hi-ōgi* dated 877 found inside a statue of Kannon at Tōji Temple is considered to be the oldest in Japan. There are many references to fans belonging to members of the imperial court during the Heian period, and by the end of the period even the common people were using them. Painted wooden fans, scented sandalwood fans, lacquered fans with decorations in gold and silver, dyed silk fans, and paper fans all belong to one of Kyoto's oldest traditional crafts.

Miyawaki has fans of every description, each with its own special name: *Rikyū-ōgi*, tea ceremony fans named after the famous sixteenth-century tea master Sen no Rikyū; *hi-ōgi*, or court fans; *mai-ōgi*, fans used in traditional dance; *uchiwa*, the stiff, flat fan which originated in China; *chūkei*, used in the noh theater; and ordinary *sensu* carried by both men and women to add a touch of elegance (and a cooling breeze) to a formal kimono ensemble.

Every famous Japanese painter has decorated at least one fan in his time, making this one example of a Japanese craft that overlaps the world of fine art. The ceiling of Miyawaki is covered with forty-eight paintings by master artists, such as Tessai Tomioka and Seihō Takeuchi, which were commissioned by the Miyawaki family in 1903. (Look for the tiger fan by Takeuchi and the orchid and rock fan by Tessai.)

The building that houses the fan shop is a treasure among the old shops of Kyoto. The Miyawakis have maintained their hundred-year-old building, adding modern lighting and the comfort of air conditioning, without marring the old elegance of its style. The *batari shōgi* bench in front folds down each day when the shop opens for business to give customers a place to rest, and folds back up each evening to become a part of the storm shutters that protect the building against the elements. The deep eaves and the black entryway curtains that bear the shop's name hide the gilded fans from the damaging rays of the sun. The *mushiko-mado* windows, said to resemble a Japanese insect cage (hence the name), were ostensibly a means of ventilation, though this leads to the question of why such a restricted view was allotted to those on the second floor. One theory says that it was against the law for members of the lower classes to have their heads higher than their superiors, so these narrow slats provided a glimpse of royalty from above without being seen from below. The clever merchants always had their ways of getting around the most absurd of laws.

Miyawaki Baisen-an gives hope to those, like Chamberlain, who would like to see the best elements of the past survive. There is not a lager-beer advertisement or a train schedule in the place.

YAMATO MINGEI-TEN folk art

Tako-yakushi-agaru, Kawara-machi, Nakagyō-ku
中京区河原町蛸薬師上ル   TEL: (075) 221–2641   FAX: (075) 221–3209
OPEN: 10 A.M.–8:30 P.M. ■ CLOSED: Tuesdays ■ CREDIT: Major credit cards

*We must bring back . . . those days when all things required
in daily, ordinary life were beautiful.*
　　　　　　　—Sōetsu Yanagi, *The Unknown Craftsman*

With these thoughts one of the leaders of the Mingei, or Folk Art, Movement noted the loss of appreciation for naturally made, simple objects—brooms and baskets, bowls, buckets, and ladles—that were once commonplace in Japan. Yanagi, a philosopher and critic, Kanjirō Kawai, Shōji Hamada, Bernard Leach, and a handful of others in the 1920s attempted to save what was left of Japan's unpretentious country craftsmen by calling attention to their plight in a rapidly industrializing society which at the time was infatuated with the West.

The founders of the Mingei Movement were not interested in the individual artist-craftsmen who produced a limited number of precious objects that were more decorative than functional in purpose. These "art pieces" were affected and self-conscious, they believed, lacking the rustic beauty of unsigned works produced in rural villages across the country.

The members of the movement set about collecting the everyday objects they so much admired, making trips as far away as Korea and Okinawa to remote areas as yet unaffected by modernization. The objects they gathered are now kept in the Tokyo Folk Crafts Museum in Komaba, which Yanagi and his friends founded in 1936. They hoped to preserve a wide selection of fine folk crafts for future craftsmen to use as inspiration until long after the tiny villages from which the objects came had joined the ranks of concrete and stucco.

But the craftsmen themselves were in need of help that no museum could offer. As the population turned its back on folk crafts as crude and old-fashioned, the livelihoods of the country craftsmen declined until many were forced to seek other employment, or to use synthetic materials and mass-production techniques.

paper (*te-suki washi*) from Echizen or Kurodani, lacquered bowls from Wajima, baskets from Miyajima, blown glass from Okinawa, Nanbu teakettles from Iwate—all are made with traditional techniques and materials, and tagged with the name of the area from which they came. In keeping with Yanagi's views that *mingei* objects should also be affordable, the prices at Yamato Mingei are reasonable, considering the value of handmade objects in modern times.

The main shop faces Kawaramachi-dōri and sells a wide variety of smaller items; the nearby branch shop has larger objects—furniture from Tottori and hand-hewn stone basins and lanterns from the Kita-Shirakawa district in northeastern Kyoto. The branch shop holds monthly exhibitions which feature the works of different craftsmen or products from different crafts villages. There are also occasional exhibitions of folk crafts from around the world.

Shortly after World War II, a man named Yaei Hayashi, at the suggestion of friends in the Mingei Movement, came to the aid of the folk craftsmen of Japan by opening a shop in the middle of Kyoto that sold nothing but folk crafts from all over Japan. Now run by his daughter Akiko, Yamato Mingei-ten on Kawaramachi-dōri still sells the finest in folk crafts gathered from village craftsmen from Hokkaido to Okinawa.

The highly refined crafts produced in Kyoto itself have never been considered "folk," but many of the villages in the surrounding area (still within Kyoto Prefecture), such as Kurodani where paper is made (see Day Trips to the Countryside), number among the finest of the crafts villages in Japan.

The selection is always changing and every month different crafts from different areas can be found among the stacks of ceramics, glassware, lacquerware, basketry, and textiles in their impressive stock. Handmade Japanese

KINMATA
inn (ryokan), restaurant

407 Shijō-agaru, Gokō-machi, Nakagyō-ku

中京区御幸町四条上ル407　TEL: (075) 221–1039 (English spoken)　FAX: (075) 231–7632

CHECK-IN: 3 P.M. ■ CHECK-OUT: 10 A.M. ■ RATES: ¥¥¥¥ w/2 meals
■ RESTAURANT OPEN: 12 NOON–1:30 P.M. (last seating), 5:30 P.M.–7:30 P.M. (reservations required
at least one day in advance) ■ PRICES: Lunch ¥¥¥–¥¥¥¥, dinner ¥¥¥¥

No gambling.
No prostitution.
No mahjong.
No credit.
No noisy parties. . . .

So begins the long list of antiquarian house rules that have hung in the hallway at Kinmata since the nineteenth century. No arbitrary mandate from the innkeeper, these were the rules of the day for all Japanese inns by order of the Tokugawa shogunate, whose rigid reign proscribed the daily life of citizens down to the finest detail for over two hundred years.

Seven generations later, Haruji Ukai, the innkeeper at Kinmata, still insists on peace and quiet in his nearly two-hundred-year-old inn. Though the inn is located in the very heart of the downtown area, its interior recesses are surprisingly removed from the noise of the city.

In 1801, the year Kinmata opened for business, the most frequent guests were traveling salesmen bringing herbal medicines to Kyoto from Omi and Shiga near Lake Biwa, east of the former capital. A few old medicine peddler *kanban*,

or signboards, are kept in the entryway as mementos of the inn's first customers.

The meals at the family-run Kinmata are planned and prepared by the innkeeper himself, who worked for a time at a fishmonger's shop in the Nishiki street market just half a block away. Nishiki-kōji is where the most famous of Kyoto's restaurateurs shop for the ingredients of their elegant *kaiseki* cuisine. This proximity gives Ukai-san an inside lead on the finest of the day's catch, and the seafood meals prepared at Kinmata have become as popular as the unchanged traditional beauty of the inn itself. Several years ago, Ukai-san decided to redesign one area of the inn to serve as a restaurant open to lunch and dinner guests, as well as to overnight guests. His reputation as one of Kyoto's finest chefs has grown in recent years, and now he offers cooking classes in Japanese—a rare opportunity for aspiring chefs and local homemakers alike.

The original furnishings and decor of this old-style ryokan have been kept unchanged, despite the trend toward modern trappings among other Japanese inns. Fine lacquered *andon* lanterns and mirrored dressing stands (*kyōdai*), curved cedar handrails, and two bamboo-fenced interior gardens contribute to the atmosphere of traditional Japanese hospitality. Kinmata has only seven rooms in all and welcomes anyone who appreciates the intimate atmosphere and gracious amenities of an old-style Japanese inn (and respects the innkeeper's request for peace and quiet).

The large family-style bath (*o-furo*) downstairs is made of solid *hinoki* (cypress wood) with its own tiny windowbox garden. It can be reserved for private use by guests each evening, offering the classical Japanese "soak" that is said to relieve all the tension and stress a medicine peddler—or a modern traveler—can accumulate in a hectic day.

JŪSAN-YA combs

Otabi-chō, Shin-kyōgoku Higashi-iru, Shijō-dōri, Shimogyō-ku
下京区四条通新京極東入御旅町　TEL: (075) 211–0498 (English spoken)
FAX: (075) 252–6486

OPEN: Daily, 11 A.M.–8:30 P.M. ■ CREDIT: Major credit cards

A simple comb can be a work of art, when you consider that the man who sits on the floor before his workbench day after day filing each tooth by hand has lived in a world full of plastic since his birth. Pocket combs are disposable items in a plastic world, and who takes the time or trouble to fuss with a hand-made wooden comb that could easily be lost and just as easily replaced with celluloid for a fraction of the price?

Shinichi Takeuchi does—and has since he was fifteen. He is a fifth-generation maker of boxwood combs (*tsuge-kushi*). He says it takes over forty years to make a proper comb, giving thirty years of credit to the boxwood tree itself. After the tree is felled, another ten years are required for the drying process. The wood is cut into wedges and fumigated with smoke from its own sawdust to ensure that each comb will be durable and strong. After this process is completed, each wedge is planed by hand and ready to be sawed into teeth. Takeuchi-san uses only old-fashioned Japanese planes, saws, and

files. One item you might expect to find in his tool box is a ruler for measuring and marking the location of each tiny tooth. He doesn't have one; a steady hand and practiced eye are the only instruments he uses to space them. This process requires concentration. The Takeuchis used to do all the work in their shop on Shijō-dōri, but now all the exacting parts of the process are done at their workshop in Yamashina, a quiet suburb east of Kyoto. The present shop was opened on Shijō in 1930 at a time when the neighborhood still kept a slower pace. Before then the shop was located to the southwest of here, the one his great-great-great-great-grandfather opened in 1868.

The fine finishing process is what makes the boxwood combs worth the few extra yen they cost. Each tooth is polished with sharkskin, then with dried *tokusa* (a hollow reed with a coarse texture), and finally buffed to a golden sheen with a soft deerskin cloth. No one can convince Takeuchi-san that sandpaper and an electric buffer produce

a finer finish than techniques like these that have been used in Japan since the tenth century.

The simplest boxwood combs Takeuchi-san makes bear only his family crest engraved on the side, but there are several more decorative styles carved with plum blossom, bamboo, and other traditional designs. Takeuchi-san also sells *kanzashi*, the ornamental hairpins worn with formal kimono. Especially beautiful are the long, slender hair ornaments in the shape of a gingko leaf that come in both boxwood and cherry.

In the old days every bride received an elaborate set of boxwood combs as a necessary part of her trousseau. They were used to dress the exotic hairstyles called *marumage* worn by married women up until World War II. Today only geisha and kabuki actors require comb sets like these, but Jūsan-ya has a full display of them in a glass case at the back of the shop.

Aside from the appreciation he has for the traditional methods of making combs for everyday use, there is another reason why Takeuchi-san maintains a craft that most people consider outdated. It has been his family's responsi-

bility for generations to make the set of ninety-one combs that is offered in a special ceremony every twenty years to the goddess Amaterasu at Ise Shrine, the center of Shintoism in Japan. At this time, the main buildings at Ise Shrine are rebuilt and a new set of treasures is donated. The need for a new set of treasures is what keeps many of the crafts involved alive. Until the Meiji period, the old set of treasures was transferred to a small museum and the previous set donated forty years before was burnt. No longer do they burn old sets but instead keep them in the museum permanently. It is fortunate that there are twenty years between each rebuilding of the shrine because that is how long it takes the Takeuchis to make the exquisite set of combs. The last set was made by Shinichi's late father, Michikazu, who was working on it when I first visited the shop in 1985. How did it feel to devote two decades to the making of a perfect set of combs? In the old days these would have been destined for destruction just forty years later. "It's wonderful," the late Michikazu explained to me back then, "the greatest honor of my life."

TAKASEBUNE
tempura

188 Sendō-chō, Shijō-sagaru, Shimogyō-ku
下京区四条下ル船頭町188　TEL: (075) 351–4032
OPEN: 11 A.M.–3 P.M., 4:30 P.M.–9:30 P.M. ■ CLOSED: Mondays ■ PRICES: ¥–¥¥

Today the Kamogawa River runs calmly through the middle of Kyoto like a reliable old friend, but in its youth the river definitely had a mean streak. In the old days it stormed through town drowning citizens and destroying homes and shops with a vengeance, always unexpected, always devastating. Floods followed by plagues, droughts followed by famines—the Kamogawa River was incorrigible. But the city always forgave it, like a helpless parent does an intractable child, until one day in the early seventeenth century when a wealthy merchant named Suminokura Ryōi decided to teach the spoiled child a lesson. Suminokura ran a shipping trade to ports in Southeast Asia (a daring venture in its day) and wasn't about to let one ruffian river stand in his way. With permission from the shogun, he dug a canal that drained the river of its wild juices and enabled his boatmen to carry their loads to Fushimi and on to the port city of Osaka in the south without further harassment.

The Takasegawa Canal runs along the western edge of the Kamogawa River all the way to Fushimi, where it joins the Yodogawa River six miles to the south. Until the late nineteenth century, boatmen plied their long flatboats up and down the canal carrying firewood, charcoal, rice, salt, and prisoners off to exile. The area between Nijō and Gojō on the canal is known as Kiyamachi, a name derived from the many charcoal and firewood merchants whose shops provided a much more somber backdrop for the old canal. At present the canal is the heart line of a glittery entertainment district filled with restaurants, bars, and hostess clubs from one end to the other.

When modern transportation came to Kyoto in the form of streetcars and trains around the turn of the century, the backbreaking job of boatmen on the Takasegawa Canal became obsolete. The system of carrying merchandise downstream was not such an arduous task, but the boatmen had to drag the heavy barges back up the river using poles and ropes which they manipulated from the banks of the canal.

When the late Shōtarō Okajima opened his restaurant on the west bank of the canal thirty years ago, he named it Takasebune after the flatboats his father once pulled up that same river. Shōtarō's son Hideo now carries on his father's business, a small family place whose tempura *teishoku*, a table d'hôte meal, includes a generous bowl of miso soup, rice, and pickles, along with a basket of crisply batter-fried tempura shrimp, fish, and vegetables. The amazing thing about Takasebune's tempura meal is that it is delicious and inexpensive at the same time.

Apart from the lunch menu, Takasebune specializes in a variety of fine fish dishes, with a new menu penned each night by Hideo himself. A seat at the tiny counter where you can watch all the culinary activity is the most fun, though private tatami rooms are available upstairs and in the back.

The fish they serve comes from Torizane, a bit further north on Kiyamachidōri, the best fish market in Kyoto, according to Hideo. He should know. Before the restaurant opened, the family were fishmongers themselves in a small shop on the same site that was run by his grandfather after he retired from his job as a Takasegawa boatman (an old photograph of him and his boat hangs just inside the entrance). They decided to offer the local people a decent midday meal of tempura at a reasonable price. That's the spirit of Takasebune; even the deluxe full-course dinners served in the evening are not geared to earn them a fortune.

The shop is on an alley east of Hankyū Department Store and can be identified by the boat oar that leans against the side of the building out front (prompting foreign residents to nickname the place "The Oar").

Notice the short curtain that hangs above the counter, where there is an inscription that reads, "Came down the river through Kyoto on a boat, just me and the cows." The haiku poet Ryūshi Akamatsu wrote the message—a pun about the owner having been born in the year of the cow. Somehow it sets the mood of the whole place.

NOTE: A replica of one of the original Takasebune boats is moored near the head of the canal where Kiyamachi-dōri meets Nijō-dōri.

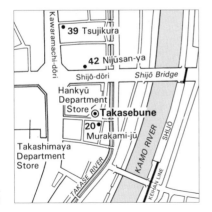

MURAKAMI-JŪ
pickles

Shijō-sagaru, Nishi-Kiyamachi, Shimogyō-ku
下京区西木屋町四条下ル　TEL: (075) 351–1737

OPEN: 9 A.M.–7 P.M. ■ CLOSED: New Year's holidays

"Feed not autumn eggplant to your daughter-in-law."

Don't spoil your son's blushing bride with needless luxury . . . a spiteful old saying, which (unlike the eggplant itself) is hardly worth preserving, except perhaps as a reminder of what was wrong with "the good old days."

The best locally grown vegetables, picked at the height of the season, have always been considered a delightful extravagance, especially in the form of Murakami's *tsukemono*, or pickles. Pickled eggplant is one of over twenty varieties of *tsukemono* found at this 150-year-old shop. Parting the dark brown shop curtain which bears the cross and circle crest of Murakami-jū (the cross symbol is also the character for the number ten, or *jū*, in Japanese), you enter a spacious shopfront with rough-hewn stone floors and two giant wooden pickle barrels brimming with the day's selection of fresh *tsukemono*. A set of small ceramic crocks on the counter contain samples from which to choose—*senmai-zuke* in winter (paper-thin slices of white radish seasoned with red pepper and lightly sweetened with kelp), *nanohana-zuke* in spring (flowers from the rapeseed plant lightly pickled in rice vinegar), or Nara-*zuke* in summer (a variety of vegetables salt-pickled and soaked in saké lees).

As basic to the Japanese diet as antipasto to the Italians, *tsukemono* was originally the primary source of nutrition in less prosperous times when a bowl of rice and a few pickled vegetables made up the entire meal for most Kyoto townsfolk.

Located far from the sea and surrounded on three sides by mountains, the citizens of Kyoto had to develop methods of preserving food in a humid, mildew-producing climate. These methods formed the basis of *Kyō-ryōri*, the sophisticated local cuisine, developed out of an assortment of salted fish and pickled vegetables, elaborately presented in an endlessly imaginative repertoire.

The most often served pickle is called *takuan*, the crisp, round, deep-yellow slices that accompany the simplest meals in any family-style Japanese restaurant. *Takuan* is said to be a good digestive

and the tale goes that no matter how much raw fish or how many bowls of white rice you eat, a few slices of *takuan* will pull you through. The name may have come from the sixteenth-century priest Takuan, who is said to have devised this method of pickling. The radishes are first dried in the sun, then placed in a wooden barrel with rice bran and salt, with a large stone placed on the lid to act as pressure. On the contrary, some say the priest never touched a pickling barrel in his life, and that the name simply comes from the strange resemblance Takuan's tombstone bore to an ordinary pickling stone.

Though the making of *tsukemono* used to be a chore every housewife took for granted, *daikon* drying on rooftops is a sight only seen these days in the countryside. The process is not complicated, however, with *tsukemono* falling into two basic categories: *furu-zuke*, pickles fermented for a time in a rice-bran mash with salt, which can be kept longer, and *asa-zuke*, pickled in dry rice bran and salt, which must be eaten within a few days. Plain salt-pickling (*shio-zuke*) and vinegar-pickling (*su-zuke*) are two other, simpler methods, but the rice bran gives the pickles a subtle depth of flavor the other methods lack. The advantage of *asa-zuke* is that no preservatives are added, though once the package is opened, they only last two or three days. Murakami-jū has not succumbed to using artificial colors to entice supermarket housewives who tend to be attracted to the most eye-catching fluorescent pink *tsukemono* and who pay no attention to expiration dates on packages (forcing major food suppliers to load their products with preservatives). Hundreds of regular customers at Murakami-jū make the brief side trip necessary daily to buy

tsukemono they know is made fresh on the premises, with the color, flavor, and fragrance of vegetables straight from the garden. Unlike the sharp tang of Western pickles, *tsukemono* retain the crisp, natural taste of the vegetable itself.

Apart from their regular customers, Murakami-jū draws visitors from all over Japan, who make a special stop on their sightseeing tours to buy a package of the famous Kyoto-style *tsukemono*. On a busy day, especially during one of the two gift-giving seasons (*o-chūgen* and *o-seibo*, in midsummer and mid-winter), you may have to wait to be served. But the thoughtful cup of tea that appears, and the exquisite floral spray that fills a giant ceramic urn in the center of the room help to pass the time painlessly. Tōru Murakami, the proprietor, believes in old-fashioned Kyoto hospitality and service, and spends much of his time coaching his youngest clerks in the proper way to sell a Kyoto pickle—graciously, honestly, and with style.

MORITA WAGAMI
handmade paper

森田和紙

Bukkō-ji-agaru, Higashi-no-tōin-dōri, Shimogyō-ku

下京区東洞院通沸光寺上ル　TEL: (075) 341–1419

OPEN: 9:30 A.M.–5:30 P.M. ■ CLOSED: Sundays, holidays

Writing is easy; all you do is sit staring at a blank sheet of paper until the drops of blood form on your forehead.

—Gene Fowler

Blank sheets of paper have been frightening artists and writers for a very long time. The Chinese were the first to suffer the silent taunting of the empty page: they've been writing poetry on paper longer than the West has been numbering years. The Japanese had paper in production for over five hundred years before the Moors opened the first paper mill in Spain in the twelfth century. By the end of the Edo period in 1868, the Japanese had figured out a way to use it for everything: lanterns, doors, windows, fans, candy wrappers, love letters, government orders, umbrellas, and even raincoats. The Tokugawas wrote their daily edicts on it, and it was no doubt a simple paper plot that finally brought the shogunate down. Paper has been absorbing mankind's mistakes and schemes, ideas and feelings, images and dreams for centuries. And nowhere more beautifully than in Japan.

Morita Wagami has a cure for nervous writers and artists everywhere—paper so peerless it's encouraging. They deal exclusively in handmade Japanese paper (*washi*), with a catalog of over eight hundred kinds from papermaking villages all over Japan.

Although there are regional variations, the three main materials used in Japanese papermaking are *kōzo*, *mitsumata*, and *ganpi*. *Kōzo*, or mulberry, is the heartiest, most common variety; *mitsumata*, a cultivated flowering shrub, produces a more delicate paper; and *ganpi*, stripped from plants in the wild, gives the highest quality and smoothest finish of the three.

There are five basic techniques used in the making of decorative paper: *suki-zome*, a process in which the paper is made from pre-dyed materials; *shitashi-zome* or *wa-zome*, in which the paper is dyed with natural colors; *hake-zome*, or stencil-dyed paper; and *hanga*, which utilizes the woodblock printing technique.

Particular regions in Japan have become famous for the production of special kinds of paper. Echizen to the northeast of Kyoto is known for the finest white *hōsho*, used as official stationery by the imperial court during the Edo period. Kurodani (see Day Trips to the Countryside), a small village about two hours northwest of Kyoto, produces a rustic paper with a quality Morita-san calls *"majime-sa"*—honesty or earnestness. Everyone in the village is related, and a local wedding often stops production until the festivities are over.

Morita Wagami has *washi* for formal Japanese *shodō* calligraphy, contemporary Nihonga painting, and *hanga* printmaking. They even have paper to accommodate the current preference among contemporary Japanese painters toward large-scale works: a single sheet five by five-and-a-half meters can run to over ¥50,000. Though many calligraphers use the less expensive Chinese papers for practice (sometimes five hundred tries are needed to produce a single character suitable for mounting), Morita-san stresses that Japan produces the very best and most durable handmade paper in the world today, essential for professional artists who cannot afford to risk using paper that may yellow or crumble. He suggests that paper be stored for a year after purchase; like a fine burgundy, it will improve with age if kept in a dry place.

Morita has a gift shop adjoining its paper warehouse where browsers will find a variety of paper products—from stationery, postcards, and notebooks to round *uchiwa* fans and miniature folding screens (*byōbu*). The catalogue on the counter contains the full range of undecorated papers offered. The shelves hold the largest selection of decorated *chiyogami* paper in Kyoto. *Chiyogami*, or "long life," paper was originally used by the aristocracy to wrap gifts of congratulations. One less-than-certifiable tale has it that the name comes from Princess Chiyo, whose obsession for brightly printed paper has apparently made a niche for her in Japanese folklore. It is certain, however, that *chiyogami* was one of many luxuries reserved for the nobility of feudal Japan.

During the eighteenth and nineteenth centuries, *chiyogami* was considered a precious gift or souvenir by people returning to their homes in the countryside from a trip to Kyoto or Edo (now Tokyo). It is interesting to compare *Kyō-chiyogami* (Kyoto style), with its reserved patterns and subdued colors, with the flamboyant designs and colors of *Edo-chiyogami*. The contrast between the restrained tastes of the people of the ancient capital and the riotous preferences of the townsfolk of Edo is apparent in matters as simple as package wrapping.

SHŌYEI-DŌ
incense

C22

松 榮 堂

Karasuma-dōri, Nijō-agaru, Nakagyō-ku
中京区二条上ル烏丸通　TEL: (075) 212–5590 (English spoken)
OPEN: 8:30 A.M.–5:30 P.M. (opens at 9 A.M. on Saturdays, Sundays and holidays)
BOULDER, COLORADO BRANCH: http://www.shoyeido.com

Life goes up in smoke: fleeting; gone before you know it, it rises, fades, and disappears. *O-kō*, or incense, is a reminder of that evanescent quality of life in Buddhism. For those practicing Zen meditation, it is a way to mark the passage of time, without the necessity of dividing it into minutes and seconds. The dying stick of incense defines an interval of silence, the composure of meditation, the moments that are, as the saying goes, "so quiet you can hear the powdered ash of incense fall."

Incense appeals to the senses, possessing age-old associations with the pursuit of pleasure. The wide range of scents developed over the centuries throughout the world appeal to the vulnerable human psyche with everything from the excitement of an aphrodisiac to the quieting effects of a midnight snowfall.

The first recorded discovery of incense in Japan was in 595 A.D. when the people of Awaji Island used a piece of aloeswood found on the beach for firewood, and were amazed by the fragrant aroma of its smoke. They presented some of the wood to the empress Suiko, whose regent, Prince Shōtoku, recognized it as the precious wood burned as incense in Buddhist rituals. Buddhism had been introduced to Japan via the Korean peninsular by the middle of the sixth century, and along with it had come incense use, although it was only known to the upper classes.

The enjoyment of incense in Japan has evolved into a refined and subtle art. Long before the tea ceremony came into practice, the nobles of the imperial court in Kyoto played a "parlor game" called *kō-awase*, in which participants tried to identify different scents as they were passed around one by one by the host. The aromatic woods and spices that were combined to create these fragrances were expensive and difficult to obtain in the days of Prince Genji. Rare ingredients were imported from Asia and the South Seas, including Java, Sumatra, and India, as none of the raw materials are indigenous to Japan. It was not until much later, in the Muromachi period, that the game became formalized into a ritual called *kōdō* (the

Central Kyoto

Way of Incense) that reached a peak of popularity in the Edo period.

Shōyei-dō has been making fine incense for three hundred years, and is one of the oldest and most respected makers in Japan. The company was founded in 1705 by Rokubei Hata, who worked at the Imperial Palace and had access to the court's secret traditions of incense making, hitherto known only to royalty. Shōyei-dō's incense is created using a combination of these traditional recipes, and modern, innovative techniques. Located near the Imperial Palace on the former site of Rokubei Hata's residence, the building that houses the shop has been modernized though the original beams have been preserved. Once in the neighborhood, the fragrance lingering in the air will guide you in the right direction.

Masataka Hata is the twelfth generation head of Shōyei-dō, and it was his great-great-grandfather who first introduced Japanese incense to the West when he took samples of cone incense, one of his own inventions, to the World Exposition in Chicago in 1894. Hata-san shares his knowledge of incense with the West by performing kōdō to appreciative audiences around the world.

Incense used for personal enjoyment today is derived from aromatic woods, and from herbs, spices, and flowers. Perhaps the most intriguing of these are the aromatic woods. Sandalwood (byakudan), aloeswood (jinkō), and resinated aloeswood (kyara) are the three main kinds. Sold in chips or granules, some of these woods are taken from root sections, some from green wood, and some from pieces found buried for a thousand years. The older the piece, the more earthy, subtle and expensive the fragrance.

Unlike senkō (the stick form of incense), wari-byakudan or wari-jinkō (the wood-chip varieties) must be burned in small charcoal-incense burners. Fine blends of incense in stick form are available, though many of them are more pungent and insistent than the natural woods, which are a bit more troublesome to burn. A lighted piece of charcoal (sumi) is placed in the center of a mound of ash in a ceramic or metal kōro burner. Over this, a small square of transparent mica is set to shield the incense from touching the charcoal directly. The mica is then covered with ash, leaving just a small opening in which to place the incense, which is heated, rather than burned, affording the longest lasting, most delicate aroma.

The language of fine fragrance defies words. The verb kagu, to smell, is not used to refer to incense. The Japanese prefer to use kiku, to listen —perhaps in an effort to describe an experience that appeals as much to a sixth sense as it does to any of the other five.

DAIKOKU-YA
buckwheat noodles (soba)

281 Minami-kurumaya-chō, Kiyamachi
Tako-yakushi Nishi-iru, Nakagyō-ku
中京区木屋町蛸薬師西入ル南車屋町281
TEL: (075) 221–2818
OPEN: 11:30 A.M.–11 P.M. ■ CLOSED: Tuesdays
■ PRICES: ¥ ■ CREDIT: Major credit cards

Located in the heart of the downtown
shopping district, Daikoku-ya is the
perfect place to stop for a bowl of *soba*
noodle soup. Made fresh daily, even
the buckwheat flour is ground on the
premises in the old stone mill just
inside the doorway! The giant red paper
lantern out front is impossible to miss,
even amid all the modern neon along
this busy downtown side street. The
staff are friendly and the food is excellent. Be adventurous and try the *nishin
soba*, a Kyoto specialty topped with an
exquisitely marinated piece of herring.

ICHIHARA HEIBEI
SHŌTEN   chopsticks

Sakai-machi, Shijō-sagaru, Shimogyō-ku
下京区四条下ル堺町
TEL: (075) 341–3831
OPEN: Daily, 10 A.M.–6:30 P.M.; Sundays 11
A.M.–6 P.M.

With three hundred years of history
behind it, Ichihara has the most extensive selection of finely crafted *o-hashi*
(chopsticks) in Kyoto and perhaps in all
the world. With more than four hundred types to choose from, Mr. Ichihara
numbers many of Kyoto's finest chefs
among his devoted customers. Whether
lacquered and inlaid with mother-of-
pearl, or carved from painstakingly finished natural wood, the rows and rows

of colorful chopsticks are a feast for the
eyes, and a perfect (and compact) Kyoto
souvenir to take home to friends.

IKAWA TATEGU-TEN
paper-covered doors

Karasuma Higashi-iru, Ebisugawa-dōri,
Nakagyō-ku
中京区夷川通烏丸東入ル
TEL: (075) 231–2646   FAX: (075) 231–2646
OPEN: 9 A.M.–6 P.M. ■ CLOSED: Mondays

One aspect of the Japanese house is
the versatility of the space within. In
the winter months, heavy sliding paper
doors called *fusuma* divide the space
into smaller rooms that can be easily
heated. In the summer the *fusuma* are
removed and replaced by beautiful sliding reed doors called *yoshi-shōji* which
allow for ventilation through the humid
Kyoto summers. Ikawa also sells *shōji*,
the wood-framed, sliding doors covered
with translucent white paper. The shop
specializes in refurbishing old *fusuma*
and *yoshi*, gathered from the many old
homes that are now facing the bulldozers. Ask to see the catalog of interesting *fusuma* door pulls called *hikite*
in a wide range of styles from simple
brass fittings to elaborate designs edged
in silver and gold.

OWARI-YA
buckwheat noodles (soba)

Nijō-sagaru, Kurumaya-chō, Nakagyō-ku
中京区車屋町二条下ル
TEL: (075) 231–3446   FAX: (075) 221–6081
OPEN: 11 A.M.–6:30 P.M. ■ CLOSED: Wednesdays ■ PRICES: ¥

One of the oldest buckwheat noodle
(*soba*) shops in Kyoto, Owari-ya is located

in a neighborhood worth wandering through, for northeast of Karasuma-Oike is a section of town that is not included on most of the tourist maps, but is full of interesting old shops of all kinds (an ancient Chinese medicine shop specializing in eye remedies is just a few doors north on the opposite side of the street). The old two-story building with its creaking stairways, tables wedged into nooks and crannies, and private rooms that overlook a tiny garden is worth the small price of a bowl of delicious home-style *soba*.

SEIKA-DŌ
metalwork, pewter

Nijō-saguru, Teramachi-dōri, Nakagyō-ku
中京区寺町通二条下ル
TEL: (075) 231–3661 (English spoken)
FAX: (075) 231–6542

OPEN: 10 A.M.–6 P.M. ■ CLOSED: Sundays, holidays ■ CREDIT: AE, MC, UC, VISA

Teapots and tea utensils in pewter and other metals done by noted local craftsmen. Mr. Yamanaka has provided not only an outlet for the sale of traditional objects, but a showplace in recent years for a fine collection of one-of-a-kind works by both aspiring young craftsmen and old masters. Mr. Yamanaka is one of the kindest shopkeepers in Kyoto and will introduce you to the little-known art of Japanese pewter ware in English.

ŌIWA
kushikatsu kebabs

Nijō-saguru, Kiyamachi-dōri, Nakagyō-ku
中京区木屋町通二条下ル
TEL: (075) 231–7667 (English spoken)
OPEN: 5 P.M.–10 P.M.; Sundays and holidays, 4 P.M.–10 P.M. ■ CLOSED: Wednesdays ■ PRICES: ¥–¥¥ ■ CREDIT: JCB, VISA, AE

An old *kura* treasure house at the head of the Takasegawa Canal on Kiyamachi near the Fujita Hotel, serving *kushikatsu*, skewered meats and vegetables which have been breaded and deep fried. The folk-style interior has a long counter where you can order either one delicacy at a time or *omakase*, a full course of thirty different skewers that will not leave you bankrupt (or hungry). If you prefer, you can take a booth in the room in the back where you will be seated around a low table on tatami. For many people, the word *kushikatsu* brings to mind a boys' night out spent munching greasy snacks over

a mug of beer, but at Ōiwa the cook was once a chef in a French restaurant in Tokyo, his skewers are *magnifique*, and the atmosphere is comfortable. (Have a look at the old flatboat moored in the canal in front of Ōiwa; it's a replica of a *Takasebune* boat, in which goods were ferried down the Takasegawa Canal to Osaka for hundreds of years.)

KYŪKYO-DŌ
incense, stationery, brushes

Ane-kōji-kado, Teramachi-dōri, Nakagyō-ku
中京区寺町通姉小路角
TEL: (075) 231–0510 (English spoken)
OPEN: 10 A.M.–6 P.M. ■ CLOSED: Sundays

This spacious shop opened originally in 1774 as an herbal medicine shop. It now specializes in incense, brushes, and ink sticks, with a large selection of handmade paper and tea ceremony utensils. A great shop to browse around in. Try a small bag of *wari-byakudan*, chips of sandalwood incense for use in a charcoal brazier. Some people toss a pinch into their fireplaces to add a subtle aroma to the whole room. Electric braziers made of porcelain eliminate the fuss of lighting small, round pieces of charcoal each time you wish to burn some. The stick variety of incense (*senkō*), though easier to use, is more pungent and is mainly for religious purposes. Unlike the overpowering, heavily-perfumed stick incense from India, Japanese aromatic wood incense, *byakudan* or *jinkō* (aloe), adds just a subtle aura to a special occasion. A complete line of paintbrushes for *sumi-e* (ink painting) are made by Kyūkyo-dō's own craftsmen.

FUNDŌ-YA
footwear (tabi)

Sakai-machi-kado, Sanjō-dōri, Nakagyō-ku
中京区三条通堺町角
TEL: (075) 221–2389
OPEN: 9:30 A.M.–6:30 P.M. ■ CLOSED: Sundays, holidays

Tabi, the split-toed socks worn with thonged Japanese footwear, are custom-made to fit your foot here, where many of Kyoto's kabuki actors and tea masters order the dozens of pairs of *tabi* they need to perform (only immaculately white *tabi* are formally acceptable). Colored fabrics are used to make *tabi* for casual or work wear. Ready-made *tabi* are also available in standard Japanese sizes (meaning small).

HIROTA
guest house

Nijō Tomino-kōji Nishi-iru, Nakagyō-ku
中京区二条富小路西入ル
TEL: (075) 221–2474 (English spoken)
CHECK-IN: 3 P.M. ■ CHECK-OUT: 11 A.M. ■ RATES: ¥¥

Owned by Harumi Hirota, a professional Kyoto guide, this charming little guest house is a hidden treasure, located behind the family residence in their former *kura* storage house. The downstairs room opens directly onto the garden and is available with or without kitchen facilities. It is popular with visiting scholars and those in search of a quiet haven in a very central location. Hirota-san is a charming Kyoto lady, fluent in English and full of sightseeing suggestions and advice. There is a midnight curfew, but who would want to be anywhere else? Book well in advance, as the tiny two-room guest house books up quickly each year.

C32

MACHIYA SHASHIN-KAN
photo gallery

Moto Seiganji-sagaru, Ōmiya-dōri, Kamigyō-ku

上京区大宮通元誓願寺下ル

TEL: (075) 431–5500

OPEN: 11 A.M.–5 P.M. ■ CLOSED: Sundays ■ CREDIT: Major credit cards

For more than thirty years, photographer Katsuhiko Mizuno has been renowned for his uncanny ability to capture the heart and soul of Kyoto temples, gardens and scenery through a camera lens. In 1995, he opened a gallery in a carefully restored 130-year-old *Kyō-machiya*. Mizuno-san has been a strong proponent of saving the *machiya* from the wrecker's ball. The purchase of one of his remarkable photographs of Kyoto is a delightful way to remember the unique beauty of this city for years to come. Open every day except Sunday, but it's best to call ahead first.

C33

MENAMI
obanzai home-style cooking

Kiyamachi, Sanjō-agaru, Nakagyō-ku

中京区三条上ル木屋町

TEL: (075) 231–1095

OPEN: 5 P.M.–11 P.M. ■ CLOSED: Sundays ■ PRICES: ¥¥ ■ CREDIT: Major credit cards

It would not be fitting to leave Kyoto without trying *obanzai ryōri*, or Kyoto family-style cooking, and Menami is the place to sample some of the best. Take a seat at the counter (if you get there early enough), and it is easy to select your courses from over a dozen beautiful porcelain serving bowls lined up along the counter top. Served on little plates not unlike Spanish tapas, the menu changes with the season at this lively and popular local eatery. A pitcher of saké, a bottle of beer, and a nibble of something quintessentially "Kyoto" won't set you back a fortune either.

C34

KUSHIKURA
grill restaurant

Takakura-dōri, Oike-agaru, Nakagyō-ku

中京区高倉通御池上ル

TEL: (075) 213–2211

OPEN: 11 A.M.–2 P.M., 5 P.M.–11 P.M. ■ CLOSED: At lunchtime on Saturdays, Sundays, and holidays ■ PRICES: Lunch ¥, dinner ¥¥

This grand one-hundred-year-old *Kyō-machiya* was once the home of a successful Kyoto merchant. In the 1990s, it was reborn as an elegant yet reasonably priced restaurant serving delicious *yakitori* (grilled chicken) and *kushiyaki* (skewered meats, fish and vegetables grilled over a charcoal fire). Take a seat at the long counter or in one of the private rooms on the ground floor, each of which has a view of the lovely courtyard gardens. Kushikura was one of the first restaurants to open in a restored *machiya* in Kyoto.

C35

TACHIKICHI
ceramics

Tomino-kōji-kado, Shijō-dōri, Shimogyō-ku

下京区四条通富小路角

TEL: (075) 211–3143

OPEN: 10:30 A.M.–7 P.M. ■ CLOSED: Wednesdays ■ CREDIT: Major credit cards

Since 1752, Tachikichi has been selling fine *Kyō-yaki*, or Kyoto ceramics, noted particularly for either a delicate blue or multicolored painting on porcelain, often edged in gold. The present shop is a modern though elegantly designed four-story building (on Shijō-dōri about a seven-minute walk west of Kawara-machi) that has become Kyoto's exclusive emporium for fine ceramics. Traditional wares for serving *kaiseki*, tea sets, vases, tea bowls, and everyday dishware in a wide range of prices are all here. Offerings include everything from an inexpensive set of five beer glasses delicately etched in bamboo, plum, and pine branch motifs to a costly but incomparable Kiyomizu-ware tea bowl stamped with the master's seal in its own signed wooden box. You can also arrange to have items shipped safely anywhere in the world.

C36

ARITSUGU
cutlery, kitchenware

Gokō-machi Nishi-iru, Nishiki-kōji-dōri, Nakagyō-ku
中京区錦小路通御幸町西入ル
TEL: (075) 221–1091 (English spoken)
OPEN: Daily, 9 A.M.–5:30 P.M.

In business since 1560, Aritsugu deals in fine hand-wrought cutlery and traditional kitchenware of all kinds, from sushi knives to vegetable peelers. Everything you need to prepare a formal meal in the Kyoto-style tradition is here—strainers, ladles, confectionery molds, bamboo steamers, wooden buckets, copper teapots, large soup pots, tempura pots, radish graters and hand-twisted copper tea strainers. For almost four hundred years Aritsugu was located a few blocks south of Shijō-dōri, but it

moved to the heart of the colorful Nishiki-kōji twenty-five years ago, becoming a landmark shop along the lively old market street unanimously acclaimed "Kyoto's kitchen."

C37

HŌRAI-DŌ
tea, tea utensils

Shijō-agaru, Teramachi-dōri, Nakagyō-ku
中京区寺町通四条上ル
TEL: (075) 221–1215   FAX: (075) 213–2505
OPEN: 10 A.M.–8:50 P.M. ■ CLOSED: 2nd, 12th, & 22nd of every month ■ CREDIT: Major credit cards

An old tea shop just half a block north of Shijō-dōri on Teramachi-dōri amid a jungle of shiny new clothing boutiques that have popped up in recent years. Not only do they have fine Uji teas, both in leaf (*sencha*) and powder (*matcha*) which you can order by the gram, but they also offer a limited selection of utensils used in the tea ceremony—tea bowls, whisks, bamboo spoons, ladle rests, and tea caddies—at reasonable prices. (A price list is now available in English.) The friendly family shop has all the charm of traditional Kyoto and refuses to give in to the downtown trend toward modernization. Now that almost every other traditional business has succumbed to redevelopment to serve the modern tourist trade along Teramachi-dōri, Hōrai-dō is much to be praised as one of the last traditional wooden shops along Teramachi to have held fast to its belief in the beauty of the traditional *machiya*.

ONO KUNGYOKU-DŌ
incense

Nishi Honganji-monzen, Horikawa-dōri, Shimogyō-ku

下京区堀川通西本願寺門前

TEL: (075) 371–0162

OPEN: 9 A.M.–7 P.M. ■ CLOSED: 1st and 3rd Sundays ■ CREDIT: Major credit cards

Ono Kungyoku-dō began dealing in fine incense over four hundred years ago. Located beside the east gate to Nishi Honganji, Kungyoku-dō is a part of the *monzen-chō*, or temple-gate town, that has provided worshipers with religious articles for centuries—Buddhist statuary, portable home shrines, prayer beads, candles, brocade banners, and altar pieces: all the finery a rural priest or pilgrim might ever need to pursue a path to the True Pure Land of the Jōdo Shinshū sect.

Kungyoku-dō specializes in a special house-blended incense in pellet form called *kun-kō*, and the recipe is a well-kept family secret. Mr. Ono also carries a wide selection of temple incense and *rōsoku* candles. The *rōsoku*, noted for its unique tapered shape, is made of plant products only, as the use of animal tallow goes against the Buddhist prohibition on killing animals. Hand-dipped in bright red or white in the same neighborhood, the *rōsoku*'s paper wick burns with a tall, pulsating flame.

TSUJIKURA
lanterns, umbrellas

Shijō-aguru, Kawaramachi-dōri, Nakagyō-ku

中京区河原町通四条上ル

TEL: (075) 221–4396

OPEN: 11 A.M.–8:00 P.M. ■ CLOSED: Wednesdays

Umbrellas of all kinds, both traditional Japanese ones (*wagasa*) and Western style, are the specialty at Tsujikura, though they also have a fine collection of handmade paper lanterns (*chōchin*) in a small room in back that shouldn't be missed. Round, traditional *bonbori* lanterns, and contemporary styles by Isamu Noguchi, as well as festival lanterns with *mon* crest designs painted in black on a white background, are available.

FUJINO-YA
tempura, kushikatsu kebabs

Shijō-aguru, Pontochō, Nakagyō-ku

中京区先斗町四条上ル

TEL: (075) 221–2446

OPEN: 5 P.M.–10 P.M. ■ CLOSED: Wednesdays ■ PRICES: ¥–¥¥

Enter this one-hundred-year-old tea-house and walk all the way down the dark corridor to the back, past the kitchen and the pocket-sized interior garden, to a tatami room that overlooks the river. During the summer, when all the restaurants and teahouses along this stretch of the Kamogawa River build platforms for their customers to enjoy a meal cooled by the river breezes, you can sit out over the water and relax in the knowledge that a full-course tempura dinner here is relatively inexpensive. This restaurant is in Pontochō, the old geisha quarter, which is famous for its high-priced restaurants. The food at Fujino-ya is simple and delicious, and the old Kyoto atmosphere lingers still.

and is actually a fry-it-yourself tempura meal which arrives with a cast iron kettle of hot oil. Place the skewered, batter-dipped pieces of shrimp, vegetables, and meat in the kettle one by one yourself—with soup and rice, a real delight. Because of the popularity of Yamatomi, the owners continue to expand and modernize, so some of the old teahouse charm has gone. It is still a lively eatery, and the food and prices have not suffered much in the transition.

C41

YAMATOMI
teppin-age, oden stew

Shijō-agaru, Pontochō, Nakagyō-ku
中京区先斗町四条上ル
TEL: (075) 221–3268   FAX: (075) 582–2200
OPEN: 12 NOON–11 P.M. (breaks 2 P.M.–4 P.M. weekdays) ■ CLOSED: Tuesdays ■ PRICES: ¥ (English menu available)

Located about halfway up from Shijō-dōri on Pontochō before you reach the park. On a cold winter evening, try Yamatomi's *oden*, a potpourri of vegetables, eggs, tofu, and other delicacies simmered in a tasty broth. You can order an assortment (*moriawase*) or a piece at a time, choosing from the steaming open vats on the counter. If you are interested in a complete dining experience, order *teppin-age*, which will be served at a table in a tatami room

C42

NIJŪSAN-YA
combs

85 Shin-chō, Kawara-machi Higashi-iru, Shijō-dōri, Shimogyō-ku
下京区四条通河原町東入ル新町 85
TEL: (075) 221–2371
OPEN: 10 A.M.–8:00 P.M. ■ CLOSED: 3rd Wednesday

Boxwood hair combs (*tsuge-gushi*), both as hair ornaments and pocket combs, have been sold here since 1820. The shop itself is a work of art, with a flower arrangement by a local *ikebana* master always on display in the front window. Their combs are now made in Osaka since their last Kyoto craftsmen retired. Nijūsan-ya also has a number of barrettes and hair clasps for modern hairstyles as well as the traditional hair ornaments worn by geisha.

Gojō-Rakuen and the Bargain Inns

The Takasegawa Canal runs through this now quiet neighborhood like a theme— one whose tune has definitely changed. For decades, the canal was lined with brothels, in all the old-fashioned sense of the word. No barkers hawk their "wares" beneath spasmodic neon tombstones as they do further north along Kiyamachi-dōri. Dimly provocative doorways frame the old "mama-san" who sit silently beside their gurgling fish tanks, waiting for the few patrons who prefer anachronism to rhinestones. Though such areas in other countries could expect their share of shady characters and crime, the police box on the corner is seldom troubled with more of a problem than putting the occasional drunk into a cab to send him home. There is even a kindergarten amid it all. In days gone by, it was known as the Gojō-Rakuen, the Fifth Street "amusement park." Today, it is better known for its inexpensive inns than for the few remaining "teahouses" that dot the canal. Many of these inns are registered with the Japanese Inn Group, an organization that encourages tourists to "experience the real Japan" by taking a room in an inexpensive, family-run ryokan, or inn. Popular with young travelers, the inns offer some of the lowest rates in town; they are clean, comfortable, within walking distance of downtown, and a very good place to meet other travelers and find out what's going on. Three of the most hospitable are listed below (C43–C45).

RIVERSIDE TAKASE
inn

Shōshinji-chō, Kaminokuchi-aguru, Kiya-machi-dōri, Shimogyō-ku

下京区木屋町通上ノ口上ル聖真子町

TEL: (075) 351–7925

CHECK-IN: 3 P.M. ■ CHECK-OUT: 10 A.M. ■ RATES: ¥–¥¥ ■ CREDIT: VISA

The owners of this annex to Kyōka Ryokan (near Kyoto Station) are teachers of flower arrangement and tea ceremony, so appointments for lessons can be made easily here. The annex overlooks the Takasegawa Canal and is just half a block from the largest public bath house in the neighborhood (sauna included).

HIRAIWA
inn (ryokan)

314 Hayao-chō, Kaminokuchi-aguru, Ninomiya-chō-dōri, Shimogyō-ku

下京区二ノ宮町通上ノ口上ル早尾町 314

TEL: (075) 351–6748

CHECK-IN: 3 P.M. ■ CHECK-OUT: 10 A.M. ■ RATES: ¥–¥¥ ■ CREDIT: AE

The largest and most popular of the inns in this neighborhood, Hiraiwa is the place to go to meet people, find out what's happening, where to eat and drink—even how to get a job—on a shoestring in Kyoto. This has become a mecca for young (and not so young) travelers seeking an inexpensive and interesting stay in the city. The owners welcome foreign guests, and at Hiraiwa you can experience both the funky, old ambience of the Gojō-Rakuen district and meet people from Amsterdam or Arkansas—all in one eclectic place. (The

Central Kyoto

117

newer Iraiwa annex is fine for connoisseurs of stucco and whitewash.)

C 45

RYOKAN YUHARA
inn

188 Kagiya-chō, Kiyamachi-dōri
Shōmen-agaru, Shimogyō-ku
下京区木屋町通正面上ル鍵屋町 188
TEL: (075) 371–9583   FAX: (075) 371–9583
CHECK-IN: 3 P.M. ■ CHECK-OUT: 10 A.M. ■
RATES: ¥–¥¥

A small, inexpensive inn that overlooks the Takasegawa Canal in the quiet area south of Gojō-dōri and is within a fifteen-minute walk of Kyoto Station. Especially delightful in mid-spring when the cherry blossoms along the canal are in full bloom. The proprietress is gracious and friendly, and, though bathing requires a short jaunt to the public bath, showers are available.

C 46

HIRATA
clay dolls, folk toys

89 Higashi-monzen-chō, Tōji, Minami-ku
南区東寺東門前町 89
TEL: (075) 681–5896
OPEN: Daily, 9 A.M.–4:30 P.M. ■ CLOSED:
Periodically

A block north of Tōji Temple, this little shop is not one of the usual guidebook selections, even for Japanese. Once a saké shop, later selling ceramic bonsai planters (some of which they still have), Hirata now specializes in folk toys from all over Japan, which the owner has been collecting for over thirty years. Mr. Hirata's Miharu ningyō, delicately painted dolls of papier-mâché from Fukushima Prefecture, are exquisite and difficult to obtain. He also has Saga men, the paper masks from the Saga area (there is only one elderly craftsman who still makes them), wooden toys, and clay figures from hundreds of villages all over Japan. An expert on Japanese folk toys, he is the author of an authoritative book on the subject.

RAKU-TŌ

Eastern Kyoto

If you have but one day to spend in Kyoto, walk the paths of the elegant Raku-tō district at the foot of Higashiyama, the Eastern Mountain, that runs from Ginkaku-ji, the Silver Pavilion, in the north to Kiyomizu-dera and Sanjūsangen-dō, the hall of a thousand Kannon, in the south. This district is the home of temples, great and small, and it is here, at Nanzen-ji, where Zen became the influential force in Japanese culture that it remains today. Black-robed monks with begging bowls in hand can still be heard chanting for alms in the neighborhoods around the gates.

Kiyomizu-dera, the grande dame of Kyoto temples, has drawn pilgrims to Raku-tō since the Heian period. The cobbled paths that lead up to it are lined with ceramics shops left over from the time when this area was the main pottery district in Kyoto. The sixty-seven-ton bronze bell of Chion-in Temple has tolled the arrival of every New Year in Kyoto since the seventh century, and Ginkaku-ji, the Silver Pavilion, where the shogun Ashikaga Yoshimasa held his elegant tea ceremonies four hundred years ago, still stands as a symbol of the height of culture attained in Raku-tō so long ago.

The Philosopher's Walk, the lovely path that follows an old canal from the foot of Ginkaku-ji southward, with its cherry blossoms in spring and red maple leaves in fall is as popular today with young lovers as it once was with great thinkers.

Kyoto's most famous geisha quarter, Gion, is in Raku-tō. Here the streets are lined with old teahouses, and in the early evening the young maiko *apprentices can be seen in all their finery hurrying to entertain guests with an evening of saké and dance.*

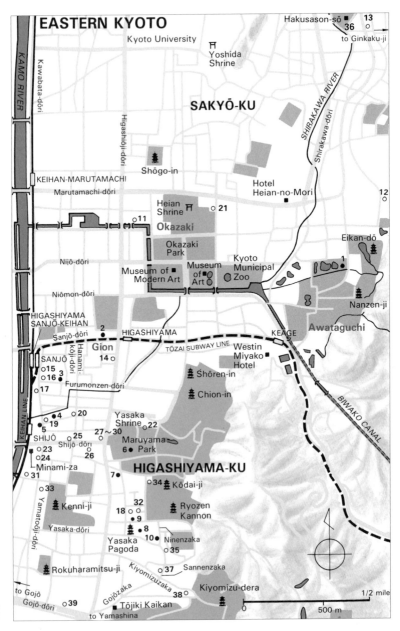

EASTERN KYOTO

Hakusason-sō ■ **13**
36 ○
to Ginkaku-ji

Kyoto University

Kawabata-dōri

KAMO RIVER

Yoshida Shrine

SAKYŌ-KU

SHIRAKAWA RIVER

Shirakawa-dōri

Higashiōji-dōri

Shōgo-in

KEIHAN-MARUTAMACHI
Marutamachi-dōri

Hotel Heian-no-Mori ■

12 ○

Heian Shrine ○ **21**

Okazaki ○**11**

Okazaki Park

Eikan-dō

Nijō-dōri

Museum of Modern Art ■

Museum of Art

Kyoto Municipal Zoo

1

Niōmon-dōri

Nanzen-ji

HIGASHIYAMA SANJŌ-KEIHAN

2

Sanjō-dōri HIGASHIYAMA

KEAGE

Awataguchi

TŌZAI SUBWAY LINE

BIWAKO CANAL

SANJŌ
○**15**
○**16** **3**
○**17**

Hanami-kōji-dōri

Gion
14○

Furumonzen-dōri

Westin Miyako Hotel ■

Shōren-in

Chion-in

KEIHAN LINE

○**4**
●**19**
5

○**20**

Yasaka Shrine ○**22**

SHIJŌ ○**25**
Shijō-dōri

27~30
Maruyama Park
6●

○**23**
○**24**
Minami-za
○**31**

HIGASHIYAMA-KU

○**33**

7●

Kenni-ji

Yamatoōji-dōri

Yasaka-dōri

○**34** Kōdai-ji

32
18 ○ ○
●**9**

Ryozen Kannon

Yasaka Pagoda

●**8**
10● Ninenzaka
○**35**

Rokuharamitsu-ji

Kiyomizuzaka
○**37** Sannenzaka

Kiyomizu-dera

to Gojō
Gojō-dōri

○**39**
Gojōzaka
● Tōjiki Kaikan
to Yamashina

38○

1/2 mile

500 m

OKUTAN
tofu cooking

Nanzen-ji main shop

86–30 Fukuji-chō, Nanzen-ji, Sakyō-ku

左京区南禅寺福地町86–30　TEL: (075) 771–8709

OPEN: 11:00 A.M.–5:30 P.M. (seating until 5:00) ■ CLOSED: Thursdays ■ PRICES: ¥¥

Kiyomizu branch (English spoken)

3–340 Kiyomizu, Higashiyama-ku

東山区清水3–340　TEL: (075) 525–2051

OPEN: 11:00 A.M.–5:30 P.M. (seating until 5:00) ■ CLOSED: Thursdays ■ PRICES: ¥¥

Making a holy pilgrimage to a revered Kyoto temple has been a praiseworthy endeavor in Japan for hundreds of years. Travel was difficult and took much time, and for a hard-working agricultural populace, time was more than money; it was life. Taking time off from toil in feudal Japan (almost as difficult as it is today) required an iron-clad excuse, but who could doubt the sincerity of a religious man? Undertaking a holy pilgrimage was a chance to see the world, and still is—a fact you'll notice when busloads of faithful travelers from the countryside unload before the gates of Nanzen-ji, one of Kyoto's most popular religious attractions. In the Middle Ages, people would undertake a pilgrimage to one thousand temples and shrines in a circuit that led from one holy site to another, often under the patronage of a particular deity. People marked the completion of each step in such a circuit by affixing stickers imprinted with

their names (*senja fuda*) to the gateway of each temple or shrine they visited. Entering the main gate at Nanzen-ji, you can count the hundreds of *senja fuda* whose namesakes have long since ended their pilgrimages through life. Aside from the joy of traveling, many people undertook such pilgrimages to pray for sick relatives or for success in special endeavors. The higher up on a gateway the sticker was placed, the more likely it was to come to the attention of the gods. During the Edo period, pilgrims used long, retractable walking sticks to reach the heights of spiritual achievement, as it were.

During the eighteenth century, when such excursions were at the height of popularity, the constant influx of pilgrims prompted the opening of dozens of inns and teahouses along the roads that lead to temple gates. *Monzen-jaya*, the name by which these rest stops were known, provided simple, nourishing

meals (vegetarian-style, in keeping with the spirit of Zen).

Near the gates of Kiyomizu-dera, Yasaka-jinja, and Nanzen-ji, three of the most popular destinations for pilgrims, there are still a few old *monzen-jaya* which serve "temple-gate" fare. Okutan, inside the north gate at Nanzen-ji, is one of the finest. For thirteen generations this small teahouse has served *yudōfu*, an old Zen recipe for fresh tofu simmered in a big ceramic pot, with a soy sauce for dipping and an array of vegetable dishes on the side. At Okutan, the side dishes include *yasai* tempura (batter-fried vegetables) and *tōfu dengaku* (skewers of grilled tofu with sweet miso sauce).

Rustic cedar-shingled tatami rooms open on one side to face a stone walkway overlooking a garden that seems to be at its best in every season: cherry trees in spring, brilliant greenery in summer, red maple leaves in fall, and the possibility of snowfall in winter.

Though every season is beautiful, perhaps winter is the best—with or without the snowflakes. *Yudōfu* was meant to warm chilled bones on a frosty afternoon in January when each breath hangs a split second in the air—hot tofu, the heat from a charcoal hibachi, surrounded by a natural setting of trees as old as the nearby hills. In warmer weather, the menu features *karashi-dōfu*, a spicy tofu dish, and *hiya-yakko*, chilled tofu sprinkled with green onions and ginger.

Just outside the entrance to the original Okutan you can see the great Sanmon Gate of Nanzen-ji, the "gateless gate" of Zen—leading ever inward, locking no one out. A notorious sixteenth-century thief named Ishikawa Goemon (a kind of Oriental Robin Hood) once hid from the wrath of the warlord Hideyoshi here on the veranda atop the great Sanmon. Knowing he was close to a violent end, he surveyed the rooftops of Nanzen-ji below and the slopes of the Higashiyama Mountains all around him and composed this poem:

> Splendid . . . splendid!
> The view from here
> Is worth more than
> A thousand pieces of gold!

Quite a recommendation for a man who spent his life in pursuit of gold coins. He met his fate (like a pot of simmered tofu, and much less pleasantly) on the banks of the Kamogawa River, where Hideyoshi had him and his son boiled in oil not long thereafter.

If you are near Kiyomizu-dera to the south, visit Okutan's southern branch, housed in the former villa of a wealthy merchant. Located where Ninenzaka meets Sannenzaka, this secluded location serves the same excellent *yudōfu* menu and welcomes guests to traditional tatami-mat rooms overlooking a luxurious landscape garden—as much a pleasure to view as the temple gardens at the main branch of Okutan at Nanzen-ji.

KAGOSHIN
bamboo

籠
新

Shichi-ken-chō, Ōhashi-higashi 4-chōme, Sanjō-dōri, Higashiyama-ku
東山区三条通大橋東四丁目七軒町　TEL: (075) 771–0209　FAX: (075) 771–0209
OPEN: 9 A.M.–6 P.M. ■ CLOSED: Monday mornings

The proudest day of Shintarō Morita's life was in 1920 when he climbed into the imperial roadster that would carry him to the old palace to receive a special award from the emperor for his role in the introduction of bamboo ware to the West. Since 1862, he had been making some of the finest bamboo basketry in Japan and had drawn the attention of buyers in the West to an art form previously overlooked abroad. His old bamboo shop still clings to the same spot on the north side of Sanjō-dōri where it first opened for business, though it is engulfed today in modern buildings and mid-town traffic.

During the Edo period, Sanjō-dōri was the last stretch of the Old Tōkaidō Highway which connected Kyoto with Edo (now Tokyo), three hundred miles to the east. There were many bamboo shops here beside the highway one hundred years ago, as it was a direct route for transporting bamboo from the lush forests of Shiga. Much of the bamboo supply in Shiga has been depleted over the years and only a few of the old bamboo shops in this area remain.

Now Morita-san's grandson must go all the way to Mukō-machi in the southwest of Kyoto where a good supply of bamboo, though dwindling, is still available. Of the 118 varieties of bamboo in Japan, over fifty special types are used in the fine basketry done at Kagoshin, and some rare varieties are brought from rural areas such as Hokuriku, Wakayama, and Shimane. With an island climate just right for growing bamboo, the Japanese have explored every possible use for the flexible material, from water pipes to umbrella ribbing. One old account lists over fourteen hundred uses in all. Basil Hall Chamberlain in 1904 remarked that "so extensive is the part played by bamboo in Japanese domestic economy that the question is rather, what does it not do?"

Times have changed, however, and aluminum and plastics now perform most of the everyday jobs bamboo once handled so gracefully. Today Kagoshin offers fine bamboo baskets primarily for tea-ceremony utensils and flower arrangement, as well as a variety of ornamental *sode-gaki* garden fence "sleeves."

One of the most interesting types of bamboo used in basket weaving is called *susu-dake*, bamboo taken from the soot-darkened ceilings of old Japanese farm houses. The rich, natural patina this *susu-dake* acquires is highly prized when woven in fine basketry, and the limited supply makes it quite expensive. It can be distinguished from artificially stained bamboo by the alternating dark and light areas on each strand which are the result of the bamboo having been lashed to the roof beams with hemp cord.

Bamboo basketry is not the simple craft it may appear to be. Freshly cut bamboo must be dried for two years before it can be worked, to which the ever-present stacks of drying stalks at the back of the shop (some several yards long) attest. Each individual stalk must then be evaluated for shape and quality. A single stone in the path of a sprouting bamboo shoot is enough to create a permanent groove that renders the stalk useless for ordinary basketry, though some tea ceremony enthusiasts do look for single-stalk bamboo vases with unusual twists and gnarls. For basket weaving, each stalk must be split and shaved to the appropriate width and thickness to suit the particular design. No two stalks of bamboo are identical, and the most difficult part of bamboo craftsmanship, according to Morita-san, is that each piece has an irrepressible character of its own that must be dealt with individually.

Apart from the baskets you see in the shop, special designs can be made to order. In fact, most of the baskets Morita-san makes are special orders for tea masters and department stores, but much of what you see in the front of the shop can be purchased directly. Many of his regular customers just describe the shape and size of basket they want, and Mr. Morita tries to match the design with the most suitable type of bamboo for the shape. At no time of the year will you find Morita-san dozing. There are always new baskets from the more than one hundred designs he makes at various stages of completion in his workshop, which opens right onto the busy street.

When asked if he hadn't considered remodeling the 120-year-old shopfront to save himself from the street noise and air pollution, he replied, "How could I tear this place down? My customers like the old atmosphere here and I would never hear the end of it, if I did! And besides, that room upstairs is where my grandfather made a bamboo chair for the emperor on his coronation day! How could I possibly destroy a room like that?"

Fortunately for Kagoshin, the legacy of this fine family lives on with the help of a new generation. Tsuyako Morita now works side by side with her proud father.

NAKANISHI TOKU SHŌTEN antique dolls

中西徳商店

359 Moto-chō, Yamato-ōji Higashi-iru, Furumonzen-dōri, Higashiyama-ku
東山区古門前通大和大路東入ル元町359   TEL: (075) 561–7309

OPEN: 10 A.M.–5 P.M. ■ CLOSED: Periodically ■ CREDIT: AE, VISA

A half smile, the faultless restraint, the delicate features, the irreproachable whiteness: like a noh mask, the face of a Japanese doll silently reveals the soul of an ancient ambiguous land. These dolls are windows to the past, and the image they pose is a half-forgotten ideal of beauty. They demonstrate in three dimensions how people lived, what they wore, what was important to them, what they felt and did not say. They recount a thousand years of history without the complication or inadequacy of language.

Kyoto is the place where the finest of Japanese dolls originated, and Nakanishi Toku Shōten on Furumonzen Street specializes in antique Kyoto dolls (*Kyō-ningyō*) of all kinds.

In Japanese, *ningyō*, the word that describes these figures, has a thousand-year-old history with its roots in the spirit world. Records from the Heian period show that figures called *hitogata* (another reading of the Chinese characters for the word *ningyō*) were used to draw evil spirits and illness away from afflicted human beings. Throwing the contaminated figure into a nearby stream was believed to rid the person of his misfortune. Paper figures used for the same purpose can still be found at shrines in Japan today. Another kind of *ningyō* was placed near the head of a newborn baby to act as a surrogate, absorbing misdirected mayhem and giving the new arrival a starting chance. These figures were enshrined in a place of honor and offerings were made to them, particularly on March 3 each year, the day of an ancient purification ritual which is known today as *Hina Matsuri* (the Doll Festival).

Over the centuries, the figures became more and more elaborate, and by the mid-Edo period, the festival was one of the major celebrations of the year. *Hina ningyō* were displayed in pairs, dressed as a nobleman and his lady, attended by servants and an assortment of miniature household furnishings (if your household happened to be regal, that is). Tiny flowering trees adorned the shelves as symbols of the season and of the imperial court.

The delicate domestic festival became a special day of celebration for girls—a

day on which they learned what it meant to a woman in Japan. The qualities *hina ningyō* portrayed were those of refinement and elegance, contentment, and restraint: exactly what Japanese society had in mind for its future wives and mothers.

The old custom has evolved into a display of wealth and status in recent years with a top-of-the-line set of dolls costing well over a million yen. Still, the celebration of *Hina Matsuri* and the eloquence of the earlier *hina ningyō* have much to teach the modern observer about the customs and background of old Japan.

So do the Nakanishis. Mr. Nakanishi was once a fan maker by trade. Now the few fan makers that remain in business are faced with increased material costs, the necessity of higher wages for their employees, and the low retail price of fans. Thirty-five years ago, Nakanishi-san decided to turn his long-time hobby of collecting antique Japanese dolls into a full-time business, and today his shop on Furumonzen Street is one of the only shops in Kyoto that deals exclusively in antique Japanese dolls. Though there are many antique dealers in the neighboring Shinmonzen district who handle dolls as a side interest, the Nakanishis specialize only in the finest quality dolls available. Collectors of fine dolls come from all over the world to buy dolls at their little shop.

The most popular kind of doll they sell is still the *hina ningyō*, but the *musha ningyō*, or samurai doll, is also in demand. In addition to these, the Nakanishis carry a wide variety of other antique Japanese dolls, many of which are rare even in Japan, including dolls made of clay or porcelain. Most of the festival dolls, like the *hina* and *musha ningyō*, are made with wooden or composition base heads that have been painted with white *gofun*, a powdered seashell paste, which is often mistaken for ivory or porcelain. Their elaborate brocade costumes are specially woven with patterns reduced to fit the miniature proportions of the dolls.

Mr. Nakanishi carves Buddhist statues from wood in his spare time, a hobby he took up some years ago "to keep my mind alert." He feels that the wooden Buddhas he carves are a natural outgrowth of his interest in antique dolls . . . after all, Buddha too had a human form.

SHIRAUME
inn (ryokan), restaurant

Shirakawa-hotori, Gion-shinbashi, Higashiyama-ku

東山区祇園新橋白川畔　TEL: (075) 561–1459

CHECK-IN: 3 P.M. ■ CHECK-OUT: 11 A.M. ■ RATES: ¥¥¥–¥¥¥¥ (w/2 meals) ■ RESTAURANT OPEN: 12 NOON–3 P.M. (last order 1:30), 5:30 P.M.–10 P.M. (last order 7:30) ■ PRICES: Lunch ¥¥–¥¥¥, dinner ¥¥¥–¥¥¥¥ ■ CREDIT: JCB, MC, VISA, AE

Kani kaku ni
Gion wa koishi
neru toki mo
makura no shita o
mizu no nagaruru.

No matter what they say,
I love Gion.
Even in my sleep
I hear the sound of water
Flowing beneath my pillow.
　　—Isamu Yoshii (1886–1960)

Gion . . . stone bridge over the old Shirakawa Canal, willows weeping like jilted lovers, their long, wispy limbs draped sadly over the shallow water, silhouettes half-concealed behind the *sudare* reed blinds hinting at the intimate rendezvous of a geisha and her patron on a warm, spring night . . . Gion. When Yoshii wrote the verse that is now engraved in stone beside the river, he must have been much in love with this floating world.

Ukiyo-e, "pictures of the floating world," allude to a world of passion that dissolves in the morning light: seduc-tive, unpredictable, exotic. Shiraume Ryokan, the "White Plum Inn," hugs the south bank of the old canal in the heart of Gion. The only way to reach the entrance is to cross the narrow foot-bridge over the stream. Part the *noren* curtain with the plum blossom crest, and step into the courtyard garden where a maid in kimono will greet you with "*Oideyasu,*" a word of welcome in the gentle Kyoto dialect so often heard in Gion.

Shiraume was once a famous tea-house called Dairyū, the "Big Willow," that was turned into an inn shortly after the war. During the Meiji period Dairyū was the popular haunt of novel-ists and poets who spent their nights lingering over cups of hot saké, lan-guishing in the melancholy night breeze with their favorite geisha in attendance. Isamu Yoshii was one of those men.

An *o-chaya,* or "teahouse," has little to do with tea, though most geisha dis-tricts started out as rest stops near shrines or temples where pretty girls served tea to weary pilgrims looking for salvation of a more temporal nature. In

Kyoto, an *o-chaya* is a house in which geisha parties are held. The proprietress, often a former geisha herself, arranges for geisha to meet guests who have made reservations for an evening of drinking, eating, and entertainment. Elaborate meals are prepared by special caterers. The geisha usually live in an *okiya*, a geisha house, which supplies them with room and board, a wardrobe of costly kimono, and an allowance. The word *ryōtei* refers simply to a first-class traditional restaurant to which geisha are often called to entertain guests.

The geisha world is complicated and has an air of mystery and intrigue, but these days it bears little resemblance to times past when impoverished farm girls were sold by their desperate parents into a life of servitude and prostitution. The word geisha means "artiste," referring to licensed professional entertainers who pride themselves on their artistry in music and dance. Although sexual favours are still a part of this exclusive world, today it is more a matter of personal choice.

Strolling down the cobblestone path beside the Shirakawa Canal in the evening, you are likely to pass a young *maiko*, an apprentice geisha, on her way to a nearby *o-chaya* to entertain guests. Dressed in elaborate multilayered kimono, her gold embroidered *obi* sash trailing behind, she'll clip-clop past on her platform geta, face painted white and hair fastened primly with lacquered combs and elaborate ornaments. She probably won't look your way—often a bit pouty, tired of cameras and flash bulbs before she turns twenty.

Shiraume is in the northern sector of Gion, in a historic district called Shinbashi, a triangular block famous for the unchanged ambience of rows of old *o-chaya*, some of which are still in use today for geisha parties as they were a hundred years ago.

As a former *o-chaya*, each room at Shiraume is different, some large enough to accommodate a party of ten, some just right for two. The room to ask for is downstairs at the end of the corridor with *shōji* doors that open right onto a small garden with a stone lantern and a thick stand of bamboo.

Shiraume serves full course *kaiseki* meals, *nabemono* (one-pot stews), sukiyaki and tempura. As in most *ryokan*, the price of accommodation is charged per person including breakfast and dinner, but Shiraume also offers a room for two with a Western breakfast at a reduced rate for their foreign guests. Either way, "the sound of water flowing beneath your pillow" is free. Unlike most Kyoto inns which close at 10 or 11 P.M., Shiraume has no curfew. How could a former Gion teahouse close its doors to those who love the night?

HIRATA
blinds

平

田

Shijō-agaru, Yamato-ōji, Higashiyama-ku
東山区大和大路四条上ル   TEL: (075) 561–1776
OPEN: 10:30 A.M.–6 P.M. ■ CLOSED: Sundays and holidays

Just after sunset Gion begins to stir with Kyoto's own special brand of night life—*maiko* in their trailing *obi* sashes, kitchen maids hurrying back to their inns with last-minute purchases for dinner, businessmen on expense accounts gathering a second wind after work for a night of serious drinking at their favorite club. *Sudare* blinds flapping gently in the breeze on the windows of teahouses that line the old stone canal in Gion are a symbol of the geisha world they half conceal.

Sudare hide the private evenings inside the teahouses from the curious eyes of passersby, adding to the sense of intimacy and mystery in Gion. Particularly in the Shinbashi district, one of the few historic preservation districts in Kyoto, *sudare* blinds are considered an essential design element of the façades of its buildings.

A block south of Shinbashi on Nawate-dōri is the shop that makes many of the famous *sudare* of Gion. Hirata has been making bamboo and reed blinds for over two hundred years, but the present proprietor, Yoshio

Hirata, the seventh-generation screen-maker, had no chance to learn his trade from his father. Hirata-san was only twelve years old when World War II broke out and his father was drafted into the imperial army. Kyoto lost many of its finest craftsmen to the war, and Yoshio's father was one of them. The day before the surrender was declared, without the head of the household present to defend it, their shop building was torn down "in the interests of the war effort." Hirata-san learned his trade after the war from other craftsmen who (unlike his father) returned home safely.

Before the war, *sudare* blinds were a necessary part of everyday life in Kyoto, where summers are hot and humid and the constant plague of mosquitoes is a perennial problem. *Sudare* allowed the paper *shōji* windows to be removed in summertime for ventilation, while shading the rooms from the heat of the sun. They also afforded a bit of privacy along the crowded streets in the pleasure quarter.

With the introduction of aluminum sash windows and metal screens after

Eastern Kyoto

the war, *sudare* became a luxury item used primarily for decorative purposes.

There are several different kinds of *sudare*, classified according to use and materials. The heavier outdoor type are called *hi-yoke sudare*. They come in a variety of materials including *take* (bamboo), *yoshi* (a hollow, jointed yellowish reed), *gama* (a solid beige reed without joints), and *hagi* (dark brown branches of a flowering shrub).

Sudare for interior use in tearooms and as room dividers during the summer months are called *zashiki sudare*, the kind with a fabric border in brocade or linen. The reeds of *zashiki sudare* are usually of bamboo, though more finely split than those for exterior use. Often when the material used is jointed, like bamboo, the joints are laid out to create a pattern on the finished blind— the more intricate, the more costly.

A third type of blind is called a *misu*, the very finest variety, formerly used to hide the emperor from the eyes of the public. Now they are used mainly in temples or shrines. As with many of the accoutrements of court life, the making

of *misu* was regulated by official protocol, which determined every detail— the number of reeds in each, the type of patterns their joints formed, and the kind of brocade used to border them.

The average *sudare* is about a yard and a half long by a little over a yard wide. Hirata will make blinds to fit any space required by special order, though at busy times you can expect to wait a month or more. If you wish to choose your own trim from fabric samples in his catalog, a standard-size order can be filled in a couple of days, since Hirata-san makes each blind himself here at the back of his shop on a machine that can be seen from the counter. English is not spoken, however, and it is suggested that you bring an interpreter to make a special order.

Other products sold at Hirata include *nawa-noren*, the hand-twisted hemp-rope curtains often seen in kitchen doorways or at the entrances to restaurants in Kyoto. Also available are *tsui-tate*, the single-panel standing screens that are placed inside entrances for decoration or to screen the recesses of the house from public view.

NAKAMURA-RŌ
restaurant

中村楼

Inside Yasaka-jinja, Gion, Higashiyama-ku
東山区祇園八坂神社内   TEL: (075) 561–0016～8   FAX: (075) 541–6738
OPEN: 11:30 A.M.–7:00 P.M. (last order, 6) ■ CLOSED: Last Thursday ■ PRICES: Lunch ¥¥, dinner
(kaiseki) ¥¥¥¥

*Standing on the bridge at Shijō I see a light: Is it Yasaka
Shrine . . . or can it be the lanterns of Niken-jaya?*

—Anonymous

Nobody remembers how long people have been stopping for a cup of tea and a bite of tofu beside the stone *torii* gate at Yasaka Shrine in Gion. But by the end of the sixteenth century, the pair of teahouses known as Niken-jaya were already famous. Only one has survived the four hundred years since then—Nakamura-rō, said to be the oldest restaurant in Japan. Rather than tearing down the tiny one-room hut that made them famous, the twelfth-generation owner of what is now a luxurious restaurant and inn guards the humble teahouse as the precious family heirloom it is.

Sliding open the *shōji* paper doors in midwinter, you become a part of a world that no longer exists. A worn stone floor, a wood-burning clay *kamado* stove with a sputtering kettle of water on for tea, the rough-hewn stone tofu basins, the old clay charcoal grill for heating the skewers of tofu, a stone well so deep you cannot see the bottom, with a lid so heavy that no one lifts it anymore, and a pair of imperturbable ladies in kimono who seem to be a part of the same frozen moment in time.

In summertime, the doors disappear completely, opening onto the graveled walkway to the shrine, and the shop looks much as it did in an old Edo-period woodblock print with pilgrims, foreigners, and itinerant priests gathered round waiting for their order of *tōfu dengaku* (skewers of tofu covered with miso sauce) to be placed on the low benches before them. Customers stopped in centuries ago to listen to the *shamisen* players strum to the rhythm of the chopping knives of beautiful ladies, who sliced the tofu to precise dimensions (seven slices lengthwise, three crosswise; 16 mm x 19 mm x 50 mm—exactly). A bowl of *o-usu*, the powdered tea of the tea ceremony, and a platter *of tōfu dengaku* still make a fine afternoon snack, no matter which century you belong to.

Late in the nineteenth century, an inn and formal restaurant were added to accommodate the number of *daimyō* (feudal lords) who flocked to Kyoto, which had become the focal point of a struggle to overthrow the shogunate and reinstate the emperor as ruler of Japan. Tales of clandestine meetings, by plotters on both sides, held in the banquet rooms and parlors of Nakamura-rō are legendary and easy to imagine as you walk down the long, narrow corridors that lead up and down stairways to the inner recesses of the inn. One royally appointed room at the back of the inn, now famous for its screen paintings by Ogata Kōrin, was once the temporary residence of Arisugawa no Miya, brother of the emperor Meiji.

All the rooms (some of which are guest rooms, some for private dinners, and others for large banquets) overlook a magnificent central garden that is beautiful throughout the year, with cherry trees in springtime, followed by azaleas, hydrangeas, maple leaves, chrysanthemums, and camellias, depending on the season. The inn is still a popular

retreat for poets and writers, who have been making annual pilgrimages to Nakamura-rō for decades.

Noted primarily as a *ryōtei* (a first-class restaurant), Nakamura-rō serves elegant private dinners and large banquets with *kaiseki*-style meals. It is not unusual to see geisha from neighboring Gion arriving to entertain a group of guests with an evening of *shamisen* music and dance.

Nakamura-rō is owned by Masamitsu Tsuji, who belongs to one of Japan's most famous families of chefs. He is the son of the late Shigemitsu Tsuji, the renowned author of an authoritative volume on tofu cuisine. At Nakamura-rō, the menu is strictly Kyoto style. Tsuji-san believes that focusing on the natural flavor of the ingredients is the secret to fine cooking, and he uses much less seasoning (salt, sugar, soy sauce, or spices) than chefs in other regions of Japan.

Apart from the full-course *kaiseki* dinners offered at Nakamura-rō, both the teahouse and the main restaurant serve a superb, but reasonably priced, *bentō* box lunch between 11 A.M. and 3 P.M. every day for a sampling of the type of cuisine offered in one of Kyoto's oldest restaurants.

In Kyoto today, the younger generation often sets about modernizing the venerable old antiques left them by their parents, whether they be houses or restaurants. When the elder Tsuji passed away in the 1980s, the mourners who attended the funeral, many of them old customers, implored the young son not to change a thing in the cherished old inn. Much to their continuing delight, Masamitsu Tsuji continues to uphold the family tradition.

27 Kasagen
28 Kazura-sei
29 Miura Shōmei
Hirano-ya
22
Maruyama Park
Shijō-dōri
Yasaka Shrine
30 Izujū
Nakamura-rō
Higashiōji-dōri
7 Minokō
34 Rakushō

MINOKŌ
cha-kaiseki cuisine

480 Kiyoi-chō, Shimogawara-dōri, Gion, Higashiyama-ku
東山区祇園下河原通清井町480   TEL: (075) 561–0328   FAX: (075) 561–1349

OPEN: 11:30 A.M.–2:30 P.M., 5 P.M.–9 P.M. (last order, 8) ■ CLOSED: Periodically ■ PRICES: *Bentō* lunch ¥¥, *cha-kaiseki* ¥¥¥¥ ■ CREDIT: Major credit cards

Just below the stone *torii* gate at the south and main entrance to Yasaka Shrine, there is a quiet neighborhood of innkeepers and restaurateurs that forms the eastern fringe of Gion, the old pleasure quarter of Kyoto. A stroll down the narrow cobblestone path called Ishibe-kōji in this area with its high rock walls and impressive old villas might lead you to believe that this is an exclusive residential district belonging to the privileged few. Many of these fine structures were indeed the villas of wealthy Kyoto merchants, but after World War II when many families lost their fortunes, most of the residences were turned into inns or "teahouses" (*o-chaya*), catering to the same affluent class that once inhabited them. The area, like Gion, now only comes alive at night. While retaining the dignity of former days, the teahouses and inns of Shimogawara-chō now have the added hint of intrigue that surrounds the world of the geisha of Gion, who are frequently called here to entertain.

Just before you get to the narrow alley that leads to Ishibe-kōji, you'll find one

of these former villas, a *ryōtei* called Minokō, that has combined these two worlds and added yet another dimension—that of *cha-kaiseki*, the elegant multi-course meal served at formal gatherings for the tea ceremony. *Cha-kaiseki* differs from banquet-style *kaiseki* not only in the characters that form the name, but in both style and purpose. In *cha-kaiseki*, *cha* means tea, *kai* means pocket or fold, and *seki* means stone, referring to the heated stones which Zen priests placed inside the folds of their garments to warm their bellies against the chill of unheated temples in winter. The meal served with the tea ceremony is intended to be "just enough to keep you warm," a reference to the Zen-like discipline and restraint sought as one of the primary goals of the practice of the tea ceremony. When served in conjunction with the tea ceremony, *cha-kaiseki* is a highly formal affair. At Minokō you have the chance to experience the same meal in the relaxed atmosphere of a private room.

Banquet-style *kaiseki* is written with different characters that mean banquet

seat and refer to the series of snacks that accompany a bottle of saké at drinking parties in a much less formal mode. This type of *kaiseki* is also available for groups who visit Minokō for events like *bōnenkai*, the let-your-hair-down year-end parties that are intended to help weary office workers "forget the old year."

At Minokō, *cha-kaiseki* is served with a bowl of thick green tea as the first course to stimulate the appetite, in a setting with all the natural beauty and simple elegance of a formal tearoom, but without the accompanying ceremony and its exactingly formal etiquette.

At lunch time, Minokō serves an informal box lunch called *chabako-bentō*, named for the elegant container in which it is served. These beautifully lacquered boxes resemble the kind that are used to carry tea utensils to outdoor tea gatherings. Lunch guests are served in a spacious tatami room overlooking a tea garden with stone lanterns and the sound of trickling water from a stream. The occasional turtle ambling from one rock to the next in this peaceful garden adds to the sense of rustic beauty so admired by aficionados of the tea ceremony.

In the evening, by reservation only, guests are seated in private tearooms with a view of the same lovely garden and are served in the height of *cha-kaiseki* style. One course after another of carefully arranged seasonal delicacies arrive on square porcelain trays, bamboo platters, and lacquered bowls chosen to complement the mood of the season. Kōjirō Yoshida remembers well the lessons his father Kazuo taught him about the seasonal appropriateness of items on each evening's menu. He never serves egg dishes in the summertime, for example, as his father had cautioned him often that Kyoto's humid summers are "a difficult time for the chickens."

The first time I arrived at Minokō to talk with the Yoshidas, it was early in the morning and I noticed a questionable looking substance strewn across the gleaming hardwood floors. Upon discreet inquiry, I was informed that these were damp tea leaves left over from last night's banquet and that every morning the maids sweep them gently across the hardwood floors to bring the surface to a deep, rich sheen. At Minokō, they wouldn't think of using anything else.

BUNNOSUKE-JAYA
amazake (a sweet beverage)

文の助茶屋

373 Yasaka-kamimachi, Shimogawa-dōri Higashi-iru, Higashiyama-ku
東山区下川通東入ル八坂上町373　TEL: (075) 561–1972
OPEN: 10 A.M.–5:30 P.M. ■ CLOSED: Wednesdays ■ PRICES: ¥

There were once scores of shops selling *amazake*—a sweet drink made from saké lees and served hot to weary travelers along the path that leads from Yasaka-jinja to Kiyomizu-dera. Though *amazake* has the aroma of the "real thing," it contains no alcohol and is said to have been the invention of Buddhist nuns. Kōdai-ji, a former nunnery just down the road from Bunnosuke-jaya, may be the reason this *amazake* shop still exists at all.

Kōdai-ji was the scene of one of the most tragic stories in Japanese history. After the death of the great military leader Toyotomi Hideyoshi, his widow vowed in grief to escape the cruel world by entering a nunnery. Perhaps in remorse for his own role in overthrowing Hideyoshi, Tokugawa Ieyasu in 1606 presented the distraught widow with Kōdai-ji, where she lived out the rest of her life. He even ordered that the Sōmon Gate of Hideyoshi's Fushimi Castle be moved here to comfort her. Not ten years later Ieyasu would wipe out every last member of the Toyotomi line.

The original site of Bunnosuke-jaya sat across the street from Kōdai-ji, just inside the precincts of a small shrine to Daitoku-ten, the god of wealth (and one of the seven gods of good luck so popular in Japan). Daikoku-ten was Hideyoshi's patron saint, and his widow is said to have brought the jolly deity with her to this site from Osaka Castle.

The shop was named after Katsura Bunnosuke, one of the great traditional entertainers of his generation, founded Bunnosuke-jaya there in the early days of the last century. He was master of the art of *rakugo*—humorous, often bawdy stories, in which the storyteller takes the role of multiple characters, with a single fan as his only prop.

The popularity of *rakugo* began to decline when the trend for sophistication and urbanity took hold of Japan around the end of the nineteenth century. Rickshaws went out with the advent of roadsters, and *rakugo* went out with talking pictures. By the end of the Meiji period, Bunnosuke had had enough of empty theaters and took early retirement to refurbish a rundown *amazake* shop that seemed to be fighting the same battle for survival as he was in a rapidly modernizing Japan.

When Bunnosuke-jaya shut its doors more than ten years ago, everyone in Kyoto mourned its apparent loss. But not for long. Today the popular *amazake* shop has re-opened on the street leading east from Yasaka Pagoda on the site of a former potter's house in this district known for the production of fine ceramics. Fire regulations now prohibit the use of wood-fired ceramic kilns in this district, and Bunnosuke-jaya took advantage of the site before it too was lost to history.

A seat at Bunnosuke-jaya for cup of *amazake* and a plate of *warabi-mochi*, a popular Kyoto confection, provides a front row seat for a viewing of one of the most bizarre collections of art and trivia in Japan. First, find the photo of old Bunnosuke and his wife taken in the Meiji period (1868–1912) for a glimpse at the flamboyant character behind this whole affair, for this eclectic spot seems more like a *rakugo* story in three dimensions than an ordinary tea shop. The shop overflows with mishmash of old Meiji clocks, *tansu* chests, wooden

tobacco boxes, kites, and souvenir folk dolls collected by Bunnosuke's successor, the late Etsuzō Yamada, on his many train trips around the countryside. There are even several interesting samples of Japanese folk erotica tucked here and there, and a woodblock print that Yamada-san swore was a masterpiece by Hokusai himself.

On my first visit to the original Bunnosuke-jaya in 1985, I discovered that the old shopkeeper had his father's sense of humor. I watched in amazement as he placed a giant carved phallus the size of a cannon barrel, in the hands of an unsuspecting young lady sipping her sweet drink on his porch. "Well, what do you think of that?" he beamed, anticipating with glee her giggled response.

Then in his late seventies, Yamada-san spent much of his time in the backroom with his TV set and his beloved photo albums full of Tamasaburō, his favorite kabuki actor and friend. It took a good deal of cajoling to persuade him to come out and tell stories. But when the gaunt old fellow in his somber striped kimono finally begrudgingly sat down on the *zabuton* cushion out front, adjusted his tobacco box, lit a long-stemmed *kiseru* pipe, and began one of his stories, I'd have sworn that *rakugo* was something in the blood.

Etsuzō Yamada is gone, but Bunnosuke-jaya lives on in its new incarnation to delight another generation of travelers who stop for a cup of *amazake* and a smile at this colorful footnote to Kyoto history.

IKKYŪ-AN
Zen vegetarian cuisine

Kōdai-ji Minami-monzen, Higashiyama-ku
東山区高台寺南門前　TEL: (075) 561–1901

OPEN: 12 NOON–8 P.M. (seating until 6:30) ■ CLOSED: Tuesdays ■ PRICES: Lunch ¥¥, deluxe courses and dinners ¥¥¥ ■ CREDIT: JCB, DC, VISA, DN

*Ten years in the brothels—hard to wear out desire; I force
myself to live in empty hills, a dark ravine. Those pleasant
places—countless miles of clouds shut them from me now.
Tall pines—harsh in my ears, wind above the roof.*

—Ikkyū Sōjun (1394–1481)

Legends about the "mad Zen monk," as Ikkyū Sōjun, the famous fifteenth-century priest came to be known, can probably only hope to come close to depicting the riotous life of one of Kyoto's most colorful monastics. The son of an emperor and one of his concubines, Ikkyū was to embarrass the haughty temple priests in whose charge he was placed at the age of five by his remarkable ability to answer all their "unsolvable" Zen riddles. By the age of twelve, he astounded his teachers by writing poetry in the sophisticated Chinese literary style he had come to the temple to study. At sixteen, he set out to find the enlightenment the temple fathers failed to show him. Under the harsh discipline of a disillusioned priest who shunned the corrupt hierarchy of Kyoto's Daitoku-ji Temple, he found enlightenment one day when the cry of a crow broke through his evening meditation on a boat in Lake Biwa.

From there he struck out again on his own, this time to the saké shops and bordellos of Sakai, carousing and challenging the piety of the pompous Kyoto abbots. He wound up as abbot of Daitoku-ji (whose lax priests he had most vehemently criticized), ironically becoming one of the temple's most revered abbots.

He never lost that edge of "madness," however, as can be seen in a series of poems written at the age of seventy-three about the blind singer Mōri with whom he had fallen in love. In spite of a long Buddhist tradition of celibacy, Ikkyū apparently continued to explore the spiritual possibilities of eroticism all the way to his grave. He died (happily, no doubt) fourteen years later.

Ikkyū-an, a quiet vegetarian restaurant at the foot of the Higashiyama Mountains, chose this endearing character as its mascot, and the server who comes to greet you at the door even wears the white robes of a priest in Ikkyū's time. Ikkyū-an serves *fucha ryōri*, an eight-course Chinese-style Zen meal, in a beautiful building that was once a part of Kōdai-ji Temple, beside whose south gate it stands. The full course includes *goma dōfu* (sesame tofu), vegetables in a delicate sweet sauce, *nasu dengaku* (eggplant with miso sauce), vegetable tempura, a variety of greens in vinegar or broth, soup, and rice. There is no need for a menu, as Ikkyū-an specializes only in this one particular type of meal. More expensive versions of the same meal can be ordered, the difference being the number and variety of courses served.

Fucha ryōri, unlike the Japanese-style Zen meal called *shōjin ryōri*, features thicker Chinese-style sauces, and is often served from large family-style platters rather than in small separate bowls.

The amazing thing about Zen vegetarian cuisine in Kyoto is the endless variety of flavors and textures in vegetarian cooking that have been explored in the Buddhist Orient. Dishes like *fu* (a wheat gluten dumpling), *yuba* (skimmings from soy milk), and tofu—however plain they may sound—offer a remarkable range of textures (in addition to the protein they provide) and are intended to absorb the flavor of delicate sauces and soups, solving the problem of monotony in a strictly vegetarian diet. Reservations are required at Ikkyū-an to insure that every dish is fresh and nothing is left over, in the spirit of Zen.

Apart from the cuisine, Ikkyū-an itself is something of a sensory treat. The bell-shaped windows in the southeast room on the second floor are typical of Zen-style architecture. They overlook the old Yasaka Pagoda on one side and the lush greenery of the Higashiyama Mountains on the other. Each small tatami room has a *tokonoma*, or alcove, with a scroll painting, a flower arrangement, and an image of Daikoku-ten, the god of wealth and happiness, and the guardian spirit of Ikkyū-an. Notice the beautifully carved transoms (*ranma*) above the sliding doors that separate the rooms.

Ikkyū-an was established as the result of a dream in which the astonished founder saw himself making Zen meals in a temple building on this site—an incongruous role for a retired Kyoto merchant in those days. Fortunately, he took his dream seriously, and opened Ikkyū-an, Kyoto's first *fucha ryōri* restaurant in 1915.

KASAGI-YA
tea and sweets

かさぎ屋

349 Masuya-chō, Kōdai-ji, Higashiyama-ku
東山区高台寺桝屋町349 TEL: (075) 561–9562
OPEN: 11 A.M.–6 P.M. ■ CLOSED: Tuesdays ■ PRICES: ¥

Amatō no sudōri dekinai Ninenzaka
(The sweet-lover's downfall, Ninenzaka.)
　　　　—by the poet Tenmin, on the wall at Kasagi-ya

Copper kettle sputtering over the hibachi coals . . . the proprietress prepares a bowl of *o-usu*, the strong powdered green tea, whisking it to a froth with elegance and ease. Carrying it gracefully across the tiny room with its sagging stone floor, she turns the bowl clockwise so that the *shōmen*, or "face," is directed toward her guest and places it on the table with a bow, just as the host would do at a formal tea ceremony. Although Kasagi-ya is not a formal tearoom, the graciousness and hospitality that is the essence of the tea ceremony is carried on here—quietly, lovingly, and in the spirit of humility that Sen no Rikyū sought to evoke in his *wabi-cha*, the aesthetic of unaffected refinement in *sadō*, the Way of Tea.

When asked about which school of tea she attended, Toshie Hayakawa is hesitant to reply. "Well, my father Hirozō studied at Omotesenke (the aristocratic branch of the Kyoto tea schools), but

following his example, we just serve tea and sweets the way we think is best," she says as she walks over to light another chip of natural sandalwood in an incense burner in the corner.

Toshie and her assistants make fresh *o-hagi* every morning the way her mother used to do. *O-hagi* is a very homey Kyoto sweet made with a sticky rice center and a coating of sweet red *azuki* beans (or vice versa.) *O-hagi* were originally served during the celebration of the autumn equinox. The name comes from a willowy bush clover that flowers only in the fall. At Kasagi-ya, the *o-hagi* are made fresh while you wait, and served warm, a rare treat in Kyoto today. They are sweet (but not cloyingly), a complement to the astringent flavor of *o-usu*.

Kasagi-ya is located at the foot of the steps that lead from Ninenzaka to Sannenzaka, the cobbled paths that lead up the hill to Kiyomizu-dera. The one-room shop seats no more than ten people and has been serving refreshments to visitors to the famous temple since 1914.

The sloping, stone-paved lanes that lead up to Kiyomizu-dera have been worn smooth over the centuries by the constant flow of pilgrims to the great temple dedicated to Kannon, the goddess of mercy. Almost thirty years ago, this neighborhood was designated Japan's first official historic preservation district. It is dotted with ceramic shops, antique shops, and inns (some old, some new) that make this area a mecca for tourists.

One of the most noted customers at Kasagi-ya was a Taishō-period painter named Yumeji Takehisa (1884–1934), whose female portraits are said to be the melancholy image of the frail woman he lived with in the old house next door to Kasagi-ya. A victim of tuberculosis, she died young, leaving Yumeji haunted with the memory of her fragile beauty. Their famous love affair was doomed from the start by the young woman's domineering father and a disease that was then in epidemic proportions across Japan. One of Yumeji's

rare landscape scenes hangs on the wall to the left of the entrance.

Aside from *o-usu* and *o-hagi*, Kasagi-ya serves other sweets and beverages to complement the season, such as *o-shiruko*, a smooth sweet bean soup, and *zenzai*, sweet whole red beans in a lighter broth, both popular in winter. Summer treats include *kōri-mizore*, shaved ice with sweet syrup on top or *kōri-uji*, shaved ice topped with green tea syrup.

The interior of Kasagi-ya, with its antique lamp shades, its old wooden tobacco boxes, the wicker stools, and the *senja-fuda* stickers bearing the names of former visitors (some famous actors and artists), is still redolent of days gone by. While other shops have completely remodeled to accommodate the throngs of tourists who flock here to soak up the atmosphere of "old Kyoto," Kasagi-ya quietly holds what its shinier neighbors lack: the genuine warmth and hospitality of a family business that can't be recaptured with a new coat of paint.

ROKUSEI NISHIMISE

Kyoto "box lunch"

71 Nishi-tennō-chō, Okazaki, Sakyō-ku

左京区岡崎西天王町71

TEL: (075) 751–6171 (English spoken)

FAX: (075) 761–6172

OPEN: Tuesday–Friday 11:30 A.M.–3 P.M., 5:00 P.M.–9:00 P.M.; Saturday and Sunday 11:30 A.M. –9 P.M. (last order, 8) ■ CLOSED: Mondays ■ PRICES: ¥¥–¥¥¥ ■ CREDIT: Major credit cards

Rokusei began as an exclusive *kaiseki* catering service in the year 1900 and later expanded to its present site on the west side of Heian Shrine overlooking the canal. The building is modern, with polished marble floors and contemporary Japanese interior design. A lunch-time favorite with both local residents and out-of-town visitors, Rokusei's *te-oke-bentō* box lunch offers the perfect sampler of Kyoto-style cuisine, beautifully presented at your table in a handcrafted cedar "bucket," a word too ordinary to describe the beauty of the natural wood finish and elegant design.

KANŌSHŌJU-AN

tea and sweets

Tetsugaku-no-michi-iriguchi, 2–1 Nyakuōji-chō, Sakyō-ku

左京区若王子町2–1 哲学の道入口

TEL: (075) 751–1077   FAX: (075) 751–1078

OPEN: 10 A.M.–5 P.M.; lunch 11 A.M.–2 P.M.; tea ceremony 10 A.M.–4:30 P.M. ■ CLOSED: Wednesdays ■ PRICES: Lunch ¥–¥¥ (reservations necessary for mini-*kaiseki*), tea ceremony ¥

Walk along the scenic Philosopher's Walk that runs from the foot of Ginkaku-ji to Nanzen-ji, and you will find this traditional-style teahouse across a narrow private bridge over the Shirakawa Canal. Kanōshōju-an is the Kyoto branch of a famous sweet shop in Shiga Prefecture beside Lake Biwa to the east of Kyoto. This is one of the best places in town to sample beautifully handmade Japanese sweets, with ceremonial green tea prepared for you in a traditional tearoom. For this you must say, "*O-cha no o-temae o haiken shitai no desu ga.*" You will then be led to a softly lit room where an elegant lady in kimono will prepare tea for you in traditional tea ceremony manner to accompany your sweets. The quiet, intimate environment allows you to enjoy the formal experience in a relaxed and comfortable atmosphere.

OMEN

wheat noodles (udon)

74 Ishibashi-chō, Shishigatani-dori, Ginkaku-ji-michi-sagaru, Sakyō-ku

左京区銀閣寺道下ル鹿ヶ谷通石橋町74

TEL: (075) 771–8994

OPEN: 11 A.M.–10 P.M. ■ CLOSED: Thursdays ■ PRICES: ¥

The name Omen means "honorable noodle," and this hospitable, country-style restaurant is famous for its thick, white *udon* noodles, served in broth and accompanied by a platter of beautifully-cut fresh vegetables topped with a sprinkling of sesame seeds. The interior of the shop is in the style of a farmhouse from the Kyoto countryside, and the pottery and baskets on which the delightful noodles are served are all handmade, from villages throughout Japan. Stop for lunch or dinner, but arrive early or late to miss the crowds at this wildly popular place located within walking distance of Ginkaku-ji.

TAZAWA KOBIJUTSU-TEN antiques

Sanjō-sagaru Nishi-gawa, Higashi-ōji, Higashiyama-ku

東山区東大路三条下ル西側

TEL: (075) 561–3009 (English spoken)

OPEN: Daily, 11 A.M.–6:30 P.M.

On Higashi-ōji just north of Shinmon-zen, the popular antique district for tourists, Tazawa is one of several interesting antique shops. The Tazawa family are noted experts in Meiji-period Japanese glassware, though they are also known abroad for their fine selection of Japanese dolls. Tazawa-san speaks English and is very knowledgeable not only about Kyoto dolls, but also about glass and other fine antiques.

NAKAMURA CHINGIRE-TEN textiles

Sanjō Minami-iru, Nawate-dōri, Higashiyama-ku

東山区縄手通三条南入ル

TEL: (075) 561–4726   FAX: (075) 531–6709

OPEN: Daily, 10 A.M.–7 P.M. ■ CREDIT: Major credit cards

Just south of Sanjō Station in the antique district that runs parallel with the river below Sanjō. In business for over a hundred years, the Nakamuras sell antique textiles, including hand-painted silks and stenciled cottons from all over Japan. Handbags, coin purses, neckties, and other accessories made from antique fabrics are also available, as well as an assortment of antique woven bamboo baskets for flower arrangements.

YAMAZOE TENKŌ-DO

scroll paintings

Nawate-dōri, Sanjō-sagaru, Higashiyama-ku

東山区三条下ル縄手通

TEL: (075) 561–3064 (English spoken)

OPEN: 10:30 A.M.–6 P.M. ■ CLOSED: Sundays

Just off Nawate-dōri, dealing in fine scroll paintings, Mr. Yamazoe's shop has been open since the Meiji period and his customers have always been students and scholars from universities both in Japan and abroad. Inexpensive unmounted paintings are displayed in wooden boxes right on the street. Some of his scrolls hang on a display rack inside, but the finer pieces are stored in individual wooden boxes on shelves in the back of the shop. Mr. Yamazoe will unroll one for the serious shopper to examine. He will provide an explanation in English if you should decide to purchase one.

KONJAKU NISHIMURA

antique textiles

36 Benzaiten-chō, Sanjō-sagaru, Yamato-ōji, Higashiyama-ku

東山区大和大路三条下ル弁財天町36

TEL: (075) 561–1568 (English spoken)

OPEN: 10 A.M.–7 P.M. ■ CLOSED: Wednesdays ■ CREDIT: Major credit cards

A one-hundred-year-old shop (not far from Nakamura Chingire-ten) also specializing in old textiles. Everything, from swatches of handwoven fourteenth-century indigo-dyed cottons to elaborately embroidered *obi* sashes and printed-silk kimono, is on display. Also offers a variety of small purses, neckties, and belts made by local seamstresses from antique fabrics.

E 18

AUNBO restaurant

Shimogawara-chō, Yasaka-toriimae-chō-sagaru, Higashiyama-ku

東山区八坂鳥居前町下ル下河原町

TEL: (075) 525–2900

OPEN: 12 NOON–1:30 P.M., 5:30 P.M.–10 P.M. (last order 9:30) ■ CLOSED: Wednesdays ■ PRICES: Lunch ¥¥, dinner ¥¥–¥¥¥

Located just two blocks south of Yasaka-jinja, Aunbo is a treasure among traditional Kyoto restaurants—good food, cozy atmosphere, friendly service, reasonable prices. The name includes the first and last cosmic sounds of the universe ("Ah" and "Un"). The restaurant is run by the very Zen-looking Hiro Tajima, famed for both his fine cuisine and his *maru-bozu* shaved head. Take a seat at the *hori-kotatsu* counter (seating on the floor, with a comfortable well to put your feet down), or ask for the tiny tatami room at the back with its own mini garden. Order the popular *ichijū-sansai* fixed menu with three delicious dishes, soup and rice, or try the *shukō sanpin omakase*, a sampler of three dishes.

E 19

KAPPA NAWATE
robata-yaki grill

Sueyoshi-chō, Higashi-kita-kado, Shijō-dōri, Nawate-agaru 2 suji-me, Higashiyama-ku

東山区縄手上ル2筋目四条通東北角末吉町

TEL: (075) 531–4048

OPEN: Daily, 6 P.M.–4 A.M. ■ PRICES: ¥

A lively *robata-yaki* grill in which you sit elbow to elbow around a crowded counter and order dishes like grilled seafood, sashimi, and *oden* (vegetables and other foods simmered in broth) from a large menu available in English. Inexpensive if you order carefully. Lots of fun and a chance to experience the raucous Osaka-style workingman's hang-out in a Kyoto shop that is used to handling foreigners because of its location on the corner of a main street in Gion.

E 20

YAGENBORI Kyoto cuisine

Sueyoshi-chō Kiritōshi-kado, Gion, Higashiyama-ku

東山区祇園末吉町切通し角

TEL: (075) 551–3331

OPEN: Daily, 12 NOON–2 P.M., 5 P.M.–11 P.M. ■ PRICES: *Bentō* lunch ¥–¥¥, dinner ¥¥¥

Yagenbori is right in the heart of the Shinbashi district where old teahouses line the Shirakawa Canal in Gion. They serve Kyoto cuisine (*Kyō-ryōri*) which can be ordered *ippin* style (a la carte) or in full-course meals. The building has a long counter where you can watch the cooks at work, tatami booths along the edges, and private rooms upstairs. It is

decorated in a folk-art style with dark woods and beautiful ceramics. The food is excellent and prices are not unreasonable for the authentic country-style Kyoto atmosphere and the delicacy with which each dish is prepared.

E21

RAKUTŌ-SŌ BEKKAN
inn

89 Okazaki, Irie-chō, Sakyō-ku
左京区入江町岡崎89
TEL: (075) 761–6333   FAX: (075) 761–6335
CHECK-IN: 2 P.M. ■ CHECK-OUT: 10 A.M. ■
RATES: ¥¥

Nestled along the eastern wall of the elegant gardens of Heian Shrine, Rakutō-sō Bekkan, known as the Three Sisters Inn Annex in English, has been a carefully guarded secret among Kyoto insiders for many years. The original inn is located about two blocks north of the annex, and is also an excellent choice. But the annex—formerly a private residence—is set back from the street down a narrow, bamboo-lined passageway, and makes you feel as if you are a guest in someone's home. The Three Sisters Inn Annex does not advertise, but with lovely tatami-mat rooms and traditional surroundings, it is a Kyoto gem in a wonderful location. Stroll to Heian Shrine after breakfast—an inspirational way to start a day in old Kyoto. Reservations are accepted by fax, but book well in advance.

E22

HIRANO-YA   restaurant

Chion-in Minami-monzen, Maruyama Kōen, Higashiyama-ku
東山区円山公園知恩院南門前

TEL: (075) 561–1603   FAX: (075) 525–1781
OPEN: Daily, 10:30 A.M.–8 P.M. ■ PRICES: ¥–¥¥

Just inside the north gate to Maruyama Park near Chion-in is the hundred-year-old Hirano-ya serving *imobō*, a dish that literally comes from the roots of Kyoto cuisine. A bowl of delicious *ebi-imo* (an unusual variety of shrimp-shaped potatoes imported originally by Buddhist priests from China) and *bōdara* (a kind of preserved fish from the Japan Sea) are served with soup, rice, and the ever-present Kyoto pickles. Delicious and inexpensive, though not the standard tourist fare, this is a chance to sample "real" Kyoto-style cuisine. In a city located a two-day's walk from the nearest sea, the people of Kyoto invented a seemingly endless variety of ways to serve dried and salted fish. Though it may sound unappealing at first, most people are pleasantly surprised. The restaurant has dozens of small rooms along a narrow stone walkway from which you can watch a score of kimono-clad ladies as they scurry to and fro with their trays of *imobō*. Peek at the old-style kitchen, and don't miss the restrooms—complete with large stone basins into which water trickles down from a bamboo spout. Hirano-ya is both visually and gastronomically a place from out of the past.

MATSUNO eel restaurant

Minamiza-higashi 4-ken-me, Shijō-dōri,
Higashiyama-ku

東山区四条通南座東4軒目

TEL: (075) 561–2786

OPEN: 11:30 P.M.–9 P.M. (last order 8:30) ■
CLOSED: Thursdays ■ PRICES: ¥ ■ CREDIT:
Major credit cards

The sign in English says Mrs. Matsuno's
Kitchen and describes the specialty of
the house as broiled eel. Mrs. Matsuno's
unagi (eel), grilled in a delicious sauce
and served at reasonable prices, has
made this a favorite haunt of theater-
goers for over a century. Just four doors
east of the Minami-za Kabuki Theater,
the folk-style restaurant retains all of its
original "theater-door" atmosphere. Try
a simple bowl of *unagi donburi* (grilled
eel over rice) or splurge on the full-
course *unagi teishoku* to sample the
range of possibilities this exotic Kyoto-
style cuisine has to offer.

GION TANAKA-YA

footwear (geta)

Yamato-chō, Shijō-sagaru, Yamato-ōji,
Higashiyama-ku

東山区大和大路四条下ル大和町

TEL: (075) 561–1993 (English spoken)

FAX: (075) 561–1993

OPEN: 10 A.M.–5:30 P.M. ■ CLOSED: Wednesdays ■ CREDIT: Major credit cards

Geta are wooden clogs for casual wear
whose *"karan-koron"* sound once provided city music with natural percus-
sion. Worn these days most often by
cooks (some pairs even raise the wearer
five inches off a soggy kitchen floor) or
summer festival goers, *geta* were everyday footwear in Japan until World War

II. Tanaka-ya has extra-large sizes to fit
the big-footed foreigner, although a
proper fit in Japanese footwear is said
to leave at least three-quarters of an
inch of heel hanging off the back for
better balance. *Geta* come in men's and
ladies' styles, the men's usually with
black thongs and the women's with a
variety of colors on either black lacquered or natural wood-finished bases.
Whereas the average sushi maker goes
through a pair of *geta* every month, a
good pair, with ordinary use, will last
years. *Zōri* are for more formal occasions and are made of specially coated
leather, grass matting over cork bases,
or even ostrich leather for the really
stylish wearer. Again, a "proper" fit
seems too narrow and short to the
Western foot. *Zōri* are the accepted
footwear for formal Japanese occasions
such as weddings or tea ceremonies,
and can be worn indoors on carpeted
floors, where the coarser *geta* cannot.

KAGIZEN YOSHIFUSA

Kyoto confectionery

264 Gion-machi Kitagawa, Higashiyama-ku

東山区祇園町北側 264

TEL: (075) 561–1818, 551–1948

FAX: (075) 525–1818

OPEN: 9 A.M.–6 P.M. (Saturdays and Sundays
until 7) ■ CLOSED: Mondays

Kagizen is one of the few remaining
places on Shijō-dōri in Gion where great
pains have been taken to preserve the
traditional beauty of the old shop while
upholding a reputation as one of the
best *o-kashi-ya*, or Japanese sweet shops,
in Kyoto. Most sweet shops in town sell
only takeout sweets in gift-wrapped
boxes, but at Kagizen there is also a room
upstairs where you may order *o-usu*,

the thick tea ceremony tea, and *nama-gashi*, fresh sweets to be eaten on the premises. Notice the exquisite cabinetry by the late Tatsuaki Kuroda, who was a Living National Treasure. The ceramic pieces are by the late master potter Kanjirō Kawai, who was offered the same honor but refused it, believing in the "anonymous craftsman" as the true hero of the Japanese folk art tradition. (See A Few Special Places to Hide.)

MONJU lacquerware

Hanami-kōji Higashi-iru Minami-gawa, Shijō-dōri, Higashiyama-ku
東山区四条通花見小路東入ル南側
TEL: (075) 525–1617   FAX: (075) 525–1665
OPEN: 10:30 A.M.–7:30 P.M. ■ CLOSED: Thursdays ■ CREDIT: Major credit cards

Lacquered trays, bowls, boxes, incense containers, and chopsticks that come with their own carrying cases. Unlike the quasi-lacquerware you'll find elsewhere in town, Monju sells nothing but the real thing. (Recently, some makers have been coating plastic bases with lacquer.) The wide price range you'll notice at Monju in bowls, for example, is not due to the difference between plastic and wood. The lower-priced bowls are made of a wood-chip composition base, rather than turned, solid wood. The composition-base pieces are actually much better suited for daily use. Most Japanese use expensive lacquerware only once a year at New Year's. Beautiful pairs of lacquered chopsticks in hand-finished wooden carrying cases make wonderful gifts for ardent sushi fans.

KASAGEN Japanese umbrellas

284 Gion-machi Kitagawa, Higashiyama-ku
東山区祇園町北側 284
TEL: (075) 561–2832   FAX: (075) 561–2832
OPEN: Daily, 10 A.M.–8 P.M. ■ CLOSED: Wednesdays

Selling handmade oiled-paper umbrellas since 1861. There are three basic varieties: *bangasa*, the large, bamboo-handled rain umbrellas used at inns and traditional restaurants, often with their names written on the rim in Chinese characters; *janome*, the delicate ladies' umbrella usually decorated with printed geometric or floral designs, suitable for kimono; and *higasa*, the hand-painted, unoiled paper parasols. Don't hesitate to use Kasagen's umbrellas in the rain. Dry them by hanging them up (opened) indoors overnight—not in the sun, which would fade the lovely colors—and they will last several years. In the old days when Raku-tō was still an uncrowded suburb, the craftsmen at Kasagen used to set their umbrellas out to dry in a field below Yasaka-jinja, but with no fields left nearby, they have moved their workshop to Gifu Prefecture, where most of the *wagasa* in Japan are made today. Kasagen is the oldest umbrella shop in Kyoto. Souvenir shops along the Shin-kyōgoku arcade down-

town sell cheaper versions, but most are imported, and the paper is generally of lesser quality, as is the workmanship. Expect to pay more here, but know you have purchased the real thing.

E28

KAZURA-SEI   hair ornaments

285 Gion-machi Kitagawa, Higashiyama-ku
東山区祇園町北側285
TEL: (075) 561–0672
OPEN: 9:30 A.M.–7 P.M. ■ CLOSED: Wednesdays ■ CREDIT: AE, DC, MC, MIC, UC

The north side of Shijō-dōri has many shops that cater to the geisha in Gion: one that started out as a hairdresser's shop for actors and dancers in 1865 now makes and sells exquisite hair ornaments (*kanzashi*) in lacquer, natural woods, or tortoiseshell. This is Kazura-sei, where you'll find a wide selection of lacquered combs in every shape and size, some inlaid with mother-of-pearl and sprinkled with gold dust in a technique called *maki-e*, which dates from the eighth century. Don't miss the elaborate human-hair wigs dressed in Edo-period geisha styles. Miniature wigs on display stands for collectors are also available, styled by traditional doll makers, each with tiny *kanzashi* of their own. Try a bottle of the shop's camellia oil shampoo, used in Gion to give the long hair of geisha a lacquer sheen.

E29

MIURA SHŌMEI   lanterns

284 Gion-machi Kitagawa, Higashiyama-ku
東山区祇園町北側284
TEL: (075) 561–2816   FAX: (075) 541–4048
OPEN: 10 A.M.–8 P.M. ■ CLOSED: Sundays, holidays ■ CREDIT: Major credit cards

Specializes in hand-crafted paper lanterns—traditional and contemporary Japanese lighting fixtures of all kinds. The shop itself has been remodeled, but all products are handmade by individual craftsmen exclusively for Miura Shōmei. Hanging paper *akari* lanterns designed by Isamu Noguchi are available here, as are bronze cast *tōrō* garden lanterns, bamboo and unfinished wood wall lamps, *andon* floor lamps with classical cone-shaped paper shades, and bamboo table lamps.

E30

IZUJŪ   sushi

292–1 Gion-machi Kitagawa, Higashiyama-ku
東山区祇園町北側292–1
TEL: (075) 561–0019
OPEN: 11:30 A.M.–8 P.M. ■ CLOSED: Wednesdays ■ PRICES: ¥

Established in 1892, this small sushi shop is right on the corner of Shijō-dōri and Higashi-ōji-dōri in Gion. They specialize in *saba-zushi*, specially prepared mackerel from the Japan Sea, a traditional Kyoto favorite from a time in which only preserved fish could survive the long journey from the coast. They also offer the standard seasonal selection of sushi in a very old-style shop which has dozens of antique, ornate Imari bowls and platters on shelves

overhead to enjoy while you dine (sushi to go is also available). Look for the double diamond pattern in dark wood on the white wall out front.

E31

TAKOCHŌ   oden stew

Higashi-kita-kado, Donguri-bashi Higashi-zume, Kawabata-dōri, Higashiyama-ku

東山区川端通団栗橋東詰東北角

TEL: (075) 525–0170

OPEN: 6 P.M.–10 P.M. ■ CLOSED: Wednesdays ■ PRICES: ¥¥ ■ CREDIT: Major credit cards

This 135-year-old *oden* shop, the best in Kyoto, has room for only fifteen customers. Behind the counter where you sit are steaming vats of *oden* broth, filled with a variety of simmering treats, like cabbage rolls and tofu, from which to choose. Order piece by piece or a *moriawase* (assortment) and dip each mouthful into a spicy Chinese mustard—a great combination with saké, particularly in the winter.

Located on the narrow street that runs beside the Kamogawa River, south of the Minami-za Kabuki Theater, the white and black walls and Meiji-style wrought iron lantern out front make Takochō an easy landmark on the corner by the first bridge south of Shijō-dōri.

E32

TAMAHAN   inn (ryokan)

477 Shimogawara-chō, Gion, Higashiyama-ku

東山区祇園下河原町477

TEL: (075) 561–3188

CHECK-IN: 3 P.M. ■ CHECK-OUT: 11A.M. ■ RATES: ¥¥¥¥ (w/2 meals)

This former home of a wealthy Osaka merchant has been welcoming over-night guests since 1929. Famed for its exquisite cuisine, the inn has a fabulous courtyard garden that is a haven away from the bustling city and a delight to visit year round. Tamahan has an annex (*bekkan*) that opens right onto Ishibe-kōji, a narrow, cobbled street that harkens back to Kyoto in an age gone by. Within walking distance of Kiyomizu-dera and the bustling Sannenzaka district, Tamahan is known for its quiet elegance and hospitality.

E33

KINNABE   one-pot cooking

Hakata-chō, Yamato-ōji Shijō-sagaru, Higashiyama-ku

東山区大和大路四条下ル博多町

TEL: (075) 531–4188   FAX: (075) 551–3403

OPEN: Daily, 5 P.M.–8 P.M. ■ PRICES: ¥¥¥–¥¥¥¥ ■ CREDIT: JCB, VISA

The restaurant has a beautiful traditional entry courtyard and an antique *maneki-neko* cat welcoming guests. It is open for dinner and specializes in *shabu-shabu* and *mizu-taki* served in a unique style called *kaminabe*. A bamboo strainer lined with special handmade paper is filled with beef or chicken and lowered into a pot of simmering broth in this unusual Kyoto-style meal. The atmosphere and cuisine are authentic—not the typical tourist fare—and Kinnabe is located on Yamato-ōji south of Shijō, right in the heart of very traditional Gion. Don't expect any of the usual concessions or Western conveniences provided in restaurants which cater to the tourist trade.

RAKUSHŌ   tea and sweets

Washio-chō, Kōdai-ji Kita-monzen,
Higashiyama-ku

東山区高台寺北門前鷲尾町

TEL: (075) 561–6892   FAX: (075) 541–1235

OPEN: Daily, 9:30 A.M.–5:30 P.M. ■ CLOSED:
Periodically ■ PRICES: ¥

Peek through the slatted gate at the fabulous garden, pond and waterfall of this remarkable little tea and coffee shop. Take a seat beside the sliding glass doors and watch the prize-winning *koi* carp glide through the water below. This former villa of a wealthy local merchant serves green tea, coffee, and a variety of local sweets. Just south of Maruyama Park, it is a refreshing spot to pause in your travels.

Sannenzaka Kyō-no-yado
KIYOMIZU SANSŌ   inn

3-341 Kiyomizu, Higashiyama-ku

東山区清水3-341

TEL: (075) 551–3152   FAX: (075) 561–6109

CHECK-IN: 4 P.M. ■ CHECK-OUT: 9:30 A.M. ■
RATES: ¥¥ (w/2 meals) ■ CLOSED: Periodically

This tiny, well-preserved inn is tucked away on Sannenzaka, the slope that leads to Kiyomizu-dera through a popular historic district lined with old shops and restaurants. The very reasonable rates include two fine meals in an atmosphere that is pure Kyoto. With only six rooms available, reservations are an absolute necessity.

HAKUSASON-SŌ
restaurant and garden

37 Ishibashi-chō, Jōdo-ji, Sakyō-ku

左京区浄土寺石橋町37

TEL: (075) 751–0446

OPEN: Garden 10 A.M.–5 P.M., lunch 11:30 A.M.
–2 P.M. ■ PRICES: lunch ¥¥ (plus admission fee
to garden)

Hakusason-sō is one of the special treasures of Kyoto (see A Few Special Places to Hide). If you are fortunate enough to stop by the garden for lunch when the beautiful proprietress, Tae Hashimoto, is present, you are in for an experience of true Kyoto hospitality and graciousness. Hashimoto-san opened Hakusason-sō as a restaurant more than ten years ago, and her delicious *yudōfu-zen* and seasonal *kisetsu-no-gohan* lunches are served in a room overlooking the spectacular pond and garden built by her late father-in-law, Kansetsu Hashimoto, one of Kyoto's greatest painters, whose studio and stroll garden are open to the public daily. Start with a walk through the remarkable grounds, and then leave your shoes behind and step up into the former villa to eat. Not to be missed on your way to Ginkaku-ji, the Silver Pavilion, on the hill at the end of the road.

HYŌTAN-YA gourd flasks

Kiyomizu Sannenzaka, Higashiyama-ku
東山区清水三年坂
TEL: (075) 561–8188
OPEN: Daily, 9 A.M.–6 P.M.

A sixth-generation craftsman of the unusual art of making *hyōtan*, or gourd flasks, which were once used to carry saké to picnics. A small hole is drilled near the top of the gourd and a tiny long-handled scoop is used to remove the contents. It is then soaked in water, dried in the sun, and left to hang for five years in a room upstairs above the shop before the surface is laboriously hand-polished. *Hyōtan* are said to improve the flavor of saké, but be sure to pour hot *bancha* tea into a new gourd and let it sit for twenty-four hours before using it. This removes the pungent odor the gourds have before they have been used. Though *hyōtan* appear to be fragile, they have been known to "bounce back" more than once when dropped by an inebriated picnicker. Prices vary according to size, color, weight, and shape (unusually-shaped gourds are popular as flower containers for tea ceremony and some are extremely expensive).

ASAHI-DŌ ceramics

1–280 Kiyomizu, Higashiyama-ku
東山区清水1–280
TEL: (075) 531–2181 (English spoken)
FAX: (075) 531–2185
OPEN: Daily, 8:30 A.M.–6 P.M. ■ CREDIT: Major credit cards

Asahi-dō was established in the Meiji period, and became a purveyor of Kyoto-style ceramics to the imperial household. Although now housed in a modern building, Asahi-dō offers the widest selection of Kiyomizu ceramics in Kyoto—all produced by local potteries in a wide range of prices. Kiyomizu ware is noted for its delicate *some-tsuke* blue painting on white porcelain, as well as for its multicolored overglaze enameled ceramics often edged in gold.

RAKUSHI-EN ceramics

Gojō-bashi Higashi 4-chōme, Higashiyama-ku
東山区五条橋東4丁目
TEL: (075) 541–1161
OPEN: 9 A.M.–6 P.M. ■ CLOSED: Wednesdays ■ CREDIT: AE, DC, JCB, UC

Located on Gojōzaka, which has been famous for pottery in Kyoto for hundreds of years, Rakushi-en offers the highest quality ceramic ware from small kilns all over Japan. The owner shows a limited selection of work by individual potters, rather than the mass-produced variety from large potteries—Oribe by Kōji Nagae, Kiyomizu ware by Rishō Katō, and Chinese-style celadon by Kei Tsukamoto. Note the paper-thin translucent porcelain Kiyomizu-ware teacups at Rakushi-en. The owner says one way to judge the quality of fine porcelain is to pick it up (carefully!)—the best is always lighter than it appears to be.

RAKU-HOKU

Northern Kyoto

Raku-hoku is almost as much "country" as Kyoto has left. Once, it was an area famous for its vegetables and rice fields, but those days are largely a part of the past.

Raku-hoku boasts two old and famous shrines that existed before the city was founded here in the eighth century—Shimogamo and Kamigamo shrines. Both are pleasant places for a stroll to catch a glimpse of what remains of rural Kyoto.

Daitoku-ji, the oldest Zen temple in Kyoto, just above Kita-ōji, has dozens of sub-temples and gardens to visit, and is known among gourmets for the fine Zen vegetarian fare (shōjin-ryōri) available both on the premises and outside its eastern gate.

Far to the north, nestled beside rivers in the mountain passes that lead to the Japan Sea, are several small villages that can be reached by bus or train. These are popular among visitors and city dwellers alike who wish to escape for a day. Kibune for lunch in the summertime on a table built right over a clear mountain stream . . . Kurama for a stroll through an old post town whose traditional shops and houses still retain the sense of a rest stop for weary travelers . . . Ōhara for a classic mountain village with small temples (see Day Trips to the Countryside).

Raku-hoku, though now a popular suburban area for merchants who have grown weary of sardine life in the crowded city, still has the air of country living in some of its hidden corners, though the famous symphonic croaking of frogs in its rice fields has now been reduced to a quiet sonata.

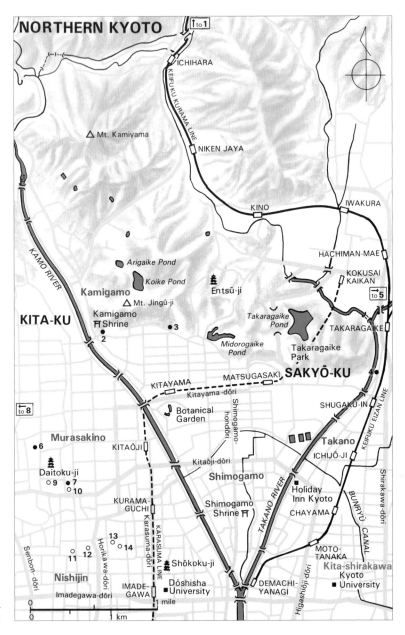

NORTHERN KYOTO

↑ to 1

ICHIHARA

KEIFUKU KURAMA LINE

△ Mt. Kamiyama

NIKEN JAYA

KINO

IWAKURA

HACHIMAN-MAE

KOKUSAI
KAIKAN

→ to 5

Arigaike Pond

Koike Pond

Kamigamo

Entsū-ji

△ Mt. Jingū-ji

KAMO RIVER

Kamigamo
⛩ Shrine

● 3

*Takaragaike
Pond*

TAKARAGAIKE

KITA-KU

2

*Midorogaike
Pond*

Takaragaike
Park

SAKYŌ-KU

● 4

KITAYAMA

MATSUGASAKI

Kitayama-dōri

SHUGAKU-IN

← to 8

🎋 Botanical
Garden

Shimogamo-
hondōri

KEIFUKU EIZAN LINE

Murasakino

● 6

KITAŌJI

Kitaōji-dōri

Shimogamo

Takano

ICHIJŌ-JI

Shirakawa-dōri

Daitoku-ji

○ 9   ● 7
    ○ 10

KURAMA-
GUCHI

Shimogamo
Shrine ⛩

■ Holiday
Inn Kyoto

CHAYAMA

TAKANO RIVER

BUNRYŪ CANAL

Senbon- dōri

○   ○
11   12

13
○
○ 14

Horika wa-dōri

Karasuma-dōri

KARASUMA LINE

🏯 Shōkoku-ji

MOTO-
TANAKA

Kita-shirakawa
Kyoto
■ University

Higashiōji-dōri

Nishijin

Imadegawa-dōri

IMADE-
GAWA

Dōshisha
■ University

DEMACHI-
YANAGI

0 _____ 1 mile

0 _____ 1 km

SAGENTA

sōmen noodles

左源太

76 Kibune-chō, Kurama, Sakyō-ku

左京区鞍馬貴船町76　TEL: (075) 741–2146 (Sagenta) / (075) 741–1068 (Ugenta)

OPEN: 11:30 A.M.–7 P.M. ■ CLOSED: Periodically in winter ■ PRICES: Seasonal *bentō* ¥¥–¥¥¥, *kaiseki* ¥¥¥–¥¥¥¥ ■ CREDIT: JCB, VISA

Deep in the Kitayama Mountains north of Kamigamo Shrine is a village called Kibune, where old inns and restaurants hug the banks of a stream beneath tall cedar and maple trees that have been enticing escapees from city life for generations.

According to legend, Kibune got its name over two thousand years ago when Tamayori-hime (the mother of Jinmu Tennō, the first emperor of Japan) traveled up the Kamogawa River on a yellow (*ki*) boat (*fune*), and, when she arrived at the river's source, she ordered that a shrine be constructed there. Kibune is now written with different Chinese characters, so the origin of the name is obscure. At any rate, a shrine has existed in Kibune since before the Heian period, and it is here that the god of water dwells.

A thousand years ago, before the river was tamed with a network of canals, floods and droughts were a constant threat to the people in the valley below. The townspeople went to Kibune, then considered the source of the unreliable river, to pray to the water god for mercy.

In times of flood a white horse was offered at Kibune Shrine; in times of drought, a black one. (In those days the northern mountains were mysterious places inhabited by goblins called *tengu*, with long noses and supernatural fighting skills.)

Kibune Shrine and the water god are still revered by the people of Kyoto, who celebrate a rain festival on March 3, a shrine festival on June 1, and water festival on July 7 as they have for centuries.

But the main attraction in Kibune today are the many beautiful inns along the roadside that serve meals all summer long on tables built right out over the river, giving Kyotoites a place to escape the torturous humidity of July and August.

Kibune is at least five degrees cooler than Kyoto, which is enough to draw hundreds of hot city dwellers here each summer (and enough to keep them away in winter, so this is also an ideal hideaway to spend a snowy New Year's soaking in the steamy *iwa-buro*, or rock baths, at one of Kibune's inns). Most

inns feature *botan nabe*, or wild boar stew, in the winter months and seasonal *kaiseki* meals year round. Though summer is by far the most popular season in Kibune, the maple trees in fall and cherry trees in spring are worth the short thirty-minute train ride from Keifuku Demachi Yanagi Station to Kibuneguchi. Walk across the bridge and through the orange *torii* gate that leads left from the train station and up the road that follows the stream.

Sagenta, the last shop on the river side at the north end of the narrow road, serves a summer treat called *nagashi sōmen*, or "flowing noodles," which is exactly what they are. Thin white noodles flow down into a boat-shaped trough through a bamboo pipe which carries them in a stream of ice-cold water from the kitchen in the main building above. Seated outside on a platform over the cool river (close enough to reach down and splash), you overlook a fern grotto on one side of the stream and the stone walls and thatched roof of Sagenta covered with bright green moss on the other. Enjoy your *nagashi sōmen* surrounded by nature—not the artificial, planned variety found in the temple gardens of the city below, but the overgrown, shady, breezy kind that reassures you that the whole island is not "landscaped."

Sagenta and *nagashi sōmen* are primarily a summer treat, and reservations for a seat out over the river at any of the restaurants in Kibune can be difficult to obtain. But there are over a dozen fine places to eat in Kibune depending on your taste and budget. Some can be quite expensive, offering elaborate full-course *kaiseki* meals and deluxe overnight accommodations.

Ugenta, the partner of Sagenta, is located further down on the opposite side of the road, and has new accommodations popular with larger groups.

Hiroya and Fujiya are the two most prominent inns and restaurants along the river. Lunches are relatively affordable, but dinner can be a costly affair, particularly in the peak summer season.

Tochigiku, an inn at the southern end of this stretch of the river, is a friendly place to stay overnight any time of the year or just to stop by for lunch or dinner. Tochigiku is just next door to Beniya, and is actually an offshoot of the older, more expensive inn, but the hospitality, cozy accommodations, and originality of their talented chef make this an annual place of pilgrimage for many of Kyoto's younger generation, to whom the prestige of staying in one of the more famous local inns doesn't mean as much as comfort, economy, and a fine meal.

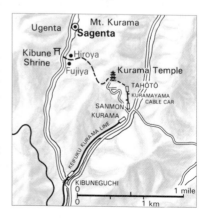

NARITA pickles

35 Yamamoto-chō, Kamigamo, Kita-ku
北区上賀茂山本町35   TEL: (075) 721–1567   FAX: (075) 281–5956
OPEN: Daily, 10 A.M.–6 P.M.

The twilight dim, the gentle breeze
By Nara-no-Ogawa stream
The splash of worshipers who wash
Before the shrine, all seem
A perfect summer's dream.
　　—Fujiwara Iyetaka, *Hyakunin Isshu*
　　(Single Poems by 100 Poets), 1237

Kamigamo Shrine, through which the legendary stream still flows, was founded by the Kamo clan in the early sixth century and is located in a strategic position in the north of Kyoto beside the Kamogawa River which afforded protection against possible invasions from provincial clans beyond the northern mountains. During the Heian period the court awarded the shrine priests with many estates, and a line of head priests who were descendants of the imperial family was established to ensure strong permanent ties.

By the seventeenth century, the area around the shrine had come to be known as a *shake-machi*, literally a "shrine family township," with 275 houses in the area belonging to the families of the shrine priests. Today the area along

the old canal that carries the gentle breeze down from Nara-no-Ogawa, the little stream beside the shrine referred to in the poem, has been declared a historic district, and the walled *shake-machi* houses that line it still retain much of the rural atmosphere that Kamigamo Shrine has kept for centuries.

Narita's pickle shop, a part of the *shake-machi* that runs along either side of the canal, originally belonged to one of the *shake* families. The Naritas have done more than just maintain the impressive two-hundred-year-old structure. They have restored it to its former glory and then some. The stone and clay walls that surround Narita are typical of the *shake* houses in this area, as are the sweeping tile roofs and white-washed walls of the main building. A stone path leads through the gateway across a graveled courtyard and past a large stone water basin at the edge of the garden beneath the bamboo and pine trees. Step over the threshold onto the black slate–tiled floors, and have a look at the stunning Edo-period *kuruma-dansu* (chest-on-wheels) in the waiting area on the left, and the large Meiji-period kitchen cabinet. In the raised tatami room on the right is part of the fine collection of *mingei* (folk art) furniture pieces owned by the Narita family, a different set of which is always on display.

The rough-hewn rafters that support the massive tile rooftop are masterpieces of construction themselves. Fitted together with complicated Japanese joinery entirely without nails, the exposed beams have been blackened over the long years from the soot that used to rise from the open hearth below. On the outskirts of the city now, the Kamigamo area was once considered "country," and many of the houses here share methods of construction used in traditional farmhouses.

It is their pickled *suguki* (a turnip-like vegetable), or *suguki-zuke*, that made the Narita family famous in Kyoto. In 1780, the family started raising *suguki* and pickling them to serve the priests of Kamigamo Shrine. Then in 1804, they started selling pickles to restaurants all around Kyoto. In the 1980s, the Kamigamo *shake-machi* was recognized as a historic district, and it was

then that the Naritas opened a shop to sell their pickles to those that had begun to flock to this picturesque area on the weekends.

The *suguki* are salt pickled in a process that is similar to that of making sauerkraut. It begins with the late fall harvest and takes about a week for each batch. After being peeled, salted, and left to set overnight, the *suguki* are then washed, salted again, and placed in giant wooden barrels over which lids are tightly pressed down with long lever-like poles that are weighted with stones (a method still followed at Narita, while most other makers have switched to modern machinery). Narita-san believes that the old ways produce the best-tasting pickles, and his many devoted customers agree. Restaurant owners and housewives as well as tourists take the extra time required to get to this out-of-the-way location to be able to serve Narita pickles at their tables. No preservatives are used at Narita, making this one of the few pickle shops in Kyoto that hasn't succumbed to the modern trend for chemical food additives.

If you wander into the neighborhood on the west side of the Kamogawa River to the south of Kamigamo Shrine, you may come across someone pulling a heavy cart full of vegetables grown in this area. Each vegetable peddler has her own route to follow. The house that is the last stop on the vegetable lady's route inevitably ends up with whatever she has left over for free. Ordinarily this works to one's advantage, but even the most inventive Kyoto housewife would have trouble dealing with a whole box of leftover burdock root, I would think.

AZEKURA restaurant

30 Okamoto-chō, Kamigamo, Kita-ku
北区上賀茂岡本町30 TEL: (075) 701-0161

OPEN: Lunch 11:30 A.M.–2 P.M., dinner 5:30 P.M.–8:00 P.M. ■ CLOSED: Mondays ■
PRICES: Lunch ¥, dinner ¥¥

Not far from Kamigamo Shrine on an old road which leads to Midoriga-ike Pond there is a three-hundred-year-old saké warehouse (*kura*) that was saved from the jaws of progress by a very thoughtful kimono merchant named Mikio Ichida forty years ago. When I first visited Azekura in 1985, the late Ichida-san told me the amazing story of how this enormous wooden structure got to Kyoto all the way from Nara over twenty-five miles to the southeast. Hearing of plans to destroy the *kura* to make way for what is now the Kintetsu train station, Ichida-san purchased it, had it disassembled piece by piece, brought to Kyoto, and rebuilt on the Okamoto estate in northern Kyoto, the site of the former home of one of the oldest samurai families in the Kamigamo Shrine district. It took nearly a year to complete the move; every beam and crosspost was fitted together as it had been originally.

Azekura is a masterpiece of Japanese joinery, as you will note by the massive roughhewn cypress posts and crossbeams which support the heavy tile roof high above. This giant *kura* was originally a brewery and storehouse for a saké establishment called "Kikuya" that was built during the early Edo period in Nara. Saving Azekura is particularly significant today, when wooden buildings on this immense scale can no longer be constructed due to the scarcity of timber of this size.

The name Azekura is written with characters that express the owner's appreciation of fine textiles—A, love; *ze*, dyeing; *kura*, storehouse. Ichida-san turned the old saké storehouse into a special place where invited guests could attend private exhibitions of fine kimono, and the public could drop by for a simple *soba* noodle lunch and a visit to the folk museum across the courtyard which displays hand tools and brewery equipment from the building's previous incarnation. Visitors are also welcome to follow the path up the hill behind the courtyard to the teahouse, which holds tea ceremonies on special occasions, or to peek inside the Hida House, a reconstructed farmhouse from the Hida-Takayama district on the hill

Northern Kyoto

behind Azekura, and watch the group of weavers at work on their hand looms.

When Mikio Ichida passed away at the turn of the millennium, his son Shunsuke was determined to carry on his father's legacy—but with a surprising twist. The noodle shop is now a fashionable Italian restaurant, a transition, like many in Kyoto, where "tradition" often means adapting to the changing tastes of the day.

Between Azekura and Kamigamo Shrine, there is another, smaller spiritual site called Ōta Shrine. This is a quiet place to experience what Shintoism means to a Japanese community. Surrounded by towering cypress, some over sixty feet high, Ōta Shrine has the sense of being in the midst of nature that is characteristic of Shinto shrines. Even atop office buildings in midtown, you'll find that shrines which house the company's protective deities are seldom without a backdrop of greenery.

Shrines are also used as meeting places, each with a festival that brings the neighborhood together at least once a year. Each shrine is dedicated to a particular Shinto deity, such as the god of fire, thunder, or harvest. Ōta Shrine is dedicated to Ame-no-uzume-no-mikoto, the god of good harvest. It has been under the auspices of the priests and parishioners of the larger Kamigamo Shrine since the twelfth century, and the love of generations of parishioners is evident each year in late spring when hundreds of carefully tended purple and yellow irises make their annual appearance just as they have for centuries. The exact origin of Ōta Shrine is unrecorded, but over the centuries people have come here to pray not only for a good harvest, but for protection against illness, for good luck in marriage, and even for a successful career on stage. (As with most Shinto shrines, Ōta has a long list of talented deities that can be implored to help out in almost any difficult situation.)

By far the most frequent visitors to Ōta Shrine are the children. The last and perhaps most important function of the guardian spirit of a neighborhood shrine is to provide children with a safe and beautiful place to play. The woods offer splendid hiding places and Ōta Shrine is seldom without its band of renegade little people laughing and running beneath the sacred cypresses.

HEIHACHI-JAYA
inn (ryokan), restaurant

8-1 Yamabana Kawagishi-chō, Sakyō-ku
左京区山端川岸町8-1　TEL: (075) 781-5008　FAX: (075) 781-6482

CHECK-IN: 4 P.M. ■ CHECK-OUT: 10 A.M. ■ CLOSED: Wednesdays ■ RATES: ¥¥¥¥ (w/2 meals); bath only ¥ ■ RESTAURANT OPEN: 11:30 A.M.–9:30 P.M. (lunch until 3) ■ CLOSED: Wednesdays ■ PRICES: Lunch ¥¥, dinner ¥¥¥–¥¥¥¥ ■ CREDIT: DC, JCB, MC, MIC, VISA

Four hundred years ago footsore fish peddlers returning to Kyoto after the twenty-four-hour trek from the Japan Sea were relieved to find Heihachi-jaya at the foot of the mountains, just where they'd left it, welcoming them with tea and barley rice, and a place to rest their heavy loads.

Heihachi-jaya still offers weary travelers the same promise of comfort and a good meal. Hugging the east bank of the Takanogawa River, the old roadhouse on the northeast outskirts of Kyoto is now an inn and restaurant serving *kaiseki*-style freshwater fish cuisine and the barley rice and tea for which they were known centuries ago. Entering the moss-covered Kigyūmon Gate, which once belonged to a rural Zen temple, you leave the city behind and stroll through a lush garden into a quiet world that seems to belong to a different time. During the Edo period this inn was the popular haunt of samurai and wealthy merchants, who knew of the inn's reputation for the best fish cuisine in the capital. Yamabana Heihachi-jaya, the inn's formal

name, means "Heihachi Teahouse at the foot of the mountains." Located on what was once the only road between Kyoto and the best fishing spots on the Japan Sea, it was the first stop for peddlers on their return trip to the capital; hence the inn received the freshest fish. When the railroad connecting Kyoto with the coast was built in the Meiji period, the peddlers no longer had to make the arduous journey. Heihachi-jaya began serving freshwater fish around a hundred years ago, and now offers both ocean fish (*wakasa kaiseki*) and river fish (*seiryū kaiseki*) cuisine.

One of the unique features of Heihachi-jaya is the delightful *kamaburo*, an old-fashioned Japanese-style clay sauna, heated from below the floor by pine wood from the nearby forest. The *kamaburo* originated just north of here in Yase several centuries ago as a means of curing the battle scars of a young emperor. Sightseeing "battle scars" can also be cured in the comfortable temperatures of the *kamaburo*, particularly when taken in combination with a fine meal at Heihachi-jaya. Have

a relaxing sauna and bath, don a cotton *yukata* robe, stroll back through the garden to a private room overlooking the Takanogawa River and enjoy a *kaiseki* meal and the full beauty of an evening in northern Kyoto. The *sansai* (or mountain greens), fresh grilled fish, and barley rice for which Heihachi-jaya is famous taste even better after the soothing sauna.

Though most of the original guest rooms were washed away during a terrible flood in 1789, the kitchen facing the highway was saved, and the original stone floors and giant rafters are just as they were in the Edo period. Peek inside as you pass by for a glimpse of the *daidokoro*, or kitchen, the heart of a traditional Japanese restaurant, where *sashimi* is sliced and rice boiled in the same way it has been for generations.

All the amenities of sauna and private room are available not only to overnight guests, but also to guests who come for lunch only, though reservations are a good idea. Guests without reservations will be offered seats in the spacious central dining room which also overlooks the river and garden, if private rooms are not available. Away from the noise and confusion of midtown, Heihachi-jaya offers fine food, a relaxing sauna, lush gardens, and a place to take off your shoes, unwind and stay awhile.

KIKAKU-TEI
inn (ryokan), restaurant

55 Kamitakano Higashiyama, Sakyō-ku
左京区上高野東山55　TEL: (075) 781–4001

CHECK-IN: 4 P.M. ■ CHECK-OUT: 10 A.M. ■ RATES: ¥¥¥¥ (w/2 meals) ■ CREDIT: Major credit
cards ■ RESTAURANT OPEN: 11 A.M.–2 P.M., 5 P.M.–9 P.M. ■RESTAURANT CLOSED: Some
Wednesdays ■ PRICES: Lunch ¥¥¥, dinner ¥¥¥¥ (reservations required)

Yase is a small rural town that clings to the foot of Mt. Hiei in the northeast corner of Kyoto like a shy child clutching her mother's apron strings. The single, narrow road that leads to Yase and Ōhara beyond was once the only trade route between the ancient capital and the Japan Sea. The old road through the mountain pass was arduous and exhausting.

For centuries Yase has been known as a place to relax, to recover, to enjoy at the end of a long journey. The name Yase literally means "eight springs," for here a number of small streams flow into the Takanogawa River as it makes its way to the Kamogawa River in the heart of Kyoto. But local legends tell of a different origin to the village's name. Once in the seventh century after the death of the emperor Tenji, the armies of the emperor's illegitimate son fought his brother for control of the throne. The brother (later known as Emperor Tenmu) won, but not without suffering a near-fatal arrow wound in the back. The battle took place at Ōmi on the other side of the mountain near Lake

Biwa, and his men carried their dying lord over the mountains to safety in a tiny village by a river and stayed with him until he recovered. The villagers say what pulled him through was the *kamaburo*, an ovenlike steam bath in which he could lie flat on his stomach while his arrow wound healed. The village became known thereafter as Yase, or "arrow-in-the-back," when written with different Chinese characters from those used today in the town's name. Both the baths and the legend persist, however, and Yase has kept its reputation as a place to escape to, if now only from the heat and commotion of the city below.

Kikaku-tei is a *kamaburo* inn, hidden at the edge of the forest beside the Takanogawa River in Yase. It was once the elegant villa of Hiroshi Tanaka, the industrial magnate who founded the famous Miyako Hotel in Kyoto. Among other things, he owned Kyoto's first electric power company and established the Keifuku train line that runs from Demachi (where the Takanogawa and Kamogawa rivers meet in Kyoto) to

Kurama (in the mountains north of the city) and to Yase, just across the river from Kikaku-tei.

The train journey to Yase takes about twenty minutes. Climbing down from the platform you walk a few yards to a creaky old footbridge that (hopefully) takes you across the Takanogawa River to a dirt path leading to the right, past a small waterfall and on to the inn. Stone walls surround the former villa and a single tile-roofed gateway leads enticingly up the stone steps and out of the real world. In "borrowed landscape" style, the gardens, though carefully tended, seem a part of the forest on the mountainside to which Kikaku-tei clings. Giant maple trees hide the secluded inn from view as you begin to climb the mossy steps.

The rooms in the north wing are smaller and on more of a personal scale than the luxurious main rooms in the south wing. At the end of the corridor in the north wing is a beautifully designed tearoom where the former mistress of the house entertained friends at tea ceremonies overlooking the Tsurukame (Crane and Turtle) Garden with its small pond, stone lanterns, and canopy of maple trees.

The south wing (originally the main house) is separated by a long corridor leading across more garden so that every room in the villa has a sweeping view. The largest, most luxuriously appointed room is downstairs on the south side, with glass doors that face the main garden on two sides, giving it an expansive air of extravagance.

Kikaku-tei was turned into a *ryokan* after the Tanakas passed away: the transformation amounted to adding a larger kitchen and re-doing the bath. The old villa seems a bit disgruntled at having been turned into an inn. Not as

polished perhaps as some of its prima donna counterparts in midtown, Kikaku-tei speaks with the voice of an era in Japanese history, not so very long ago, when the very wealthy few lived a life of sequestered elegance and luxury away from the eyes and out of the reach of the majority of the poor.

The *kamaburo* at Kikaku-tei can be used by overnight guests anytime, before or after dinner and again in the morning, if the guest so chooses. Not as hot as a Swedish sauna, the round clay oven-shaped *kamaburo* is the original Japanese way to unwind and heal your wounds, be they sore feet or over-taxed senses.

As with most *ryokan* in Japan, the price of a room includes two meals. At Kikaku-tei, dinners feature freshwater fish in season, whether as a part of a full-course *kaiseki* meal, or in *kamayaki*, the one-pot specialty of the house—a bountiful feast of seafood, mushrooms, and vegetables simmered in a delicious broth at your table.

Kikaku-tei is occasionally used by local companies for employee retreats, so be sure to ask for a quiet room facing the garden to enjoy a peaceful evening.

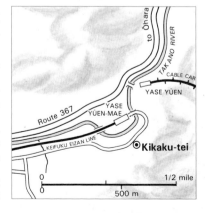

ICHIWA   rice cakes

いち和

69 Imamiya-chō, Murasakino, Kita-ku
北区紫野今宮町69   TEL: (075) 492–6852

OPEN: 10 A.M. till sunset ■ CLOSED: Wednesdays ■ PRICES: ¥

Mochi wa mochiya (Leave rice cakes to the rice cake makers)

"Old" is a relative term. Two hundred years is about as old as you can get in America; a thousand years is "pretty old" in Japan. Ichiwa, a shop that has served grilled *mochi* (rice cakes) in sweet sauce to visitors to Imamiya Shrine since the Heian period, is "pretty old" by any standard.

In her nineties as of this writing, Mrs. Hasegawa is old too, but she doesn't seem to mind. Her daughter has taken over the seat at the charcoal grill out front, but Mrs. Hasegawa still sits beside her, supervising the proper turning of the little skewers of *aburi-mochi* in winter snow and summer thunderstorm, as she has all her life. "*Bimbō hima nashi* (the poor have no time to spare)," she once told me, wiping her hands on her apron, as she welcomed customers with a hearty "*O-koshi-yasu*" and ushered them into a seat beside the little garden in back said to have been designed by Kobori Enshū, the famous tea master and landscape garden designer in the

early seventeenth century. Even the tea-caddy-shaped stone water basin in the old garden attests to Ichiwa's long association with the masters of tea. The crystal-clear water, drawn from the ancient well at the center of the shop, has been sought after by tea people for centuries. The daughter of the head master of Urasenke, the world-famous school of tea, is even rumored to have a secret sweet tooth when it comes to the Hasegawa's tasty *aburi-mochi*.

Aburi-mochi are cakes of rice flour dough, charcoal grilled, and dipped in a delicious sweet miso sauce. The bamboo skewers on which the *mochi* are placed for grilling are split by hand from green bamboo stalks whenever there is a spare moment at Ichiwa. Sixteen skewers are used with every serving, which keeps the Hasegawa family busy all the time.

Aburi-mochi has been connected with a very old festival held at Imamiya Shrine, outside the gates where Ichiwa has stood for centuries.

Yasurai Matsuri, celebrated on the first Sunday in April at Imamiya Shrine,

is another such festival dating from the ninth century, intended to pacify the spirits of the falling cherry blossoms, which were thought to cause epidemics. Dressed in red and black wigs representing demons, the participants beat their drums chanting "Flowers rest in peace" with great conviction.

Sekihan, rice with red *azuki* beans served at festive occasions (in this case with flower petals on top), and a skewer of *aburi-mochi* were said to be all that was needed to ward off disease till the following year. Ichiwa sells *aburi-mochi* every day of the year now, but its

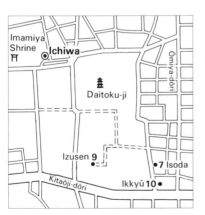

history is tied to that of this ancient shrine and the festival still held here every year in the spring. (Imamiya Shrine was dedicated in the year 1001 following an epidemic that took the lives of thousands. The death toll was so high that there is a record of bodies having been carried to Osaka, twenty-five miles to the south, to be cast into the Inland Sea.)

Aside from a chance to see this three-hundred-year-old building and taste the delicious sweet *mochi*, the Hasegawas themselves are worth the trip to the north of Daitoku-ji. When questioned about the equally old and marvelous *aburi-mochi* shop, Kasuragi, just across the way, old Mrs. Hasegawa whispers, "Yes, they're very old too, but the shop changed hands a while back" (two hundred years ago to be exact), as if she were letting us in on a recent neighborhood scandal. She is justifiably proud of her twenty-three-generation heritage, and now that her daughter has taken over, they move on to twenty-four. Unlike some of the other old Kyoto shops, Ichiwa has a future.

ISODA nattō

41 Shimo-monzen-chō, Murasakino, Kita-ku
北区紫野下門前町41   TEL: (075) 491–7617   FAX: (075) 481–7617
OPEN: Daily, 8 A.M.–7 P.M.

Even a veteran foreigner in Japan, when asked which Japanese food she could live without, will inevitably answer "*nattō*." The viscous texture and piercing odor of fermented soybeans doesn't even appeal to all Japanese, though people from Tokyo seem braver in this regard than those from Kyoto.

The specialty of the house at Isoda bears the name *nattō*, but that's where the resemblance stops when it comes to flavor. Daitoku-ji *nattō* is a Kyoto treat that comes in a small wooden box, has the salty, rich flavor of soy, keeps for a year, and will permanently ruin your taste for peanuts with beer.

In business for centuries, Isoda has no need of a flashy sign board—people who know Daitoku-ji *nattō* know where to go. Like many old Kyoto shops, Isoda never advertises. A tiny bowl of the addictive little black beans in the window to the left of the doorway is all Isoda needs to inform its customers that this is the home of Daitoku-ji *nattō* (and of the Isoda family since the late fifteenth century).

When the founder of Daitoku-ji came to Kyoto in the early fourteenth century, he brought with him an entourage of soldiers to protect the new center of the Rinzai sect of Zen. One of Isoda's ancestors was a guard who not only defended the controversial temple, but acted as a servant to the powerful priests who lived there.

After the temple was destroyed in the Ōnin War (1467–77), an eccentric Zen priest named Ikkyū supervised the reconstruction of the temple and became its forty-seventh (and most celebrated) abbot. According to legend, it was Ikkyū who introduced the Chinese Buddhist recipe for this compact, high-protein treat that could easily be taken along as a snack by mendicant priests to fortify them on their way around the countryside begging for alms.

The original recipe for Daitoku-ji *nattō* (the one still used at Isoda) is a simple, natural process: an old-style cookstove is used to boil dried soybeans in water in a giant cast-iron vat for five or six hours and then left to cool overnight; the beans are then drained and rolled in barley flour in wooden

flats where they are kept for five or six days until a fuzzy white mold forms, indicating that the fermentation process has begun; next, they are placed in large round wooden buckets and stirred with salt water (the stirring is repeated off and on for an additional five or six days). From here the beans are placed outside in the direct sunlight in the courtyard at the rear of the Isoda home. They are left to ferment and dry for one to two months, stirred several times a day until they separate into individual beans again (the viscous consistency gone) and are judged to be the proper color and texture to be packaged.

Because warm weather and natural sunlight are required, Daitoku-ji *nattō* can only be made during the summer months, most often in August after the rainy season has let up. The entire process is regulated by experience, rather than timers and gauges. There are no temperature controls or humidity regulators, and the not infrequent Kyoto summer thunderstorms keep the Isodas running around with umbrella-shaped tin lids to keep this year's batch dry. They produce enough in a few months to last all year, though they have been known to sell out by July of the following year if regular customers let their addiction get the best of them.

Even the famous tea master Sen no Rikyū is said to have been a fervent fan of the salty morsels. Because of the many tea people who frequent Isoda, they also make two kinds of dry confectionery, or *hi-gashi*, which contain tiny bits of *nattō* and are served with ceremonial tea.

Chūgo Isoda, the present owner and a seventeenth-generation *nattō* maker, still keeps an iron-pointed halberd that has been in the family since his forefathers spent their days defending the famous neighboring temple. He and his son work together each day during the sweltering Kyoto summers, boiling and stirring their beans. In the evenings they retire to the main room of their house, just behind the split curtain that separates the shopfront from the kitchen in back. But Isoda-san doesn't eat *nattō* with his evening glass of beer. "Enough is enough," he says, wiping the sweat from his brow in the midday heat. "They're great, but enough is enough."

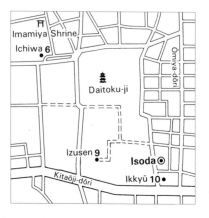

TARUDEN
buckets and casks

Sadly, Taruden, the old bucket-maker's shop, no longer exists. This page has been included in the new edition of Old Kyoto in memory of the late Hiroichi Tomii, owner of Taruden, one of the last of the traditional wooden bucket makers in Kyoto.

It is a sizzling summer afternoon in the middle of the city and Hiroichi Tomii draws an ice-cold bucket of water from his well for his foreign interviewer to refresh her face and hands. He props up an electric fan on top of a giant wooden washtub, sits me down in front of it, and asks me what I'd like to know. "Tell me about the man in the picture," I say, pointing to the emaciated figure in white robes in the photo on the wall in back. "Oh, that's my friend Sakai-san. He's a holy man." Sakai-san had just completed a thousand-day austerity, called *sennichi kaihō gyō*, in which he walked a circuit of twenty-five miles a night around Mt. Hiei (north of Kyoto) for a thousand nights over a period of seven years. During the final stage of fasting and prayer, Sakai-san carried a pair of Taruden's wooden buckets suspended on a pole over his shoulder from a well to a sacred site where a purification ritual was performed. Having made the buckets that Sakai-san carried is one of the things Tomii-san is proudest of.

You'll find Tomii-san to be a very down-to-earth person, but his family has always had a connection with the world of spirits. The family well stood inside the precincts of an old shrine at one time and provided water for the purification of its worshipers. Over 120 years ago, Tomii-san's great-grandfather started to make buckets here in this same building.

Today one of his best customers is the local Tōei Movie Studio, which places regular orders for old-style buckets to be used as props in samurai dramas (though Tomii-san would rather see his buckets used for the simple purpose for which they were intended: as bath buckets, washtubs, and saké containers).

A middle-aged neighbor appeared as we sat talking. She announced that her eighty-year-old mother could no longer bear to be without a wooden washtub. Tomii-san was out of washtubs that day and apologized. Spying the used tub on top of which the fan was perched, she said, "Well, how about that one?" Perhaps understanding how adamant an eighty-year-old lady can be, Tomii-san extricated the large tub, doused it with well water, scrubbed it down with a bristle brush, and tied it to the back of her bicycle. "I know what you mean," he said. "The old folks just don't believe that these new-fangled washing machines can get a collar clean enough." As his customer peddled off with a satisfied expression, he turned to me with scrub brush in hand and said, "I haven't been sick one day in forty years. It's because I use one of these old scrub brushes on my back!"

Both Tomii-san and his buckets are sturdy. His cedar bath buckets last thirty or forty years with daily use, if properly dried in the sun whenever possible. The lidded casks (*taru*) for storage and carrying buckets (*oke*) are made from designs and techniques described by his great-grandfather in an old notebook, one of his prized possessions. Special handmade curved planes called *kanna* form the exact angle of each curved stave, depending on the diameter of the particular bucket to be made. Like most traditional woodworkers in Japan, Tomii-san makes all his tools himself. The staves are held together by tiny bamboo dowels joining every seam. The workmanship must be perfect to create a bucket that holds water even before the bamboo or copper ring is put around it for extra strength.

Some of Taruden's buckets are used by Urasenke, the world-famous tea ceremony school just across Horikawa Street to the east, in preparation for each New Year's ceremony. Bucket-shaped flower vases are also popular with local tea masters in search of objects that possess a sense of simplicity and unpretentious dignity. Taruden makes several different shapes and sizes of flower vases in cypress (*sawara*), all with a natural unvarnished finish.

Postscript

Taruden was located in the heart of the Nishijin textile district and the rhythmic sound of looms could be heard all over the neighborhood. Most of the larger weaving companies abandoned hand-weaving for the jacquard loom nearly a century ago, and out of the twenty thousand looms in Nishijin, few remain.

Tomii-san, unfortunately, had no son and no apprentice to carry on his honorable trade. He passed away in 1998, leaving a hole in the heart of the Nishijin district where the bright red buckets out front (his only "sign board") were once a famous landmark. Life is fleeting, the Buddhist monks teach us. May you live it fully and love your work, as did Hiroichi Tomii.

MATSUNO SHŌYU

soy sauce

21 Tsuchitenjō-chō, Takagamine, Kita-ku

北区鷹峯土天井町21

TEL: (075) 492–2984

OPEN: Daily, 8:30 A.M.–6:30 P.M.

Since 1805, the Matsuno family has been producing the very best *shōyu* (soy sauce) in Kyoto. With only half the amount of salt used by most commercial makers, "*matsumaru*" soy sauce is noted for its delicate flavor. A peek in the back reveals the giant handmade wooden barrels in which this limited production soy sauce is fermented. According to sixth-generation Matsuno-san, they are the last company in Kyoto to produce fine *shōyu* the old-fashioned way. The current storehouse and factory building itself is more than 140 years old, and a landmark along the Sugisaka highway that leads out of town and into the countryside north of Kyoto. Follow Kitayama-dōri as it curves to the southwest, then turn right onto Senbon-dōri. Matsuno Shōyu is located several blocks further up the street. Beautifully wrapped gift bottles of soy sauce make memorable gifts for those who appreciate fine Japanese food.

IZUSEN
Buddhist vegetarian cuisine

4 Daitoku-ji-chō, Murasakino, Kita-ku
北区紫野大徳寺町4
TEL: (075) 491–6665   FAX: (075) 491–6615
OPEN: Daily, 11 A.M.–4 P.M. ■ PRICES: ¥¥–¥¥¥

Izusen is a restaurant that serves *shōjin ryōri*, or Zen temple meals, on the grounds of a sub-temple of Daitoku-ji called Daiji-in. The restaurant itself has facilities for large groups as well as individuals, but a delicious meal can be enjoyed at a table in the garden in quiet natural surroundings (weather permitting). Meals are served in a set of red lacquered bowls in the shape of a *teppatsu*, or priest's begging bowl, that can be stacked one inside the other when the meal is finished. On the edge of the garden which leads to Daiji-in is the "grave" of the writing brush of Murasaki Shikibu, the author of *The Tale of Genji*. Prices are reasonable and reservations are not required (but a good idea in spring and fall).

IKKYŪ
Buddhist temple food

20 Daitoku-ji-monzen, Murasakino, Kita-ku
北区紫野大徳寺門前 20
TEL: (075) 493–0019   FAX: (075) 491–1900
OPEN: 12 NOON–6 P.M. (seating until 6); shop, 9 A.M.–8 P.M. ■ CLOSED: Periodically ■
PRICES: Lunch *bentō* ¥¥, full-course meals ¥¥¥

The most famous Buddhist temple food (*shōjin ryōri*) restaurant in Kyoto, located outside the east gate of Daitoku-ji. The food is excellent, but the portions are small and the prices are higher than neighboring Izusen. The restaurant has a long history of serving the priests at Daitoku-ji, and reservations are a must.

HINODE-YA
kimono

106 Kakai-in-cho, Tera-no-uchi-sagaru, Omiya-dori, Kamigyo-ku
上京区大宮通寺之内下ル花開院町106
TEL: (075) 441–1437
OPEN: 10 A.M.–8 P.M.; CLOSED: Thursdays

In Nishijin, a district famous for the production of fine textiles since the sixteenth century, it is not easy to find a shop that sells fabric. Most of the area's looms are hired by major wholesalers, who in turn resell their goods to the *gofuku-ya-san*, the retail kimono merchants, most of whom do business from shops in the downtown area west of Karasuma and south of Oike-dōri. Hinode-ya is an exception and they have been in business here in the heart of Nishijin since the Meiji period. They sell all kinds of fabrics, primarily in the narrow width used for making kimono. Although most *gofuku-ya* sell only by the full bolt length needed to make one kimono, Hinode-ya also sells by the meter off the bolt, much to the delight of modern shoppers, most of whom no longer wear kimono. Hinode-ya also offers ready-to-wear *yukata* (light summer kimono) and *monpe* (traditional women's folk-style pants), as well as a selection of beautifully hand-dyed scarves and other fine crafts.

N12

MYŌREN-JI
temple lodgings

Tera-no-uchi Nishi-iru, Horikawa-dōri, Kamigyō-ku
上京区堀川通寺之内西入ル
TEL: (075) 451–3527   FAX: (075) 451–3597
CHECK-IN: 6 P.M. ■ CHECK-OUT: 9 A.M. ■ CURFEW: 10 P.M. ■ RATES: ¥ (w/breakfast and ticket for public bath)

Friendly lodgings in a thirteenth-century temple of the Hokke sect. The old bell tower is noteworthy, and the rooms of the *shukubō* (lodgings) overlook a sand and stone garden of which the temple is proud. Popular with young travelers from around the world, it is best to make reservations by postcard well in advance, as temple activities take precedence over outside lodgers. Sutra reading (*o-kyō*) is conducted in the main prayer hall from 6:30 A.M., a fine way to start the day, but not mandatory.

N13

SEISHŌ-DŌ YAMASHITA
tea utensils

Tera-no-uchi-agaru, Ogawa-dōri, Kamigyō-ku
上京区小川通寺之内上ル
TEL: (075) 431–1366

OPEN: Daily, 9 A.M.–5 P.M. ■ CREDIT: Major credit cards

On the road which leads to the gates of the two most famous schools of tea ceremony in Japan, Urasenke and Omotesenke, Seishō-dō has been selling tea utensils since 1847. From the most exquisite antique tea bowls worth hundreds of thousands of yen to the smallest tea accessories, a set of tiny wooden forks for slicing tea cakes, Seishō-dō is the place to browse or to search for a particular item to complement a collection of tea utensils. Stroll through this neighborhood past the grounds of Urasenke, to Hōkyō-ji (famous for its exhibition of antique Japanese dolls in March and October) or to nearby Myōken-ji (see N14), which provides overnight accommodations and a sample of temple life.

N14

MYŌKEN-JI
temple lodgings

Tera-no-uchi Higashi-iru, Horikawa-dōri, Kamigyō-ku
上京区堀川通寺之内東入ル
TEL: (075) 414–0808   FAX: (075) 414–0848
CHECK-IN: 6 P.M. ■ CHECK-OUT: 9 A.M. ■ CURFEW: 9 P.M. ■ RATES: ¥

Accommodations for women only in a temple of the Nichiren sect founded over 650 years ago. You may have to share a large room with other travelers if the temple is crowded, but private rooms are available if you send a postcard ahead requesting reservations. Unlike most modern-day inns, the rooms have no TVs or other gadgetry to mar the traditional beauty. They overlook a mossy garden that's as fine as any you'll find in one of Kyoto's expensive inns. No meals are served at Myōken-ji, but bath facilities are available.

RAKU-SEI

Western Kyoto

Arashiyama . . . the name is synonymous with "autumn" in the minds of anyone who has ever visited this beautiful western ravine in November. The steep mountain slopes with their seasonal wardrobes of crimson and green have been the favorite haunt of Japanese emperors for centuries.

Togetsu-kyō, the landmark bridge that spans the wide River Ōi, marks the center of this area, and from here north, the path leads past Tenryū-ji Temple with its dragon ceiling, and on through the bamboo groves and rice fields that run all the way to the torii gate which leads to Atago Shrine.

Further to the north is Ninna-ji, with its pair of snarling carved temple guardians at the gate; Ryōan-ji, with its world-famous raked sand and stone Zen garden; and Kinkaku-ji, the Golden Pavilion, built by Shogun Ashikaga Yoshimitsu in the fourteenth century.

Raku-sei, renowned for its scenic beauty, was also a place of exile for court ladies who fell out of favor with their lords. The melancholy aura of small temples like Giō-ji, named after one such lady who shaved her head and lived out her years here in sadness, have given Raku-sei a wistful feeling of romance that appeals to the thousands of young women who flock here every year to share in the timeless sentiment of unrequited love that seems to pervade the western hills.

Once away from the modern souvenir shops that now line the main thoroughfare, the quiet paths, bamboo glens, rivers, and fields, dotted with small country temples, restaurants, and inns, make this area the best in Kyoto for a leisurely stroll away from the noisy city.

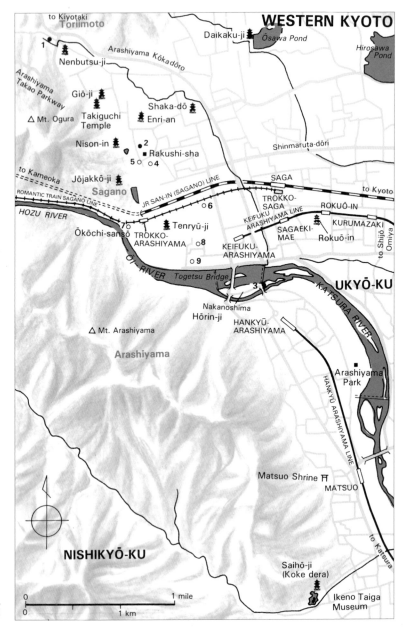

to Kiyotaki
Toriimoto

Daikaku-ji

Ōsawa Pond

Hirosawa Pond

1

Nenbutsu-ji

Arashiyama Kōkadōro

Arashiyama Takao Parkway

Giō-ji

Shaka-dō

△ Mt. Ogura

Takiguchi Temple

Enri-an

Shinmaruta-dōri

Nison-in

2

Rakushi-sha

5 ○ ○ 4

to Kameoka

Jōjakkō-ji

Sagano

SAGA

to Kyoto

ROMANTIC TRAIN SAGANO LINE

JR SAN-IN (SAGANO) LINE

TROKKO-SAGA

ROKUŌ-IN

HOZU RIVER

○ 6

KEIFUKU ARASHIYAMA LINE

KURUMAZAKI

7 ○

Ōkōchi-sansō

TROKKO-ARASHIYAMA

Tenryū-ji

○ 8

SAGAEKI-MAE

Rokuō-in

KEIFUKU-ARASHIYAMA

to Shijō Omiya

OI RIVER

Togetsu Bridge

○ 9

3

UKYŌ-KU

KATSURA RIVER

Nakanoshima

Hōrin-ji

HANKYŪ-ARASHIYAMA

△ Mt. Arashiyama

Arashiyama Park

Arashiyama

HANKYŪ ARASHIYAMA LINE

Matsuo Shrine 卂

MATSUO

to Katsura

NISHIKYŌ-KU

Saihō-ji (Koke dera)

Ikeno Taiga Museum

0   1 mile
0   1 km

HIRANO-YA
sweetfish (ayu)

16 Sennō-chō, Saga Toriimoto, Ukyō-ku
右京区嵯峨鳥居本仙翁町16   TEL: (075) 861–0359   FAX: (075) 861–0359

OPEN: Daily, 11:30 A.M.–9 P.M. ■ PRICES: *Okimari* special lunch ¥¥–¥¥¥; full-course *ayu kaiseki*
¥¥¥¥ ■ CREDIT: DC VISA

Smoke rises in the air above thatched rooftops at sunset. Below, the light of the bath fire glows in the darkness. A single cricket perseveres on the edge of winter until the sound of footsteps warns him to be silent (he is, after all, alone now). Steep-sloped mountains contain the ancient valley and the last few farmers trudge home from their rice fields, another year's work almost done.

Sagano in the western part of Kyoto was once nothing more (or less) than a country field. To find such pastoral scenes now, one must travel beyond the mountain ridges that surround the former capital city to the more remote rural areas that remain. Shūzan is one such place, Hanase another. Ōhara, though a popular tourist destination, still retains much of its rustic charm. But inside the city limits of Kyoto, there is hardly a scrap of countryside left untouched by urban sprawl. Sagano is perhaps the last area in which vestiges of rice fields and farmhouses can still be found at all in Kyoto.

Just inside the vermilion *torii* gate that leads up the mountainside to Atago

Shrine on the northwest edge of Sagano stands a four-hundred-year-old thatched teahouse called Hirano-ya.

Grilled *ayu*, a small freshwater fish, is the specialty of the house now, but long ago a cup of tea and a skewer of *shinko dango*, a popular local rice confection, were the treats for which Hirano-ya was best known. For centuries, their homemade *dango* provided shrine worshipers with the encouragement to tackle the steep, two-hour climb to the top of Mt. Atago, the home of the god who puts out fires.

Fire has always been the most dreaded affliction in Kyoto, where the houses were built of wood with shared walls on two sides. On more than one occasion fire has destroyed the entire city in a matter of hours, so it became customary for every citizen to climb the hill once a month to plead with the cantankerous god of fire for mercy.

Though this custom has given way to a once-a-year symbolic climb on July 31, the pair of old teahouses at the base of the hill beside the *torii* still offer rest and nourishment to faithful

worshipers and to anyone who enjoys a fresh *ayu* meal served in gracious traditional country style.

The *ayu* served at Hirano-ya are caught in the nearby Hōzugawa River, brought live by fishermen and placed in the large pond out back. No refrigerator is used, so each morning just enough fish are caught from the pond to last the day (a process you can watch from the open veranda where you'll be seated, overlooking not only the pond, but a backdrop of maple trees whose tiny star-shaped leaves form a jigsaw puzzle with the sky).

The smell of freshly caught *ayu* grilling over charcoal in the kitchen below and the rustic beauty of this two-hundred-year-old farmhouse with its dark, curving beams and heavy thatched roof is just about the only taste of traditional Japanese countryside this side of Mt. Atago. *Ayu* season is from May through October, and a full-course meal can be rather expensive. In the fall, however, the *yudōfu-no-okimari* lunch of tofu simmered in a ceramic hotpot at your table is much more affordable. (For a brief country pause—particularly on a tight budget—the original *shinko dango* are still made fresh every morning and served with green tea at pilgrims' prices.)

The unusual Saga paper lanterns that light each room at Hirano-ya are a special source of pride for Tamiko Inoue, the thirteenth-generation proprietress of the old restaurant. It is difficult to find rustic lanterns like these, and she must order them from the last craftsman in the area who still knows how to weave the bamboo spines and coat the handmade paper with tannin the way they were made in the old days. Giant and unevenly constructed, they glow with a soft amber light that sets the mood at Hirano-ya, a quality described

as *soboku* in Japanese, a word which refers to the artless beauty of things that belong to the countryside.

Kyoto Prefecture includes miles and miles of breathtaking farmland that extends all the way to the Japan Sea. After lunch under the high thatched roofs of the old teahouse, a short drive through the tunnel to the west (or hike over the hillside trail) will lead you to Kiyotaki, a country village from which you can begin a walk that leads along the banks of a river out into the hills beyond. Or drive up through the Takao Parkway to Highway 162 which, in three hours, will take you down winding mountain roads lined with Kitayama cedar (the trees that are so carefully groomed to decorate the interiors of Kyoto homes) to the Japan Sea. Valleys wedged between steep cedar-covered mountains reveal tiny farm villages around every bend, scenes not long for this increasingly urbanized world.

KOTŌ-EN
Shigaraki ware

小陶苑

福狸本

15–2 Chōjin-chō, Saga Nison-in-monzen-kita, Ukyō-ku
右京区嵯峨二尊院門前北長神町15–2   TEL: (075) 872–2134
OPEN: 9 A.M.–5 P.M. ■ CLOSED: Tuesdays ■ CREDIT: Major credit cards

A hundred-odd ceramic *tanuki* (the legendary barrel-bellied raccoon dogs of Japan), from six feet high to pocket-sized, lined up in a courtyard in the middle of the bamboo forests of Sagano is enough to charm any traveler to stray for just a moment from his path. That's the secret of the wily *tanuki*, who has been seducing unwary strangers with his magical powers for centuries. Able to transform himself at the blink of an eye into a beautiful maiden or a ugly old hag, the *tanuki* is not to be trusted. Mischievous, rather than evil, he has a whimsical turn to his dubious character that has managed to endear him to the hearts of even the most circumspect Japanese. A popular symbol with Kyoto merchants, the *tanuki* can often be found outside the doorways of the city's old shops, placed there perhaps in the hopes that some of the creature's crafty ways will rub off on its master.

Kotō-en, a pottery shop in the middle of Sagano in western Kyoto, is known for the comical covey of *tanuki* in its courtyard, as well as for the wide variety of Shigaraki ceramics on display inside.

Kotō-en is a Kyoto branch of the Sōtō-en kilns in Shigaraki, a famous pottery village since the Middle Ages in Japan. Built in the Edo period, the climbing kiln (or *noborigama*) at Sōtō-en is one of the largest kilns in Japan, producing glazed and unglazed stoneware from the coarse, reddish clay taken from the surrounding hillside.

Though pottery making in the Shigaraki area dates back nearly twelve hundred years, Shigaraki ware rose to its height during the Muromachi and Momoyama periods when the natural, rustic character of its ash-glazed finish came to the attention of tea masters in search of *wabi*, the simple, unaffected quality that was considered essential to the practice of tea ceremony.

Shigaraki ware still flourishes today, although it has undergone as many changes as the *tanuki* himself in the centuries it has been in production. The pottery is now popular as everyday ceramic ware (mugs, *nabe* cooking pots, and *ueki-bachi* planters), but the Shigaraki kilns still produce some of the beautiful natural-glaze tea ware

Western Kyoto

195

for which the village became famous.

A short stroll through the courtyard to the display room will introduce you to the incorrigible Tanuki-san in almost every form imaginable. Long a symbol of good luck and happiness, the *tanuki* has become a trademark of the ancient kilns at Shigaraki in recent years. Inside the shop you'll find vases, tea bowls, coffee cups, serving platters, dish sets, ashtrays, and even chopstick rests (*hashioki*), all at the most reasonable prices in town. It is possible to visit the kilns at Sōtō-en in Shigaraki by bus or train. (See Day Trips to the Countryside.)

Tanuki

The *tanuki*, apart from his legendary escapades, is a real-life creature. A member of the badger family, the *tanuki* (or raccoon dog) has often been known to pester farmers and even suburban dwellers in search of food to fill his insatiable belly. The hair of the *tanuki* is prized for use in the finest paint brushes (almost as much as its clever hide is prized by irate farmers).

His mythological reputation is even more notorious than his name as an incorrigible farm pest, and over the ages these eight special "charms" have been officially attributed to this popular character:

1. the umbrella hat—a symbol of protection against accidents and mishaps.

2. the big round eyes—a reminder to be wary of all that is around you.

3. the whimsical face—a reminder to be amiable and keep smiling.

4. the saké bottle—*tanuki* wisdom says: if you have the money to buy saké, you should have the good manners to know how to hold your liquor.

5. the credit book—reminds the heavy drinker that his local saké shop extends him credit, so he in turn should learn the importance of trust.

6. the big belly—Japanese decisions are made from the gut (*hara o kimeru*); remember to think well before making a decision and to have the courage to stick to your decision.

7. the stalwart tail—anything as determined as a *tanuki* tail is to stand straight and tall should find nothing but success ahead.

8. the privates—last but impossible to overlook, the *kinbukuro*, a word which literally means money bags, in slang refers to the scrotum— the crafty badger's last word on the subject: don't be a miser, buy a *tanuki*. . . .

NISHIKI kaiseki cuisine

Inside Nakanoshima-kōen, Arashiyama, Ukyō-ku
右京区嵐山中之島公園内 TEL: (075) 871–8888, 881–8888 FAX: (075) 872-4334
OPEN: 11 A.M.–9 P.M. ■ CLOSED: Tuesdays ■ PRICES: ¥¥–¥¥¥ ■ CREDIT: Major credit cards

The story of Ine Tanaka, the late owner and founder of Nishiki, is one I will never forget. She was ninety-one years old the year I met her. *"Obake deshō?"* her staff used to tease, joking that she was already a ghost. But Ine Tanaka was the heartiest spirit I'd ever had the pleasure to meet. For over forty years she was the proprietress of one of Kyoto's most popular restaurants, and the story of her life is as amazing as her *kaiseki* menu is delicious.

"Actually, I was born in Tokyo," she told me, "so people around here consider me kind of a foreigner. I married a man whose family owned a pair of successful tempura restaurants. He threw me out when I didn't bear him any children. That's the way it was in those days: the man's word was law. I had no choice but to leave.

"I ended up staying in Osaka with his folks, no less, to help them manage one of the restaurants. As could be expected, we didn't get along, and when I asked them if they'd consider just selling the place to me, I think they agreed just to get rid of me. They wanted

¥3,000, which was a fortune before the war. I rounded up ten people I knew and talked them into loaning me ¥300 each. In no time my place was one of the best tempura restaurants around. Until the fire bombings, that is. (Did you say you were an American, dear?) Well, they got me. The place burnt to the ground. Decided it was time to move to a quieter town. I wound up staying at a rundown old inn in Kyoto out on a sandbar in the middle of the river in Arashiyama. The old couple who owned it were looking for someone to take it off their hands, so I volunteered. (Had to borrow the money again, mind you.) Little by little I pulled the place together and opened another restaurant right here."

Ine Tanaka bustled around the corridors at Nishiki every day, bowing to customers and barking orders at the maids to straighten the shoes left by the guests in a jumble by the doorway. "You have to be on them every minute," she'd whisper. "That's the only way to be sure the place is run the way you want it." A dozen young cooks scurried

back and forth worriedly as the tiny gray-haired rear admiral in kimono scrutinized the *sashimi* slicing. Today, two generations later, the restaurant Tanaka-san so valiantly started still serves more than hundred people a day in peak season, and there is no time for mistakes.

Nishiki sits on an island in the middle of the River Ōi, across the Togetsu-kyō Bridge from the central part of the Arashiyama district. This area is part of a historic preservation district and the traditional tatami mat rooms at Nishiki sprawl low along the river bank, half hidden behind the high bamboo fence that surrounds the entire place, in keeping with the local style. Reservations are a must, though you may have a chance without them if you arrive before 11 A.M.

Like her life, Tanaka-san played her menu by ear, creating one of Kyoto's most original *bentō* lunches. It is *kaiseki* style with all the delicate courses, but presented elegantly in beautifully lacquered box. Designed after an old-fashioned Japanese workman's lunch box with drawers (a work of "found art" discovered in a neighborhood junk shop by Tanaka-san's adopted son) the *o-shuku-zen* lunch box is the centerpiece of this fantastic meal—an eclectic cross between formal *kaiseki* and a deluxe *bentō* box lunch. The name *o-shuku-zen* refers romantically to an inn which serves meals amid the cherry blossoms.

The basic seven-course *o-shuku-zen* is the most reasonably priced in town for a *kaiseki*-style lunch of such proportions. Every month the ingredients are changed completely to match the season, and a special booklet (in Japanese) is prepared describing each course with exacting detail for customers to peruse while they are waiting.

Tanaka-san's grandson Hideyuki carries on his grandmother's honored tradition at Nishiki. A sample menu for the month of July featured such seasonal treats as *ayu no shio-yaki*, small freshwater white fish, salted and grilled; *karashi-dōfu*, a spicy local tofu dish; and *age-nasubi*, fried eggplant in miso sauce, served in a silver eggplant-shaped container. The top shelf of the *o-shuku-zen* box was decorated with cross-hatched twigs of bamboo on which "bloomed" three miniature paper-thin porcelain bowls, the shape of morning glories (the flower of the season) in soft blues and pinks, filled with tiny portions of seafood delicacies such as sea urchin and baby clams.

After our long conversation that day twenty years ago, my final question to the indomitable Ine Tanaka was this: What do you think about women's lib? "Women's lib?" she cackled. "Good heavens, dear, I'm an old lady ... what would I know about a thing like that!"

FAR LEFT: Ine Tanaka at the age of ninety-one in 1985

BOAI-SŌ
restaurant

2-2 Yamamoto-chō, Saga Ogurayama, Ukyo-ku

右京区嵯峨小倉山山本町2-2

TEL: (075) 862-3785

OPEN: 11 A.M.–4 P.M. ■ CLOSED: Mondays ■ PRICES: ¥

North of Ōkōchi-sansō (see W7), walk along the path beside Ogura Pond, and watch the local fishermen try their luck. Further along the path sits Boai-sō, a lovely *Kyō-ryōri* restaurant surrounded by a stand of giant bamboo. The restaurant is in an old farmhouse owned before World War II by the famous Japanese philosopher Kitarō Nishida, who used it as a quiet retreat in which to ponder ways to blend the best ideas of East and West. This is a wonderful spot to stop for a tasty lunch in a serene setting.

SAGA NINGYŌ NO MISE
Saga dolls, clay toys

2 Saga Ogurayama-chō, Ukyo-ku

右京区嵯峨小倉山町2

TEL: (075) 871-7141

OPEN: 10 A.M.–5 P.M. ■ CLOSED: Periodically

The term Saga *ningyō*, or Saga doll, refers to an old type of wooden figure that was coated with a white shell paste, elaborately painted, and edged in gold. Though true Saga dolls are no longer made, the Iura family makes small clay figures (*tsuchi ningyō*) that retain a touch of the refinement their predecessors were noted for. The Iuras have been making these small clay figures here

beside the rice fields in front of the thatched poet's hut known as Rakushi-sha since the late Edo period. The figures are miniatures of the twelve animals of the Chinese Zodiac: the cock, the dog, the dragon, the horse, the monkey, the ox, the rabbit, the rat, the sheep, the snake, the tiger, and the boar. Each year in a cycle of twelve has the name of an animal in the zodiac. Your character is said to be related to the animal of the year in which you were born. Each little figure at the Iuras' shop is sold in a tiny wooden box with its name and the shop's stamp.

SHIGETSU
Zen vegetarian cuisine

Inside Tenryū-ji Temple, Saga Tenryū-ji, Ukyō-ku

右京区嵯峨天龍寺内

TEL: (075) 882-9725

OPEN: Daily, 11 A.M.–2 P.M. ■ PRICES: ¥¥–¥¥¥ (plus admission fee)

Tenryū-ji is one of Kyoto's most beloved Zen Buddhist temples, located in the very heart of the Arashiyama district. Shigetsu serves a wonderful lunch in a restaurant on the temple grounds, overlooking the stunning landscaped garden. One of the earliest in Kyoto, the garden was designed in 1340 by the great Zen priest, Musō Kokushi. The stroll garden and pond are in the dramatic paradise style, which originated in southern Sung dynasty China. The food is *shōjin ryōri* vegetarian style, served in the kind of red-lacquered bowls used by Zen priests. Reservations are recommended, and prices are reasonable, though admission to the temple garden is also required.

ŌKŌCHI-SANSŌ
tea and sweets, kaiseki lunch

Saga Tenryū-ji, Ukyō-ku
右京区嵯峨天竜寺
TEL: (075) 872–2233

OPEN: Daily, 9 A.M.–5 P.M. ■ PRICES: *Matcha* and sweets ¥, *kaiseki* lunch ¥¥–¥¥¥

This exquisite villa is located in the middle of a bamboo forest atop Mt. Ogura in the Sagano district, fifteen minutes on foot from the Togetsu-kyō Bridge at Arashiyama. Built by the late Denjirō Ōkōchi, one of Japan's greatest silent screen stars, the former villa sits amid five acres of land surrounded by beautiful gardens with a breathtaking view of the entire city. After Ōkōchi-san retired, he spent the remaining thirty years of his life landscaping the entire estate, an absolute wonderland of paths winding through the woods on the hillside. For a modest admission price, guests are served *matcha* and sweets in a courtyard below the magnificent building, after which they may stroll through the gardens, take a peek at the elegant main building with its curved shingled roof, and admire the magnificent view. Reservations can also be made in advance for formal *kaiseki* lunch, served in a magnificently appointed private room overlooking the most splendid view Kyoto has to offer.

SAGANO
yudōfu restaurant

45 Susuki-no-baba-chō, Saga Tenryū-ji, Ukyō-ku
右京区嵯峨天竜寺芒ノ馬場町45

TEL: (075) 861–0277, 871–6946
FAX: (075) 871–6921

OPEN: Daily, 11 A.M.–7 P.M. (last order 6:30) ■ CLOSED: New Year's holidays ■ PRICES: ¥¥ ■ CREDIT: Major credit cards

Hidden in the bamboo forest just south of Tenryū-ji is a beautifully designed restaurant serving *yudōfu*, a popular Kyoto dish featuring simmered tofu and a number of side dishes for a reasonable price. It is difficult to say whether this restaurant is in the middle of the forest, or the forest is in the middle of the restaurant—everywhere you look there are towering stands of bamboo. The walls in the main building are lined with *some-tsuke* blue-on-white porcelain bowls and platters. The gravel path that leads to the entrance is guarded by twelve large stone figures which were brought back by the warlord Hideyoshi from his sixteenth-century invasion of Korea. On the north end of the modern tile-roofed building there is a sand and stone garden that is unequalled by any in Japan—not for its extraordinary beauty, but for the submarine enshrined in the center. It is one of the suicide subs used in World War II and was placed there by the peace-loving owner of Sagano as a monument to the tragedy of war and a reminder of the importance of peace.

KITCHŌ
kaiseki cuisine

58 Susuki-no-baba-chō, Saga Tenryū-ji,
Ukyō-ku

右京区嵯峨天竜寺芒ノ馬場町58

TEL: (075) 881–1101

OPEN: 11:30 A.M.–7:30 P.M. (reservations
required) ■ CLOSED: 2nd and 4th Thursdays ■
PRICES: ¥¥¥¥

Beside the River Ōi, just far enough off
the beaten path, along the river road
that runs west of the heart of the
Arashiyama district, sits Kitchō, one of
the finest and most exclusive restaurants in Japan. Tucked quietly away
behind a woven bamboo fence, this
remarkable place is a paradise for connoisseurs of fine Japanese cuisine. Dinner can run to several hundred dollars,
and as one jaded Kyoto restaurateur
noted, customers paying top prices for
kaiseki cuisine are also paying for the
priceless dishware on which these per-
fectly prepared meals are presented.
A summer meal might appear in a
serving bowl hand painted by the famed
eighteenth-century ceramic artist,
Kenzan. A serving of the best *sashimi*
you will ever taste might arrive in a tiny
wooden boat, covered with a miniature
bamboo trellis, adorned with springs
of wisteria buds—all patterned after
the excursion boats of the princesses
who once made Arashiyama their play-
ground. An afternoon at Kitchō is a
total sensory experience—one that you
(and your pocketbook) will never forget.

RAKU-NAN

Southern Kyoto

Raku-nan is the only side of Kyoto unprotected by mountains, and the main transportation route to the old port of Sakai (now Osaka) on the Inland Sea to the south. The old highway used by samurai and peddlers in the Edo period still exists, as do the post towns along the way like Fushimi. Fushimi Inari is the home of a shrine to the rice goddess which predates the founding of Heiankyō (the original name of Kyoto) in 794 and still attracts thousands of merchants and businessmen who pray for a successful year during its festival every February. Fushimi Momoyama, formerly a castle own at the foot of Toyotomi Hideyoshi's great sixteenth-century fortress Fushimi-jō, is now one of the two biggest saké producing towns in Japan, with thirty-seven different breweries (see page 211) within walking distance of each other along a canal that was once a main thoroughfare for the flatboats that carried goods back and forth from Kyoto to Sakai. It takes just fifteen minutes to reach Fushimi by local express from Sanjō-Keihan Station, but this nonetheless puts Fushimi outside the normal tourist path.

Raku-nan belongs to the common people. It has never had the frills and finery of areas in the north that were in closer proximity to the Imperial Palace. This is where "the people" lived—and still live. Industrial, straightforward, and real, it is seldom included on tourist routes. If you are looking for a side of Kyoto that hasn't been tinted for the travel posters, Fushimi is the place to find it.

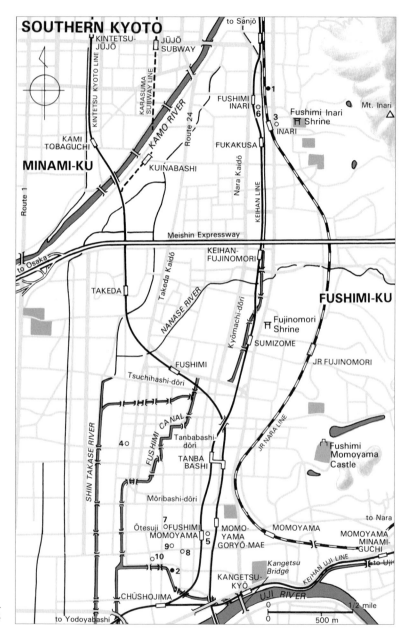

SOUTHERN KYOTO

to Sanjō

KINTETSU-JŪJŌ

JŪJŌ SUBWAY

KINTETSU KYOTO LINE

KARASUMA SUBWAY LINE

KAMO RIVER

Route 24

FUSHIMI INARI

●1

6

3

Fushimi Inari Shrine

Mt. Inari △

INARI

KAMI TOBAGUCHI

MINAMI-KU

FUKAKUSA

Route 1

KUINABASHI

Nara Kaidō

KEIHAN LINE

Meishin Expressway

to Osaka

KEIHAN-FUJINOMORI

TAKEDA

Takeda Kaidō

NANASE RIVER

Kyōmachi-dōri

FUSHIMI-KU

Fujinomori Shrine

SUMIZOME

JR FUJINOMORI

FUSHIMI

Tsuchihashi-dōri

SHIN TAKASE RIVER

FUSHIMI CANAL

4○

Tanbabashi-dōri

TANBA BASHI

JR NARA LINE

Fushimi Momoyama Castle

Mōribashi-dōri

Ōtesuji

7 ○FUSHIMI MOMOYAMA

9○   ○8

○10

●2

5

MOMO-YAMA GORYŌ-MAE

MOMOYAMA

to Nara

MOMOYAMA MINAMI-GUCHI

to Uji

KEIHAN UJI LINE

Kangetsu Bridge

KANGETSU-KYŌ

CHŪSHOJIMA

UJI RIVER

to Yodoyabashi

0   1/2 mile

0   500 m

204

TANKA Fushimi dolls

伏見人形窯元

丹 嘉

22–504 Hon-chō, Higashiyama-ku
東山区本町22–504 TEL: (075) 561–1627
OPEN: 9 A.M.–6 P.M. ■ CLOSED: Sundays, holidays

Wherever you find a pair of perky-eared stone foxes (whose inscrutable demeanor bears a suspicious resemblance to the small bushy-tailed house dogs chained to many Kyoto doorways), you know you are standing before the precincts of one of Japan's forty thousand Inari shrines. The vigilant foxes, one perched purposefully on either side of the brilliant vermilion *torii* gate, are the messengers of the rice goddess enshrined within, a revered spirit in a traditionally agrarian country whose staple food has always been rice.

Since the eighth century, Inari-san, as Fushimi Inari Shrine is affectionately known, has belonged to the common people—to the farmers, of course, whose lives once hung in balance on the basis of the number of rice bales they were able to pay the feudal lords to allow them to keep on toiling; later to the merchants whose profits helped hold society together in times of war and political upheaval; and finally to the businessmen and industrialists who run the country today. Every year in February during the shrine's annual

festival, the young *miko* priestesses literally rake up hundreds of thousands of yen in contributions to the goddess of rice, who seems to have become the goddess of yen. The hundreds of symbolic *torii* gates which lead up the mountain to the heart of the shrine commemorate sizable donations made by hundreds of local shopkeepers and national corporations alike. A walk through the brilliant tunnel of vermilion is magic enough to draw tourists and photographers to Fushimi Inari year round.

The path leading up the hill to Inari Shrine is lined from end to end with shops selling all manner of amulets and Shinto paraphernalia to pilgrims and sightseers alike. Tanka was there, long before any of the rest, making and selling Fushimi *ningyō*, the painted clay dolls that are both colorful souvenirs and symbols of good luck at the shrine.

Fushimi dolls depict characters from folk tales (Kintarō, Momotarō, and Manjūkui-no-ko) or from the Seven Gods of Good Luck (Hotei, Ebisu, or Daikoku). Some, like the heroic folk

character Kintarō, are given as gifts of congratulations upon the birth of a baby boy with the wish that he will grow up strong and honorable like the legendary character the doll represents. These, like most Japanese dolls, are not meant to be played with, but to be displayed as protective objects or symbols of good luck.

At Tanka, Ōnishi-san—a seventh-generation craftsman—makes Fushimi dolls from the same molds cut by his ancestors over four hundred years ago. These are said to have been the prototypes for all the *tsuchi ningyō*, or clay dolls, made throughout Japan today. These dolls have become popular regional souvenirs in rural towns from Hokkaido to Kyushu in hundreds of different forms and designs.

Tanka has over eight hundred original molds to choose from, and samples of many of these are displayed in a glass case that covers the entire south wall. (They are not all kept in stock, however, and although special dolls can be custom ordered, this year's selection is in a display case in the center of the room.) Each year Ōnishi-san also makes up a large order of the "animal of the year," according to the Oriental zodiac.

The dark, burnished-looking shapes that inhabit the display case on the north wall are not the goblins they appear to be, but are in fact some of Tanka's original centuries-old molds. Ōnishi-san brought out one for us to examine, pointing out the stamp on the base. Tenshō 3, it said—1576.

The shop building itself is characteristic of Fushimi-style architecture with its slightly curved, expansive tile rooftops. Note the row of roof guardian figures. Shōki (the demon queller), the bearded warrior with his sword, is the most common in Kyoto, but at Tanka, the figures include an array of chubby urchins and horned devils that only a master mold-maker like Ōnishi could have devised. Constructed over two hundred years ago, the building is older than many in Kyoto, having survived the dreadful series of fires that destroyed much of the city proper.

One of the most popular dolls at Tanka now is Manjūkui-no-ko, a standing figure of a boy who holds half of a *manjū*, or bean cake, in each chubby hand. This enigmatic figure is the perfect statement of the wisdom of an Eastern Solomon:

A young boy, wiser than his years, was asked by his quarreling parents to choose which one of them he liked best. He paused thoughtfully, picked up a knife and cut the *manjū* he was holding in his hand in two. He held out the two slices to his parents and asked: "Which half of this bean cake is sweeter?" Out of the mouths of babes....

GEKKEIKAN
saké brewery

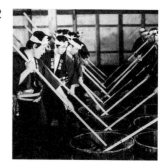

Gekkeikan Ōkura Commemorative Hall, 247 Minamihama-chō, Fushimi-ku

伏見区南浜町 247　月桂冠大倉記念館　TEL: (075) 623–2056

OPEN: 9.30 A.M.–4:30 P.M. (¥300 admission) ■ CLOSED: Mondays—except when a national holiday

Yoi niya moto suri yonaka nya koshiki

Ara, yoi-se yoi-se

Asa no araiba ga nakenya yoi

Asa no araiba ga nakenya yoi

Asa no araiba ga nakenya yoi.

So sang the saké makers of Fushimi as they toiled through the night, stirring fermenting rice with long-handled wooden paddles preparing the *moto*, or yeast mash, for the next step in the marathon task of making saké, the traditional rice brew of Japan.

The song tells of a young man who wanted all his life to be able to work in the great saké breweries of Fushimi. When his lucky break finally comes and he finds himself toiling all through the cold winter night over steaming tubs of rice, he has second thoughts. He bemoans the icy mornings when he has to wash the rice and wishes he hadn't been quite so hasty in his choice of employment. In the end, he muses, his efforts will be turned into delicious Fushimi saké, but there is a touch of

irony in his words that implies he'll never be the one to taste it.

Since the seventeenth century, the great saké breweries (*kura*) of Fushimi have hired farmers from Echizen and Tango in the cold north near the Japan Sea to come to Kyoto during their idle winter months to make what was once the saké of samurai.

The eldest, most experienced of these workers were known as *tōji*, the master brewers, who brought with them the hard-earned knowledge of generations of saké makers who spent one hundred days of constant, backbreaking work each year to make Fushimi one of the main centers of saké production in Japan today. Although some of the saké companies now have modern factories elaborately temperature-controlled to produce saké year round, many of the smaller makers still employ the *tōji* each year from the same families that have worked in their *kura* for centuries.

Gekkeikan, the number-one-selling saké in the world, hasn't forgotten the debt it owes the *tōji*, who have served the company faithfully for over three

Southern Kyoto

209

hundred years. Although it now possesses the most advanced, best-equipped brewery in the country, Gekkeikan still insists on maintaining the original old tile-roofed *kura* in which its *tōji* have worked for centuries. Beside a willow-lined canal not far from the Keihan train station at Chūshojima (fifteen minutes south of Kyoto), the huge tile-roofed *kura* of Gekkeikan still produce a limited amount of *te-zukuri*, or "handmade," saké just as they have since 1637.

When Ōkura Jiemon first opened his brewery in Fushimi 360 years ago, he was one of many competing for the favor of the Tokugawa shogunate in an area that was already one of the two biggest saké producers in the country (the other being Nada near Osaka in the south).

Fushimi is located at the convergence of three major rivers, the Yodogawa, the Kamogawa and the Katsuragawa, and was a convenient stop for boatmen and traders plying the waterways and highways between Kyoto and Osaka. Fushimi was a saké brewer's dream—it had river access with which to bring the best rice available from Himeji; it had the chilly winters necessary for

conducting the world's most finicky brewing process; and not only did it have some of the best underground spring water available, but it had a castle full of thirsty samurai, possibly seventeenth-century Japan's most avid saké fans.

In 1905, when renewed commerce with the West was in full swing, the Ōkura family named its saké Gekkeikan, a name which means "laurel wreath" (as the illustration on the label still indicates), to symbolize the Olympian heights to which the company aspired. In 1914, Gekkeikan was designated a purveyor to the imperial household.

Stop at one of the many liquor stores on the main market street that leads west from Fushimi Momoyama Station on the Keihan line. There you can find all thirty-eight brands of saké produced in Fushimi, as well as a number of gift sets from Gekkeikan. Look for a single-bottle gift box of *junmai-shu* (100 percent rice saké, with no extra sugar or alcohol), or try the beautiful two-bottle set of dry (*karakuchi*) and sweet (*amakuchi*) saké. A saké cask (*komokaburi*) complete with decanter (*tokkuri*) and a pair of matching saké cups (*choko*) makes a wonderful gift.

Wander the backstreets near the canal where Gekkeikan's old *kura* still stand and visit the company's museum, the Gekkeikan Ōkura Commemorative Hall, for a look at how saké was made four centuries ago.

SMALL BREWERIES IN FUSHIMI

Of the thirty-seven saké brewers in Fushimi, a few small places are worth a visit, although tours are available only by making special arrangements well in advance. Neighborhood liquor stores sometimes arrange annual tours with ten or so of their best customers, and a call to the brewery may help you get in on one of these. Saké is brewed only during the winter months from October through March; no tours are conducted in the off-season. Not all saké brewers have retail shops. The Tsunoyoshi Saké Shop on Nishiki Market Street in downtown Kyoto carries most Fushimi brands (and a wide selection of ji-zake, *or local saké, from small rural breweries all over Japan). A sampling of saké brewers open to the public can be found among the Fushimi shops listed below.*

S3

NEZAME-YA
yakitori restaurant

82–1 Inari Gozen-chō, Fukakusa, Fushimi-ku
伏見区深草稲荷御前町82–1
TEL: (075) 641–0802
OPEN: 9 A.M.–6 P.M. ■ CLOSED: 4 days a month ■ PRICES: ¥

For years, the enticing aroma of grilled *yakitori* has greeted travelers as they step off the Keihan train on their way to visit the magical Fushimi Inari Shrine, famed for its tunnel of vermilion *torii* gates that leads up the hill to the top of the sacred mountain. *Yakitori* literally means "grilled bird," though most often the term refers to grilled chicken. At Nezame-ya, the specialty is a bit more exotic—grilled quail and sparrow are the local delicacies most customers seek here. The skewers of *yakitori* are grilled right out on the street in front of the shop, and you can eat in, or ask for takeout (*mochi-kaeri*) at this reasonably priced little restaurant whose old Kyoto shopfront has become a landmark.

S4

SHŌTOKU saké

Shōtoku Shuzō Ltd., 16 Butai-chō, Fushimi-ku
伏見区舞台町16
TEL: (075) 611–0296
OPEN: 8:15 A.M.–5 P.M. ■ CLOSED: Saturdays, Sundays, and holidays

During the Edo period, this brewery was located at Kawaramachi-Shijō, right in the center of downtown Kyoto. It moved to Fushimi during the Meiji period, where the brewery now produces some of the finest saké in Fushimi. The owner graduated with a degree in agricultural science, and is noted for his research on the propagation of rice, a background that must come in handy to a rice-wine maker. Shōtoku *junmaishu*, or "pure saké," is noted for its pleasant aroma and slightly *karakuchi*, or dry, flavor. Many of the drinking establishments along Pontochō have been serving Shōtoku saké for generations, and Pontochō is one of the best places to sample it. Bottles may be purchased at the brewery.

S5

UOSABURŌ
kaiseki fish cuisine

187 San-chōme, Kyōmachi-dōri,
Fushimi-ku
伏見区京町通三丁目187
TEL: (075) 601–0061
OPEN: 11 A.M.–7:30 P.M. ■ CLOSED: January 1–3
■ PRICES: Lunch ¥¥, dinner ¥¥¥–¥¥¥¥

Fushimi's most elegant restaurant has been serving fine *kaiseki* cuisine on this site since 1764. The carefully restored façade of the restaurant is in true Kyoto style, with its slatted windows and understated *noren* curtain. Step inside and experience the calming effects of the best Kyoto incense welcoming the day's guests. Though the prices reflect the level of refinement and quality of Uosaburō, it is the perfect place to experience how fine locally produced Fushimi saké complements a full-course Japanese meal. The 240-year-old restaurant is renowned for its excellent fish dishes, as its name suggests ("*uo*" means fish in Japanese). Try the *hanakago gozen* lunch, served in a handmade bamboo basket. Reservations are required.

S6

MATSUDA TŌKŌ-EN
tea

Ni-bangai, Ōtesuji, Fushimi-ku
伏見区大手筋二番街
TEL: (075) 601–1017
OPEN: 9:30 A.M.–7 P.M. ■ CLOSED: Tuesdays

Fushimi is not only about saké. This little tea shop on Ōtesuji arcade has been selling fine green tea for over 380 years. Thirteenth-generation Matsuda-san is proud of her shop's heritage and happy to introduce visitors not only to her

fine assortment of green teas, but to her selection of tea bowls, tea whisks, and other utensils used in the preparation of powdered tea for the tea ceremony. The beautifully made portable *chabako* set sold at Matsuda's contains everything you need to make tea in elegant style at home or in an outdoor garden setting.

S7

AZUMA   sushi

762 Higashi-ōte-chō, Fushimi-ku
伏見区東大手町762
TEL: (075) 611–1379 (English spoken)
OPEN: 10 A.M.–7 P.M. ■ CLOSED: Tuesdays ■
PRICES: ¥–¥¥ ■ CREDIT: UC, VISA

On the arcade just west of Fushimi Momoyama Station. Serves the best sushi in Fushimi, with plastic samples of the menu outside in the display window, making it easy to order. This is an excellent place to sample Gekkeikan saké while you are in Fushimi.

S8

TORISEI
yakitori and saké

186 Kami-aburagake-chō, Fushimi-ku
伏見区上油掛町186
TEL: (075) 622–5533   FAX: (075) 622–3110
OPEN: 11:30 A.M.–2 P.M., 6 P.M.–11 P.M. ■
CLOSED: Mondays ■ PRICES: ¥–¥¥

A *yakitori* (skewered morsels of grilled chicken) restaurant that is owned by Yamamoto Honke (see S9), the maker of Shinsei saké, and shares one of the Yamamoto *kura*. For lunch they serve a chicken and rice dish called *tori-meshi*, and a chicken noodle soup called *tori-*

ramen. In the evenings they have regular *yakitori* fare. This is an excellent place to sample Shinsei saké.

YAMAMOTO HONKE

saké

36-1 Kami-aburagake-chō, Fushimi-ku
伏見区上油掛町36–1
TEL: (075) 611–0211
OPEN: 8:30 A.M.–5 P.M. ■ CLOSED: Saturdays, Sundays and holidays

In business since around 1688 as a retail shop for saké, miso, and salt, Yamamoto Honke started making its own saké during the Meiji period and is now one of the most popular brewers in Fushimi. Their brand name is Shinsei and it can be purchased at almost any liquor store in Fushimi or Kyoto, or directly from their head office around the corner from their *kura* storehouses. (To sample Shinsei, see Torisei, S8.)

TERADA-YA

historic inn

263 Minami-hama-chō, Fushimi-ku
伏見区南浜町263
TEL: (075) 622–0243
OPEN: Daily, 10 A.M.–4 P.M.

This historic *ryokan* is famous as the scene of a fight between Sakamoto Ryōma (a loyalist who sought to overthrow the Tokugawa shogunate and restore the emperor to power in 1866) and samurai troops of the shogun. His struggle was successful in the end, and marked the beginning of the Meiji Era in Japanese history. Sakamoto, however was assassinated in 1867 at the age of thirty-two—a year too soon to see his comrades-in-arms succeed. No longer operating as an inn, Terada-ya is now open as a historical museum, complete with nicks in the woodwork that commemorate the famous sword fight. Although most of the historical documentation is only in Japanese, Terada-ya is a landmark for history buffs visiting Fushimi.

Getting Around

Finding your way around an unfamiliar city can be a trying and time-consuming task, even when language is not a problem. Fortunately, the Kyoto Tourist Information office on the ninth floor of the Kyoto Station building ([075] 344–3300) can tell you everything you need to know. City maps, transportation information, listings of current exhibitions, hotel and inn reservations, and even volunteer guides are available here. The office is open from 10 A.M. to 6 P.M. every day (except the second and fourth Tuesdays of the month).

Aerial view of Central Kyoto

There are two helpful periodicals available at most hotels, and at the Tourist Information office: the *Kyoto Visitor's Guide* gives information on exhibitions and festivals and other current events in Kyoto, and the *Kansai Time Out* offers everything from movie listings to sumo wrestling matches in the Kansai area, which includes Kobe, Osaka, and Nara.

Kyoto has an excellent public transport system. It is inexpensive and easily navigable using one of the plentiful tourist transit maps available around the city at hotels, at Kyoto Tourist Information, and other outlets. The trains can be very useful for destinations on the outskirts of the city (Arashiyama, Yase, Kibune, or Fushimi) or for traveling to Nara, Osaka, or Kobe. Most of the buses, however, do not have destinations written in English, and stops are announced in Japanese. Buses are often overcrowded, and for someone with only a few days to spend in Kyoto, much time will be wasted in trying to locate bus stops, waiting for the bus, and praying you'll be able to figure out when and where to get off.

Within the city limits, taxis are a good alternative. From downtown (Kawara-machi-Sanjō) to anywhere in the city the fare will not exceed ¥3,000, and in many cases it will be less than ¥2,000. The drivers are honest, do not expect to be tipped, and are rarely guilty of taking you "the long way around." Few of the taxi drivers in Kyoto speak English, so it is a good idea to have the location you wish to reach written down in Japanese (your hotel clerk will be glad to do this for you). All of the shop addresses in this book are listed in both English and Japanese.

For exploring the backstreets, bicycles are a popular option, and there are several places that rent them. Kyoto Cycling Tour Project ([075] 354–3636) is centrally located west of Kyoto Central Post Office and offers both bicycle rental and guided cycling tours in English. Kyoto Tourist Information also has a list of other bicycle rental shops in the city. Most ex-pats travel by bicycle in Kyoto, but take care with traffic on the city's narrow streets. Be aware that bicycles parked outside designated areas are towed away periodically.

One extra piece of advice on seeing Kyoto is to not try to see it all if your time is limited. The guided tours will run you all over town from Famous Temple to Famous Temple in a thorough (and thoroughly exhausting) five hours. If you have only one day, visit Raku-tō, which has more splendid temples, shops, and museums than you could see in a week. If you have two days, try Raku-tō and Raku-chū, the central district. In three days, the western sector, Raku-sei, with Arashiyama and Sagano could be added. With more time, Raku-hoku in the north, and Raku-nan in the south would take at least a day each to explore.

Walking is by far the best way to search for the heart of Kyoto. With a comfortable pair of shoes, you can discover all the little alleyways and niches that make this city one of the most intriguing in the world. Since Kyoto is still a safe place to wander, you can stroll through any quarter without fear of having your pockets picked or being otherwise assaulted. (Even after dark in the middle of the entertainment district in Gion the streets are relatively safe.) Most of the shops in this book were found on foot, and it is the author's hope that you will use this guide to lead you into areas that you can explore on your own.

Walks through Old Kyoto

There are several old neighborhoods in Kyoto where the streets are lined with old houses and shops that have remained relatively unchanged for the last hundred years. Some of these areas have been designated historic preservation districts, and a few of the houses and shops along their narrow streets have been named cultural assets. The long blocks of old wood-frame houses that open directly onto the street in traditional Kyoto style are called machi-nami, *or urban row houses. Largely due to the efforts of local citizens (and the Department of Architecture at Kyoto University), some of these neighborhoods now have building regulations and receive financial assistance from the city or prefectural government.*

A walk through one of the historic machi-nami *districts takes you away from the bustle and traffic of the twenty-first century for a moment to experience what life was like for the citizens of Kyoto in days gone by.*

GION-SHINBASHI. The heart of Kyoto's most famous geisha quarter is within a five-minute walk of the center of town. South of Shijō along Hanami-kōji-dōri are rows of old "teahouses" to which the sound of *shamisen* music and the exotic delights of the "floating world" nighttime entertainment still belong. On the corner you'll find the rust-colored walls of Ichiriki, a two-hundred-year-old teahouse in which the leader of the forty-seven samurai is said to have plotted to avenge his master's downfall by assassinating the arrogant shogun retainer responsible. Ichiriki is one of the teahouses in Gion that requires a personal introduction from a respected customer for reservations. No amount of money will get you past the gate without it.

Wandering the side streets, even late at night, is safer now than it ever was in the raucous eighteenth century when this district was in its heyday. You may

pass an apprentice geisha (*maiko*) dressed in elaborate kimono, with her long brocade sash, her face painted white, her hair adorned with costly ornaments, clip-clopping past you in platform *geta*.

North of Shijō along the Shirakawa Canal is the Shinbashi district. Weeping willows and *sudare* blinds have become symbolic of this triangle of teahouses beside the old canal. As you walk down the narrow street one block north of the canal, you'll pass a miniature shrine to the Buddhist deity Jizō, protector of children and patron saint of every neighborhood in Kyoto. The women who run the teahouses of Shinbashi take turns tending the shrine, cleaning it carefully and offering fresh flowers each day. (Eastern Kyoto.)

HONGAN-JI. Between Nishi Hongan-ji and Higashi Hongan-ji temples, two powerful schools of the Jōdo sect of Buddhism, there is an area called a *monzen-machi*, or temple-gate town, that abounds with old shops dealing in religious articles such as prayer beads, home shrines, altar cloths, candles, and incense. The two temples are located just north of Kyoto Station and draw thousands of devotees each year on pilgrimages from the countryside, eager to buy religious articles to take back to the temples in their hometowns. Walking east from the central gate of Nishi Hongan-ji, you'll pass dozens of shops and old *ryokan* that have been offering accommodations to visitors to the temples for centuries. (Central Kyoto, south.)

KAMIGAMO. The area in the north of Kyoto that surrounds Kamigamo Shrine is one of the oldest in the city. The shrine itself predates the founding of the capital, having been dedicated to the god of thunder and rain long before Emperor Kanmu took up residence in Kyoto in 794. One of Kyoto's oldest festivals, the Aoi Matsuri, started here in the sixth century when a series of disastrous floods were thought to have been the result of the emperor's neglect of

the thunder god. Every year on May 15 an imperial messenger visits the shrine in an elaborate procession to perform solemn rites to appease the god.

The shrine was built by the Kamo clan, one of the two main clans that inhabited this valley before Kanmu arrived. According to records from the seventeenth century, over 275 households belonging to descendants of this family (who were also priests of the shrine) formed a *shake-machi*, a township that centered around the shrine to protect it and administer its affairs. The canal that leads east in front of the shrine is part of an original network of canals that acted as both a protective moat and an irrigation system. It is still lined with the clay-walled family residences of the *shake-machi*, some of which date back to the time of the first generation of priests. The area is also famous for its fresh produce, and local women with their heavy vegetable carts can still be seen making the rounds of nearby neighborhoods, particularly the Nishijin weaving district. The pond in front of Ōta Shrine, about six hundred yards east of Kamigamo Shrine, is famous for its gorgeous irises which bloom each year in May. (Northern Kyoto.)

NISHIJIN. Kyoto's famous textile district where the fabulous brocade *obi* sashes are woven and the kimono fabrics are dyed. Since the early sixteenth century

a guild of weavers and dyers has existed in this neighborhood and the dark, heavily gridded façades of their houses still line its narrow backstreets. Most of the textiles are sold under the names of famous wholesalers, though production is divided among hundreds of local craftsmen, who specialize in only a part of the whole process (like dyeing threads or preparing warps for weaving). The sound of thousands of looms no longer echoes down the narrow alleyways of Nishijin as you walk along, but a few of the workshops remain hidden behind the *senbon-gōshi*, or "thousand-fingered," wooden-slatted windows that hide the way of life of their inhabitants from public view. Peeking through half-open doorways of the remaining textile workers' homes, you may catch a glimpse behind the scenes of one of Kyoto's most treasured old crafts. (Northern Kyoto; area cordoned off by Kita-ōji-dōri and Horikawa-dōri.)

NINENZAKA and SANNENZAKA. Walking south from Maruyama Park toward Kiyomizu-dera, you'll find an area of old shops and crumbly-walled temples that is one of the most popular in Kyoto for a Sunday afternoon stroll. The cobbled slopes leading up to the thousand-year-old temple are lined with *monzen-jaya*, or temple-gate tea shops, that have been serving refreshments to pilgrims and sightseers for centuries. A recent surge of interest in the area has prompted many local shopkeepers to remodel their old shops to accommodate the influx of tourists, and many now have a coat of paint and a facelift that robs the original of the dignity and *sabi*, "the beauty of rust," they once possessed. Until recently this area was also a booming ceramics center producing Kiyomizu ware, the painted porcelain for which Kyoto is famous. Many pottery shops still exist in the area, though the kilns have all moved to the suburbs in accordance with new pollution control laws. Dozens of shops selling antiques, pottery, and Buddhist articles, and a number of fine restaurants crowd the narrow streets leading up to Kiyomizu-dera. A brief detour to the west to see Yasaka Pagoda will take you down quieter side streets in a very old neighborhood. Don't miss Ishibe-kōji, a small alley across from the entrance to Kodai-ji. This

cobbled street with its high stone walls is lined with teahouses where geisha from Gion come each evening to entertain their guests. During the daytime it is practically deserted, except for an occasional sightseer who has wandered off the main path. (Eastern Kyoto.)

SAGANO TORIIMOTO. The orange *torii* gate of Atago Shrine in the western suburbs of Kyoto is the focal point of a row of *minka*, or rural houses, many of them thatched, that line the road leading through the gate to the old shrine dedicated to the god who puts out fires. The constant danger of fire in the ancient capital precipitated a custom that encouraged everyone in Kyoto to visit this shrine once a month. A festival held once a year in July still draws believers to make the steep three-hour climb up the mountain to gain the favor of this important local deity. The two thatched teahouses on either side of the *torii* have

been there for four hundred years selling a special kind of sweet called *shinko dango* to fortify pilgrims on their uphill trek. They now serve *ayu*, a popular local river fish, grilled in *kaiseki* style (see listing for Hirano-ya, W1).

The graveyard at Adashino Nenbutsu-ji with its thousands of stone grave markers nearby also attracts a large number of visitors to this area. Take the turnoff about halfway down the road from the *torii* gate that leads to Arashiyama in the south. This road winds through rice fields and bamboo forests, past the minor temples and shrines of yet another historic preservation district noted for its rural beauty. The road leads eventually to Arashiyama and the Togetsu-kyō Bridge that marks its center. It takes a full day to walk from *torii* to bridge, so many people prefer to rent bicycles at a shop near the bridge. A leisurely ride takes you to the shrine gate in half the time. The hundreds of crimson maple trees in Arashiyama make this area a popular tourist attraction in the fall. (Western Kyoto.)

NOTE: For further information on Kyoto's historic districts, see *Kyoto: Seven Paths to the Heart of the City* by the same author.

Day Trips to the Countryside

Within a few hours by train or bus from Kyoto there are several towns and villages worth visiting, particularly if you are interested in pottery, papermaking, green tea, saké, or just beautiful countryside.

FUSHIMI. Located at the spot where the Yodogawa River meets the Takasegawa River, Fushimi was originally a rest stop for boatmen traveling between Kyoto and Osaka. The northern part of Fushimi is called Fushimi Inari and is the location of an old shrine to the god of the harvest. Every year people still flock to Fushimi Inari Shrine around New Year's to pray for a prosperous year (whether their business is rice farming or microchip manufacturing). A road that was part of the Tōkaidō Highway built by the Tokugawa shogunate during the Edo period passes through Fushimi Inari, and some of the old shops and inns still exist, practically unchanged from the days when the feudal lords and their entourages used the highway.

Fushimi Momoyama, a bit farther south, was the site of one of Toyotomi Hideyoshi's castles in the sixteenth century. The location of the Yodogawa River, the availability of fresh water, and the proximity of a castle full of thirsty samurai made this castle town, or *jōka-machi*, the perfect place for brewing saké, for which this area is still famous. The old storehouses of the saké brewers have been preserved along the canal here, and some brewers give tours (by

appointment only) for a glimpse of how saké is made. (See also S2, S4 and S9.) Terada-ya (see S10), a former inn in this area, now operates as a museum. It is famous as the hideout of Sakamoto Ryōma, one of the principal plotters of the Meiji Restoration in the 1860s, and mementos of his stay are on display throughout the museum.

Ten minutes by Keihan Line from Sanjō Station to Fushimi Inari. Fare: Approximately ¥200. Twenty minutes by Keihan Line from Sanjō Station to Fushimi Momoyama. FARE: Approximately ¥300.

KURODANI. A beautiful papermaking village two hours north of Kyoto by bus. Everyone in this village seems to be related—if there's a wedding, the whole town closes up. But when it is open you can see the village women rinsing reeds in the stream as has been done for centuries. The different kinds of paper made here are displayed and may be purchased in the Kurodani museum and gift shop. The rural setting and authentic nature of this little town make the long bus ride well worth it.

About two hours by Kyōto Kōtsū bus from Shijō-Kawaramachi Terminal (south of Hankyū Department Store). FARE: Approximately ¥2,000.

ŌHARA. Few people miss the chance to visit this small town in the northeast of Kyoto if they have even half a day extra to spend. Just a forty-minute bus ride takes you to the foot of a hill that leads to the secluded temple Sanzen-in, founded in 860. The women of Ōhara (*Ōhara-me*) are noted for the colorful farm costumes they wear and the heavy loads they once carried on their heads. Weekdays are best for trips to this popular nearby town, also well-known for its delicious home-grown pickles.

Forty minutes by Kyoto bus #16 or #17 from Sanjō Station. FARE: Approximately ¥500.

SHIGARAKI. This still-booming pottery village is one of the oldest in Japan and the site of an imperial palace in the eighth century before the capital was moved to Kyoto. The salt-glaze ceramics of Shigaraki were once among the favorites of the tea master Sen no Rikyū, who praised their rustic beauty. There is a museum in the center of town which has a fine collection of old Shigaraki ware, and several major kilns which are open to the public. All are within walking distance of the station. A few individual potters continue to fashion tea wares, while the major kilns produce everyday wares such as cooking pots (*donabe*), vases, coffee cups, saké sets, and even *tanuki* raccoon dogs and frogs as garden ornaments.

About one and a half hours from Kyoto Station. Take the Tōkaidō Line to Ishiyama. Change to a local bus at Ishiyama. TOTAL FARE: Approximately ¥1,500.

UJI. This old town forty minutes to the southeast of Kyoto has been famous for centuries for the production of the finest green tea in Japan. From the train station you can easily locate the famous Uji Bridge, the oldest stone bridge of its kind in the country, and walk up the gentle slope toward the temple Byōdō-in, one of the only examples left of the graceful architecture of the Heian period. All along the road that leads to the temple you'll find shops that sell the famous local tea. Buy a container of *sencha*, the high-quality green-leaf tea, or one of *matcha*, the powdered green tea of the tea ceremony.

Forty minutes by Keihan Line from Sanjō Station. FARE: Approximately ¥350.

A Few Special Places to Hide

A few special places in Kyoto always offer a peaceful moment or two, even in the height of tourist season—places a bit out of the way (and out of the ordinary) that come as a welcome change of pace when the city's two thousand temples and shrines start melting together in your mind.

HAKUSASON-SŌ. The private villa of the painter Kansetsu Hashimoto, built in 1916. Stroll through the lush garden, past a quiet pavilion and teahouse along the edge of a pond full of colorful *koi*. Have a bowl of *matcha* and a traditional tea cake in a tatami room overlooking the pond. Visit the small gallery in back which contains some of Hashimoto's works, and objects from his

collection of ancient European and Middle Eastern art. Note the small stone carvings under the tall bamboo between the gallery and the main house. These are mourners at the death of the Buddha, collected by Hashimoto from all over Japan. Open daily 10 A.M.–5 P.M. FEE: ¥800. ¥750 extra for tea. *See map of eastern Kyoto, page 120.* See also E36.

KAWAI KANJIRŌ MEMORIAL HOUSE. This is the home of the noted potter Kanjirō Kawai, who was one of the founders of the folk-art movement of the 1920s and 1930s. The movement was established to promote an interest in everyday Japanese crafts among the general populace, who had rejected what they considered rough country products in favor of the new objects imported from the West. His home, workshop, and kiln are open to the public as a memorial to the life of this extraordinary man who excelled not only as a potter but as a poet, essayist, and designer. The giant climbing kiln Kawai used can also be seen behind the main building which he designed himself in the manner of a traditional farmhouse. Just five minutes southwest of Gojō and Higashi-ōji-dōri. Open 10 A.M.–5 P.M. Closed Mondays and on certain days during August and the New Year period. FEE: ¥900. *See map at front of book.*

NIJŌ JINYA. Located south of Nijō Castle, this "mystery house," with its secret passageways and trapdoors, was built in the mid-seventeenth century by a wealthy merchant named Yorozuya Hiraemon as an inn for *daimyō* (feudal lords) visiting the capital from the provinces. The twenty-four-room house has hidden staircases, concealed rope ladders, and even a secret tunnel under a pond in the garden. It graphically demonstrates the political intrigues of the Edo period when the shogunate resorted to the use of a special clan of ninja spies to maintain control over the provincial warlords. Nijō Jinya has been designated an Important Cultural Property, and tours are conducted daily by appointment only. Reservations can be made by calling (075) 841–0972 (in Japanese) a day or two in advance. Non-Japanese-speaking foreigners are advised to bring an interpreter or guide. This can be arranged by calling ISC, the volunteer guide service ([075] 462–2288). FEE: ¥1,000. *See map of central Kyoto (north), page 42.*

RAKU MUSEUM. "*Raku*" has become synonymous with a hand-molded, low-fired ceramic technique, which has its roots in a type of Japanese ceramic ware associated with the tea ceremony. The name belongs to the Raku family of potters who trace their history back to the mid-sixteenth century when a man named Chōjirō began making tea bowls under the direction of the great tea master Sen no Rikyū, founder of the tea ceremony in Japan. Chōjirō received the artist's name "Raku" (meaning "pleasure") from the great military ruler Toyotomi Hideyoshi, who bestowed the title in appreciation for his exquisite work. 450 years later, Chōjirō's descendants continue to carry on the family tradition. The beautiful Raku Museum opened in 1978 beside the Raku family residence on the eastern edge of the Nishijin textile district. At any given time, a remarkable selection of tea bowls from their nine-hundred-piece collection is on display at the museum, with at least one work from each of the past generations on view to demonstrate both the continuity of the tradition and the individuality of each succeeding generation. The current successor, Raku Kichizaemon XV, has gained international renown for the personal flair shown in the abstract forms of his tea bowls, which are taking the family tradition in stunningly new directions. Include a visit to this peaceful site in your wanderings through the Nishijin textile district. Open 10 A.M.–4 P.M. Closed Mondays, and some holidays. FEE: Approximately ¥1,000 (varies according to exhibition). *See map of central Kyoto (north), page 42.*

RAKUSHI-SHA. This is the thatched hut of Mukai Kyorai (1651–1704), a student of the famous wandering poet Bashō who is said to have written his *Saga Diary* here amid the persimmon groves and rice fields in the heart of Sagano. The hut is a twenty-minute walk from the Togetsu-kyō Bridge in Arashiyama. The path to Rakushi-sha leads through bamboo forests and out-of-the-way temples and shrines to a district that has been preserved as an area of scenic beauty. Many *minka*, or country houses, with their thatched roofs and rustic clay walls still remain here, some of the last remnants of rural Kyoto. Open daily 9 A.M.– 5 P.M. (10 A.M.–4 P.M. in January and February). FEE: ¥150. *See map of western Kyoto, page 190.*

Nishiki-kōji Street Market

A street market may sound like a peculiar place to go for therapy, but if the noisy buses and inscrutable contradictions of life in Kyoto start to drown you, wander in the direction of Nishiki. It has everything you need (and several things you don't) to restore flagging senses and revive the weary mind. The aroma of fresh-roasted tea, of ovens steaming with hot bean cakes, of skewered fish dripping with soy sauce over a charcoal grill (this latter pleasure admittedly reserved for Orientally adjusted noses). The sound of shopkeepers calling out a hearty welcome, of fishmongers touting the day's catch in boisterous tones—"*Oishii yo*"—"Delicious!" Finally, the riot of color for which Nishiki-kōji, "Brocade" Street, earned its name—shiny red apples stacked in perfect pyramids beside equally impeccable towers of persimmons, green vegetables (some familiar, some obscure . . . fern fronds, *wasabi* root, and broccoli), clams, oysters, shrimp, more varieties of fish than you knew existed, freshwater and salt. Sprinkle with a few old shops selling knives and cookware, *geta* clogs, or pottery bowls, and you have Nishiki, the liveliest street market in Kyoto.

Since the Middle Ages, this street has been the site of a public market for fish, produce, and saké. It was destroyed in the Ōnin War (1467–77), but was rebuilt in the late sixteenth century and has been a popular marketplace ever since. Today the shopkeepers of Nishiki still follow some of the customs of their early merchant ancestors, as can be seen in the careful specialization of shops. Those which sell freshwater fish never deal in fish from the sea. Egg shops don't sell chicken (and vice versa). Some shops sell only shellfish, and others specialize in eel or blowfish. This division dates to the guilds that were

established in Kyoto in the thirteenth century for mutual protection and profit during those turbulent times. By the sixteenth century, this division had evolved into a strict system of government favoritism that gave particular merchants absolute monopolies on the goods they sold, including the right to pass on their trade to their descendants in exchange for taxes.

The merchants of Nishiki still work together in close cooperation with one another, and though competition exists, the almost endless variety of specialty items in the Japanese diet and the similarly endless throngs of eager customers (who continue to patronize the shops their grandparents did) make for a harmonious atmosphere in one of Kyoto's oldest marketplaces.

Most of the shops on Nishiki are open by midmorning, and it is then that you'll find many of Kyoto's most lauded restaurateurs shopping for the special foods they need to prepare elaborate *kaiseki* meals. In the afternoon, the local housewives invade the market, and by 3 P.M. Nishiki is always crowded. Working people stop by on their way home, and most shops stay open until about 7 P.M.

Nishiki is one block north of Shijō-dōri and runs from Teramachi-dōri on the east to Takakura-dōri on the west (near Daimaru Department Store). It is four hundred yards long and the red, yellow, and green awnings overhead house 141 shops. Look for Aritsugu, the cutlery and traditional kitchenware shop, on the north side of Nishiki, one block west of Teramachi. Farther east, on the corner of Fuyachō-dōri, is Jintora, a sweet shop that specializes in *kodai-gashi*, or old-style sweets. Over a dozen wooden cases with glass lids hold different-shaped sweets, each molded and colored in designs appropriate to the season—pine needles, maple leaves, plum blossoms, and hundreds more. About halfway between Fuyachō and Tomino-kōji, you'll find Tsunayoshi, a saké shop selling *ji-zake* (saké made in small villages all over Japan) and dozens of Fushimi saké from the local saké-producing area (see Day Trips to the Countryside; S2, S4, S9), some in gift sets of small painted bottles in specially made wooden boxes.

Dried beans, sea urchin jelly, cod roe, fish paste, chrysanthemums (both to arrange and to eat), seaweed, live eels, raw oysters, flakes of dried bonito for making soup, rice cakes, grilled squid . . . what more could you ask?

Afterword

New Beginnings

Kyō nite mo	Though I am in Kyoto
Kyō natsukashii ya	I miss Kyoto . . .
Hototogisu	Cry of the cuckoo

When the poet Bashō wrote these lines more than three hundred years ago, he expressed a feeling familiar to all who love Kyoto. *Natsukashii* . . . a deep longing for days past. The haunting call of a bird in the forest reminds us that our lives—and great cities, no matter how long lived—exist for only a precious moment in time.

Ten years have passed since I left Kyoto in 1995. Twenty, since I first met the cast of characters who are the stewards of the wonderful traditional shops of old Kyoto. The *people* are what old Kyoto is about—the remarkable people who year after year are still to be found on the backstreets, working dawn till dusk in the shops of their ancestors—some for generations. When I revisited the old shops for this twentieth anniversary edition of *Old Kyoto*, I discovered that Naitō-san, the old broom-maker's widow, though now in her nineties, still ventures out front at her broom shop on busy Sanjō-dōri to grin endearingly at beloved customers she can no longer see; it was a wonderful surprise.

Shinise is the word in Japanese that distinguishes establishments like those of Mrs. Naitō. A word that literally means "old shop," but implies a tradition that has been carried on in the same family for at least one hundred years and three generations. The *shinise* are the best of the best—many were purveyors to the imperial court of Japan until the emperor left Kyoto for what is now Tokyo in 1868.

Sadly, some of the older generation of my beloved Kyoto shopkeepers are gone . . . old Mrs. Kimura of Tsukimochi-ya, Kōichi Kobori of Fūka, Ine Tanaka of Nishiki, Michikazu Takeuchi of Jūsan-ya, and so many others. Miraculously, their children have carried on their traditional trades. Such was not the case, however, with Mr. Tomii of Taruden, the wonderful old bucket maker who worked until the day he died in his remarkable little bucket shop in the heart of the Nishijin textile district. He had no heir and no apprentice and his shop disappeared with the turn of the millennium. In his memory, I left Taruden unchanged on these pages, hoping to convey his extraordinary vitality and kindness. Most of the photographs of the shop owners from the first edition of this guidebook have also been left unchanged, as the people, not the objects they sell, are at the heart of this book.

It is harder to find the *shinise* now, lost amidst the trappings of the modern city, yet many of the descendants of the old families have chosen to carry on centuries-old traditions of impeccable quality and gracious hospitality. A surprising number of *Kyo-machiya* and the traditional trades they shelter remain.

Recently, a new awareness of the beauty of *machiya* has come to life among a younger generation of Kyoto people, who have begun to restore the old shopfronts and turn them into chic restaurants and boutiques, some of which have been added to the pages of this book. Through the efforts of a handful of valiant Kyoto architects and preservationists like Ryō Kinoshita, revitalization of the *Kyō-machiya* has at last caught on. Their vitality and inspiration is taking Kyoto in new directions that have roots in an aesthetic and a work ethic that refuse to die and will no doubt continue to delight new generations of travelers for years to come.

At this writing, the irrepressible Mrs. Hasegawa still sits on the stoop out front at Ichiwa, though her daughter now grills the *mochi* cakes and her granddaughter pours the tea. "*Bimbō hima nashi* (the poor have no time to spare)," she continues to grumble to the taxi drivers who stop by for tea and rice cakes, as popular now as they were in the twelfth century.

"*Banzai!*" to Mrs. Hasegawa and to all the shopkeepers of old Kyoto. May you live ten thousand years.

Diane Durston
Portland

Glossary

amazake, a sweet nonalcoholic drink made from saké lees

ayu, a small river fish that is a delicacy in western Japan

bonsai, miniature potted plants

cha-kaiseki. See *kaiseki*.

chanko-nabe, a hearty stew served in portions fit for sumo wrestlers

-chaya or *-jaya* (suffix), a shop that serves tea. See also *monzen-jaya, o-chaya.*

-chō (suffix), township

daimyō, provincial feudal lords

dango, balls of *mochi* served on skewers (*shinko dango*—the special type of *dango* served at Atago Shrine)

-dera. See *-tera.*

donabe, an earthenware cooking pot

-dōri (suffix), street

fu, wheat gluten

fusuma, sliding paper doors

futon, traditional folding bedding

-gawa. See *-kawa.*

geta, wooden clogs

happi, workmen's coats

hashi-oki, chopstick rests

imobō, a dish of preserved fish and boiled potatoes (an old Kyoto specialty)

-jaya. See *-chaya.*

-ji (suffix), temple. See also *-tera.*

jinja, a shrine

ji-zake, regionally produced saké (refers to saké made in limited quantities by small local breweries)

junmai-shu, 100-percent natural saké (no alcohol added)

kabuki, traditional Japanese drama

kaiseki (or *cha-kaiseki*), a formal Japanese meal

kamaburo, literally "oven-bath"; refers to a clay-walled steam room shaped like an old country oven

kamado, an old-style clay cookstove

-kawa or *-gawa* (suffix), river

Kiyomizu ware, ceramics from the Kiyomizu district of Kyoto

koi, carp

-ku (suffix), ward (administrative area of a city)

kura, a family storehouse; saké brewer's warehouse

kushikatsu, pieces of skewered meats and vegetables, fried or grilled

Kyō (prefix), refers to objects or traditions of Kyoto (i.e., *Kyō-ryōri*, meaning Kyoto cuisine)

machi-nami, row houses

machiya, a townhouse; refers to traditional city dwellings

maiko, apprentice geisha

maki-e, gold decoration on lacquerware

manjū, bean cakes

matcha, powdered tea-ceremony tea

miko, Shinto priestesses

mingei, folk art

minshuku, an inexpensive family-run inn

miso, soybean paste used in making soups and sauces

mizu-taki, a method of cooking by boiling in water

mochi, rice cakes

monpe, farmwomen's pants

monzen-jaya, a teahouse outside the gates of a temple. See also *-chaya*, *o-chaya*.

nabe, a cooking pot. See also *donabe*.

nabemono, a dish stewed or boiled in a pot

nattō, fermented soybeans

ningyō, doll

noh, traditional Japanese drama, which originated in the upper classes

noren, a short curtain hung in the doorways of shops and restaurants indicating that the shop is open for business

obi, a wide sash worn with kimono

o-chaya, literally "teahouse"; refers to places where geisha entertain their guests. See also *-chaya*, *monzen-jaya*.

oden, an assortment of ingredients such as potatoes, hardboiled eggs, and Japanese specialties like *kamaboko* (fish cakes) simmered in a light broth

o-hagi, confections of rice and beans

o-kashi, sweets (*wa-gashi*, Japanese sweets; *yō-gashi*, Western sweets)

o-usu, the name for tea-ceremony tea as it is served in most Kyoto shops (from *usui* meaning "weak" or "thin," as opposed to a thicker type which is also served in formal tea ceremonies)

pachinko, Japanese pinball

Raku (prefix), literally "capital"; used to refer to areas in Kyoto (i.e., Raku-chū, meaning Central Kyoto)

Raku ware, a type of pottery used in the tea ceremony which originated in Kyoto, usually black or red

rakugo, traditional storytelling

robata-yaki, a variety of fish, meat, and vegetables charcoal grilled and served at a counter

ryokan, a traditional Japanese inn

ryōtei, an expensive traditional restaurant

saké, rice wine

sashimi, raw fish

sencha, high-quality green leaf tea

sensu, a folding fan. See also *uchiwa*.

shabu-shabu, thinly sliced beef quickly dipped in boiling water in a pot at the table and then dipped in a sauce

shake. See *shake-machi*.

shake-machi, a township or neighborhood of families connected with a local shrine

shamisen, a three-stringed musical instrument

Shigaraki ware, ceramics from the town of Shigaraki, southeast of Kyoto

shinkansen, a bullet train

shinko dango. See *dango*.

Shinto, native Japanese religion that worships the spirit in natural things (gods of wind, fire, water, etc.)

shogun, a hereditary military dictator

shogunate, the office, period in office, or rule of a shogun

shōji, white, translucent sliding paper doors and windows

shōjin ryōri, Japanese Zen-style vegetarian food

soba, buckwheat noodles

soboku, rustic; unpretentious

sōmen, thin white noodles served chilled in summer

some-tsuke, blue painting on white porcelain background

sudare, reed or bamboo blinds

sukiyaki, thinly sliced beef sautéed in a slightly sweetened soy sauce

sushi, raw fish served with vinegared rice in a variety of forms

tabi, split-toed socks

tansu, chests, cabinets

tanuki, a badgerlike animal with alleged magic powers to transform itself into different shapes; the ceramic mascot of the pottery town Shigaraki and of many Kyoto merchants

tatami, woven straw floor mats

teahouse. See *-chaya, monzen-jaya*. For "teahouse," see *o-chaya*.

tempura, fish or vegetables deep-fried in batter

-tera or *-dera* (suffix), temple. See also *-ji*.

tofu, soft bean curd

tokonoma, the recessed alcove in a Japanese home used to display objects, flower arrangements, and paintings

torii, the gate to a Shinto shrine (often painted vermilion)

uchiwa, a round flat fan. See also *sensu*.

udon, thick wheat noodles

ukiyo-e, woodblock prints depicting the "floating world" of entertainment

wabi, the elegance of simplicity, an aesthetic value of the tea ceremony

wagasa, a Japanese paper umbrella

wa-gashi. See *o-kashi*.

wasabi, Japanese "horseradish"

yakitori, grilled skewers of chicken

-yama (suffix), mountain

yō-gashi. See *o-kashi*.

yuba, skimmings from simmering soy milk

yudōfu, tofu simmered in a pot at the table, dipped in a sauce, and served with side dishes

yukata, a cotton summer kimono

Yūzen dyeing, a traditional resist-dyeing process in which colors are applied with a brush

zabuton, floor cushions

Shops by Type

RESTAURANTS

SNACKS

Kasagi-ya	*tea and sweets*	E10	148
Ōkōchi-sansō	*tea and sweets*	W7	201
Rakushō	*tea and sweets*	E34	159

Alphabetical List of Shops

Aizen Kōbō	*indigo textiles*	C1	44
Aritsugu	*cutlery, kitchenware*	C36	114
Asahi-dō	*ceramics*	E38	160
Aunbo	*restaurant*	E18	153
Azekura	*restaurant*	N3	169
Azuma	*sushi*	S7	212
Boai-sō	*restaurant*	W4	200
Bunnosuke-jaya	*amazake (a sweet beverage)*	E8	142
Daikoku-ya	*buckwheat noodles (soba)*	C23	110
Fujino-ya	*tempura, kushikatsu kebabs*	C40	115
Fūka	*wheat gluten*	C3	50
Funahashi-ya	*rice crackers*	C13	80
Fundō-ya	*footwear (tabi)*	C30	112
Gekkeikan	*saké brewery*	S2	208
Gion Tanaka-ya	*footwear (geta)*	E24	155
Hakusason-sō	*restaurant and garden*	E36	159
Heihachi-jaya	*inn (ryokan), restaurant*	N4	172
Hiiragi-ya	*inn (ryokan)*	C7	62
Hinode-ya	*kimono*	N11	187
Hiraiwa	*inn (ryokan)*	C44	117
Hirano-ya	*restaurant*	E22	154
Hirano-ya	*sweet fish (ayu)*	W1	191
Hirata	*blinds*	E5	133
Hirata	*clay dolls, folk toys*	C46	118
Hirota	*guest house*	C31	112
Hōrai-dō	*tea, tea utensils*	C37	114
Hyōtan-ya	*gourd flasks*	E37	160
Ichihara Heibei Shōten	*chopsticks*	C24	110
Ichiwa	*rice cakes*	N6	178

Useful Web Sites

A wealth of information about Kyoto exists on the Internet. The following sites are particularly useful for finding out about seasonal events and the latest tourist and travel information.

The Kyoto Visitor's Guide Homepage
Monthly event listings, as well as an accommodation, dining and shopping guide.
www.kyotoguide.com

Kansai Time Out Homepage
Monthly event listings for the Kansai area, which includes the cities of Kyoto, Osaka, Kobe and Nara.
www.kto.co.jp

Kyoto City Tourism and Culture Information System
Seasonal event information.
raku.city.kyoto.jp/sight_e.phtml

Japan National Tourist Information
Travel tips for Japan and in-depth regional tourist information.
www.jnto.go.jp/eng/

japanunlimited.com
A selection of Japan-related web sites.
www.japanunlimited.com

Further Reading

Clancy, Judith. *Exploring Kyoto: On Foot in the Ancient Capital.* Tokyo: Weatherhill, 1997.

Keene, Donald. *Appreciations of Japanese Culture.* Tokyo: Kodansha International, 2003.

Kondō, Hiroshi. *Sake: A Drinker's Guide.* Tokyo: Kodansha International, 1984.

Morse, Edward S. *Japanese Homes and Their Surroundings.* Tokyo: Tuttle, 1982 (original edition, 1885).

Mosher, Gouverneur. *Kyoto: A Contemplative Guide.* Tokyo: Tuttle, 1978.

Plutchow, Herbert E. *Historical Kyoto.* Tokyo: Japan Times, 1983.

———. *Introducing Kyoto.* Tokyo: Kodansha International, 1979.

Ponsonby-Fane, R. *Kyoto: The Old Capital of Japan (794–1869).* Tokyo: Ponsonby Memorial Society, 1956.

Price, Margaret. *Classic Japanese Inns and Country Getaways.* Tokyo: Kodansha International, 1999.

Richie, Donald. *A Taste of Japan.* Tokyo: Kodansha International, 1985.

Sansom, George. *A History of Japan.* Tokyo: Tuttle, 1981.

Steward, Harold. *By the Old Walls of Kyoto.* Tokyo: Weatherhill, 1981.

Tanizaki, Junichirō. *In Praise of Shadows.* New Haven, Conn.: Leete's Island Books, 1980.

Thomas, A. F. *Commercial History of Japan.* Tokyo: Yuhodo, 1936.

Treib, Mark and Ronald Herman. *A Guide to the Gardens of Kyoto.* Tokyo: Shufunotomo, 1983.

Yanagi, Soetsu. *The Unknown Craftsman.* Tokyo: Kodansha International, 1989.

Acknowledgments

This year marks the twentieth anniversary of *Old Kyoto*, and it is thanks to the readers who have spread the word that somehow this book is about something more than tourism and that tourism is more about finding yourself in others than about bringing home exotic souvenirs from Zanzibar. You have kept my little book in print for two decades, and I thank you from the bottom of my heart.

My deepest gratitude to Barry Lancet, my editor at Kodansha International and friend for the past twenty years, without whom this revised edition would never have seen the light of day. Thanks to Cathy Layne and Michiko Uchiyama, for your hard work in editing this manuscript and to Masumi Akiyama for the jacket design. Without the dedication of Joseph Cronin, old friend and long-time Kyoto resident, up-to-date changes would not have been possible. I thank you all.

I continue to hold in my heart the many people who helped me with the original manuscript and their friendship over the years I lived in Kyoto, including Yōko Yoshikawa Couling, Mikiko Murata Schummacher, Philip Meredith, John McGee, Joseph Justice, Gary Cadwallader and Margaret O'Sullivan. Thanks to Aiko and the late Kenkichi Kuroda, the late Hirotoshi Kuwano, Yasuo Kitazawa and Kazuko Saitō, for teaching me how to think (and feel) in Japanese.

Many thanks always to Lucy Birmingham Fujii, whose beautiful pictures continue to tell more than my words; to Tsuyoshi Itō, for great photos of *machiya*; and to the Kyoto Chamber of Commerce and Industry for permission to reprint old photographs of Kyoto from their collection.

Thank you always, Donald Richie, for your friendship and advice. Thanks to Dave Jack, Tom Chapman, and Greg Starr for giving me a place to start as a writer. Thanks to Robert Singer for his friendship, expertise and advice. And first, last, and always—thanks to my husband, Stephen Futscher, whose belief in me helps me now, as then and always, to believe in myself.